הדרך יהוה
THE WAY

An introduction to modern
'Jewish-Christianity' (Talmidaism)

Book 1: Re-interpreting Jesus of
Nazareth & the history of his first
Jewish Followers
in the light of Israelite theology

by

Shmuel ben Naftali

Other books by the same author:

'The Exhortations'
(The Talmidi Israelite equivalent of the 'New Testament')

THE WAY – An Introduction to Modern 'Jewish-Christianity' (Talmidaism)
Book 2: Teaching the Talmidi Israelite faith through the words of the 'Our Father'

THE WAY – An Introduction to Modern 'Jewish-Christianity' (Talmidaism)
Book 3: God's Customs and Festivals in the Modern Talmidi Israelite Community

THE WAY – An Introduction to Modern 'Jewish-Christianity' (Talmidaism)
Book 4: Reflections, Challenges and Aspirations of an Ancient Faith in the Modern World

First edition published 10 January 2018
This 2nd, revised edition published January 2020
published under the auspices of
'LAMP HOUSE BOOKS'
(a private, non-profit foundation of
The World Fellowship of Followers of the Way)

Published through KDP on Amazon

Copyright notice: All quotations and sources cited in this book are used under the condition of 'fair use', and are not intended to infringe other author's copyright. Where known, all quotes have their authors and original works cited. Genuine apologies where the author or work is unknown. All quotations from the Hebrew Bible and New Testament are my own translations; if otherwise, I have quoted the source.

Copyright © 2018 Shmuel Beit Parzal

All rights reserved.

ISBN: 9781976844379

PLEASE TREAT THIS BOOK WITH
RESPECT, AS IT CONTAINS THE HOLY
NAME OF GOD.

PLEASE THEREFORE
DO NOT DESTROY IT.
IF YOU NO LONGER REQUIRE IT,
PLEASE GIVE IT TO SOMEONE ELSE
WHO MIGHT BE INTERESTED IN
READING IT.

DEDICATION

I ultimately dedicate this book to Yahveh our God, for the sake of whose Kingdom and Message these sermons and articles were collected over the course of the last 30 years. I also dedicate this book to the memory of the prophet Yeshua` of Nazareth, of his cousins Ya'aqov the Pious and Shim'on bar Qlofas, of the line of Nasis[a] who succeeded them, and of all those ancient Followers of the Way (both Jew and Godfearing Gentile alike), whose Jewish way of life has too long been forgotten, and whose genuine, Yahwist beliefs have too long been misrepresented and suppressed.

---

[a] pronounced nah-SEEZ (singular Nasi) – religious presidents of the ancient community of the Way

Contents

A NOTE ON THE AUTHOR xii

PREFACE xiii

GENERAL INTRODUCTION xv

Chapter One: An Overview of basic Israelite theology, with relevance to the history of the First Century C.E. 1

Introduction 1

The well-trodden road I am not going to take 2

The Way of Yahveh 4

The purpose of the Israelite religion 5

The Glory of Yahveh 6

The holiness of God 10

The effects in this world of the 'fire' of Yahveh 15

The trembling of heaven and earth 17

Misfortune and blamelessness 20

The endurance of the righteous 21

Signs of the times: the troubles in the Holy Land in the 1st century CE 22

The great and terrible Day of Yahveh 24

Repentance as a way of avoiding the Day of Yahveh 26

The role of the prophet in the Israelite tradition 28

The prophet like Elijah 30

Summary 32

Chapter Two: The Forgotten History of the Way: the Talmidi

Israelite view of the Prophet Yeshua`, and the community of his earliest Jewish Followers 34

    Introduction.......... 34

    The prophet Yeshua` 35

    The ancient community of the Way 37

    Jacob the Pious ('St James the Just') – the real first leader of the Community of the Way 40

    The Gaius Crisis and the 'Letter of St James' 45

    The Convention of Jerusalem 48

    Varieties of belief: The ancient schools of the Way 56

    Paul's bogeymen: the 'Judaisers', and those who clung stubbornly to God's Torah 59

    Jacob the Pious's edict against false teachers, and the fate of Peter 64

    The fateful result of Peter's Paullist ministry – the Nazarenes 67

    The lead-up to the destruction of the Temple 68

    Shimon bar Qlofas ('St. Symeon of Jerusalem') 69

    The Benediction of the Heretics 73

    The final demise of the community 75

    What we can learn from such a new perspective on our history 77

    Summary 80

Chapter Three: Interpreting the person of Yeshua` in the light of Israelite theology 83

    The problem of stripping away 'Jesus' to find the historical

Yeshua` 83

'But his Apostles believed he was a god!' 87

If Yeshua` were a god, then why did he pray to himself? 88

The evolution of Christian messianism.................................. 89

Paul and Messianism 91

Re-Interpreting So-Called 'Messianic' Prophecies................. 97

Why belief in a messiah-saviour is a rejection of Yahveh 99

Any Messiah Will Be Subservient To God............................. 101

Why Yeshua` was not a god-messiah: Isaiah 9:5 in context 102

Psalm 45 – God supposedly addressing the king of Israel as 'God' 105

David's 'lord' in Psalm 110... 107

The Suffering Servant: Isaiah 53 in context......................... 109

Gen 18 - The three angels who visited Abraham were not the trinity 112

Superhuman rabbi or prophet of God?................................ 113

The supposed miracles of Yeshua` 118

Giving Yeshua`'s mission its proper historical and theological context... 120

The Zealots and nationalist messianism.............................. 123

The kingdom of God as a replacement for messianism 124

Yeshua`'s ultimate fate – Yeshua`'s death 125

Examining the issue of resurrection from a Jewish perspective 130

1. Reanimation of the Dead... 130

2. Ascension of the Pious 131

3. The Final Resurrection of the Dead at the end of time ... 132

4. The Resurrection of Yeshua` 133

The impetus behind the renewal of the Apostles' faith at Shavu`ot (Pentecost) 137

The theology of Adoptionism: how Yeshua` became a divine messiah 141

Summary 144

What's waiting for you in the next three books 145

APPENDICES: General Notes On The Talmidi Israelite faith 147

APPENDIX ONE: Main Talmidi beliefs 148

Basic tenets of the Talmidi Israelite faith 149

The Twelve Central Attributes of Yahveh: 149

The Four Cornerstones of Israelite Culture: 149

The Seven Pillars of Piety: 149

The Twelve Major Negative Injunctions: 150

The Twelve Words of the Prophets: 150

In detail: The Basic beliefs of Talmidaism 151

On God: 151

On Torah and the Covenant: 152

On the viewpoint of the Talmidi Community: 152

Some Basic Talmidi affirmations: 154

Some Basic Talmidi values and emphases, derived from the teachings of the prophet Yeshua` and of Jacob the Pious: . 155

Some Voluntary Acts of Piety 156

Some Yahwist beliefs held by Talmidis 157

APPENDIX TWO: About the Mission of Talmidaism 158

Articles of Mission of the Talmidi Faith 158

With relation to God: 158

With relation to the Houses of Israel and Judah 159

With relation to the Gentile nations: 160

With relation to one another: 161

With relation to Torah: 161

With relation to Yeshua` and the Jewish tradition of his ancient followers: 161

APPENDIX THREE: CULTURAL DIFFERENCES WITH OTHER ISRAELITE/JEWISH COMMUNITIES 163

A note on relations with the wider Jewish Community 166

APPENDIX FOUR: GLOSSARY & LIST OF ABBREVIATIONS USED IN THESE BOOKS 168

SELECT BIBLIOGRAPHY & RESOURCES 181

A Final Note from the Author 188

Shmuel ben Naftali

אנכי אנכי יהוה
ואין מבלעדי מושיע

"I – and I alone – am Yahveh,
and besides Me, there is no other
saviour."

(Isaiah 43:11)

אני יהוה
הוא שמי
וכבודי לאחר לא אתן

"I am Yahveh – that is My Name;
I will not give My glory to any other
name."

(Isaiah 42:8)

A NOTE ON THE AUTHOR

Shmuel Parzal was born in Sri Lanka (then Ceylon) in 1961, and emigrated to England in February 1962 with his parents and grandparents.

He was born of mixed ancestry, mostly of Dutch, Portuguese *Converso*[a] and English lineage. He was raised as a Catholic, and during his late teenage years felt a calling to become a priest. However, due to internal spiritual doubts and a realisation that he was not yet ready to enter into ministry, he concluded that this was not to be his vocation.

Later, he spent some years with the Unitarians, during which time he acted as a lay preacher, travelling around congregations in the southeast of England to take services. He describes this time as "an important turning point in my spiritual development, when I learned to question everything, and accept nothing as given". He eventually converted to Judaism, beginning the process with the Reform Movement, and completing it with the Liberal Jewish community in London.

He now acts as Moderator for the moderate wing of the Talmidi Israelite community, a role that he has fulfilled since 1998.

A long-time researcher in early Christian and Jewish history, he has focussed his private studies not only on early 'Jewish-Christianity' (that is, Talmidaism), but also on the pre-Exile Israelite faith and its theology, as distinct from post-Exile Rabbinic theology.

---

[a] Jews who were forcibly converted to Christianity under pain of death, during the Portuguese Inquisition in the 16th and 17th centuries.

PREFACE

In 1998, I self-published my work on the reconstructed, Jewish Aramaic *'Our Father'*. Since then, I have journeyed much, encountered many different people, and learned a whole lot more. I now feel that what I have picked up in these last two decades warrants collecting it all together, and expounding it all in a set of four handbooks on the Talmidi Israelite faith. The wealth of information that I have accumulated – as well as the scepticism of those in established religion – has also prompted a change in how I present my information in these four books. Whereas in my very first book, I tried to avoid footnotes and complicated background explanation, in these new books I have included footnotes, and gone into greater depth to explain the Yahwist[a] Israelite way of thinking.

What has changed most significantly for me in the last twenty years, is that I now have the privilege of serving a unique religious community – one that tries to maintain the best of the biblical customs and traditions of ancient Israel, together with a *completely* Yahwist Israelite understanding of the teachings of Jesus of Nazareth (to whom I shall refer henceforth by his original name, Yeshua`).[b] From the beginning, we have tried to do this with godly compassion and spiritual humility. We have turned our backs on the destructive and divisive acrimony of religious fundamentalism, and value all knowledge[c] and wisdom as a blessing and gift from God.

What this theological mixture has resulted in for me personally, and for people like me, is a deeper and closer relationship with our heavenly Father. It is a relationship not mired in dogma or ritual, or in the rulings of man, but a living relationship that transforms the human heart and soul. I can honestly and humbly say that I am not the same person who

---

[a] I use the terms 'Yahwist' and 'Yahwism' to refer to the purest form of monotheistic, Israelite theology and ethics, unhindered by contemporary polytheism, or later, non-Israelite beliefs and influence; in my writings, 'Yahwism' represents the core ideal of the Israelite faith. I am aware that other authors use these terms differently.

[b] pronounced *yuh-SHOO-aah*, with the *-uh-* pronounced like the *-a* in Ti**na**, the *–oo-* like the *-oo-* in c**oo**l, and the *-aah* like the *-a-* in f**a**ther. In Aramaic there is also a glottal stop at the end of the name, but it is not necessary to attempt this.

[c] The Massorite sect of Talmidaism, for example, does not see any conflict between scientific knowledge and religious faith, and does not have a problem with the theory of evolution, or with the great geological age of the earth.

started out on this journey thirty years ago in March 1987.[a]

Lastly, I wrote my first manuscript for a general audience, aimed at anyone of any faith who might be interested in my reconstruction of the Jewish Aramaic *'Our Father'*, and in knowing a little more about the cultural background to the prayer; it was short and to the point. Over the intervening years, by giving myself over whole-heartedly to Yahwist theology – and so trying to walk each day in the living Presence of God – I have learned more and more to think like an ancient Israelite. As a direct consequence of this exercise in living history, I have taken on the ancient Israelite mind-set and worldview myself. This has enabled me to gain some extremely valuable insights – even to retrieve some lost Yahwist concepts, some of which have not seen the light of day since before the Babylonian Exile over 2,500 years ago.

I genuinely feel that these insights have helped me to understand the theology of the minds that wrote the Hebrew Bible; they have also helped me to understand the ancient beliefs and values that underscored the Israelite way of life. So this time, because of what I have learned, these four books have been written more with a Talmidi[b] audience in mind; they have virtually become introductory handbooks to the Talmidi form of Judaism – or more accurately, the Talmidi form of the Israelite faith. While this does not preclude non-Talmidis from reading them, my primary aim is to speak directly to my fellow Talmidis – to my spiritual brothers and sisters who follow the Way. Although I have written these books primarily from a Massorite[c] Talmidi point of view, I hope that the books will be readily accessible to *all* Talmidis, regardless of their sect.

Shmuel Parzal
Lincoln, England
June 2017

---

[a] 12th March 1987 - the date of my own personal 'conversion experience' to Yahwism.

[b] the modern alternative to the term, 'Jewish-Christian', pronounced taal-MEE-dee. It is used of both the ancient Jamesian community, as well as the modern 'Jewish-Christian' community.

[c] the Talmidi sect to which I belong. It is a traditionalist but moderate sect, with a defined yet flexible theology. We value scholarly learning and modern historical research. Not to be confused with 'Masorti' (a conservative sect of Rabbinic Judaism), or Masorete (the scribes who defined and fixed the text of the Hebrew Bible).

GENERAL INTRODUCTION

These four books represent nearly thirty years' worth of sermons, public talks, commentaries and web articles. They embody the sum of what I have learned so far about the ethos underlying the Jewish faith of the prophet Yeshua`, and the faith of his first Jewish followers.

I remember how I felt the first time I visited a rabbi, after my long years of isolated, private study. I had gained a deep affection for the faith of the early Israelites,[a] and tried to convey this affection to the rabbi. Imagine my dismay when I was told that the modern Jewish religion is based, not on the faith lived and practised by the ancient Israelites – nor even on the Hebrew Bible – but on the Talmud and the teachings of the rabbis of the Second Temple period. Imagine my further anguish when I was told that the Israelite religion was dead, with no further relevance to Jewish life today. Thankfully, this did not put me off – I persevered with my conversion. But my affection for the faith of the ancient Israelites never left me. From everything I had read about the Israelite religion, I had come to the understanding that the Israelite faith was meant to be an *eternal* witness to the inextinguishable Presence of the God of Israel, and I hungered to be part of that eternal witness.

Some will counter that the Israelite religion has no place in the modern world, because it was all about animal sacrifice, but this is a distraction.[b] What has been lost to us is the understanding of the rich, theological symbolism *behind* animal sacrifice, which thankfully takes us beyond the outdatedness of blood offerings,[c] and provides us with valuable insights into the nature of Yahveh, and into God's ongoing, eternal purpose for us. This loss of understanding of the most basic, pivotal Yahwist concepts, has enabled the dishonesty of Paullist theology to flourish unchallenged.[d]

---

[a] cf Jer 6:16 – *"Thus says Yahveh, "Stand at the crossroads and look about you; ask for the **ancient paths** - where the good way is, and walk in it. Then you will find rest for your souls."*
[b] Isa 43:22-28, esp v.25; it is not the blood of sacrifices that brings about forgiveness of sin, but *"I – and I alone – who blots out your transgressions for My own sake, and I will not remember your sins any more."* See also Isaiah 1:11 – *"What is the profusion of your sacrifices to Me? says YHVH. I have had more than enough of your burnt offerings . . . I take no delight in the blood of bulls or lambs or goats."*
[c] cf Isa 1:11-13, Hos 6:6, 8:13, Amos 5:22; for what God prefers instead, see Isa 1:16-17.
[d] For example, Paullist theology says that it is the blood of 'Christ' that brings about the forgiveness of sin, and only the death of 'Christ' can atone for sin;

The prophet Yeshua` is often portrayed in the gospels as overruling Torah. If Torah were only about commandments (*mitsvot*), then we might be forgiven for this impression. However, Torah is also about ethical principles (`*iqronot*),[a] and what Yeshua` was doing all along, was reaffirming the principles and ethos of the original Israelite faith – *'the old wine is good enough'*.[b] These principles give a living flexibility to the commandments, and enable them to function in a just yet fair and wise manner.[c] Modern Talmidaism[d] emphasises the importance and wisdom of *principles* as equally as *commandments*.

For most Christians, 'Jesus Christ' is the foundation of a new revelation, and for some die-hard fundamentalists, he even represents an end to Judaism. However, for ancient Followers of the Way, the human prophet Yeshua` represented instead a reaffirmation of the Yahwist heart of the original Israelite faith, and a restoration of its ideals and purpose at a time of enormous spiritual and political crisis – the impending destruction of Jerusalem and the Roman exile.

In this first book of the series, I want to present to you those aspects of Israelite belief which have relevance to the Talmidi understanding of Yeshua`'s ministry, and to the story of his first Jewish followers. I want to show you how Yeshua`'s teachings were not an end to Judaism and

---

however, in Israelite theology it is through God's infinite and merciful love that God forgives a penitent soul, and it is the fire of God's Glory which purifies and cleanses us of our sin, restoring our souls to full and perfect health (which is what atonement is in the Israelite religion).

[a] For example, the principle of hospitality is nowhere explicitly stated in Torah, but by example, the principle that a host should not abuse their guest, and that a guest should not take advantage of their host, is understood as a given in the Hebrew Bible. So also the principle that one should not abuse animals, that a parent should not abuse their children etc. People who take the bible literally, do not take biblical principles and ethics into account.

[b] S.Yesh. 14:1-2; cf Mk 2:22, Lk 5:39

[c] cf the words of Jacob the Pious: 'Mercy triumphs over judgment' (Ig.Yq. 3:10; cf Letter of James 2:13)

[d] pronounced taal-mid-DAY-izzm; from the Aramaic word *talmida*: 'student' or 'follower' (the Hebrew equivalent is *talmid*); the form of the word 'Talmidaism' is modelled after the ending of the word 'Judaism'. It has nothing to do with the Talmud; the only linguistic link is that they are both from the root *talmad*: 'to teach'. The term was coined while in secret prayer on Temple Mount in June, 1996 (Jews are otherwise forbidden to pray there).

This term refers to *both* ancient and modern 'Jewish-Christians', specifically those who hold that James, not Peter, was the head of the Jewish community which followed the teachings of the Prophet Yeshua`; that God is One; that Yeshua` was a human prophet, not a god or a messiah; that Torah and Israelite custom is to be followed; and who most of all reject the Oral Law, and the authority of Paul of Tarsus. 'Ebionism' would therefore be a sect of 'Jewish-Christianity' – that is, 'Talmidaism'.

the beginning of a new faith, but rather a legitimate continuation of the God-given faith of Abraham, Moses, David and Solomon; furthermore, that his teachings remained loyal to the message and vision of all the biblical prophets. Most of all, I want to teach you the Way that leads us to experiencing the full, unhindered Presence of the Living God of Israel – as a real, this-world phenomenon, not merely an intellectual set of beliefs, or something that can only be experienced by singing in a loud frenzy. I want to show you how the faith of the prophet Yeshua`, and the faith of the ancient Israelites, was something far greater than you could ever have imagined. And I want to show you that it is something you too can rekindle today, whoever you are – Jew or Gentile – wherever you may be. Allow the fire of Yahveh[a] to live in your heart, and make of you a new being!

---

[a] The Talmidi community uses the Holy Name in private and congregational prayer. Our convention is that we do *not* use it in argument or anger, and that we do not use it in everyday conversation. Since we do not really know the exact pronunciation of the Name, we do not argue over its exact pronunciation – it could be Yahveh or Yehovah. Our advice is that you use whichever form is more meaningful, sacred and intimate for you.

Shmuel ben Naftali

Chapter One: An Overview of basic Israelite theology, with relevance to the history of the First Century C.E.

Introduction

For many newcomers to the subject, it will be a surprise to learn that there is a dichotomy between the Gentile 'Jesus' of faith, and the Jewish Yeshua` of history. In the academic community, it is well-known that the earliest Jewish followers of Yeshua` did not accept the authority or teachings of Paul of Tarsus (or 'St. Paul'). As a result, their beliefs were very different from what is now considered to be standard Christian theology: they did not accept the virgin birth, original sin,[a] the trinity,[b] or that Yeshua` died to save us from our sins.[c] We know these things, because of the diatribes the early Church Fathers wrote against the Jewish Followers of Yeshua`.

I spent a long while engaged in some serious soul-searching, debating at what point (and even *if*) to spend time explaining basic Israelite theology – the very environment and heritage that produced people like Yeshua` ('Jesus of Nazareth'), Yochanan the Immerser ('St. John the Baptist'), and Jacob the Pious ('St. James the Just'). In the end, I felt that it was not good enough for people to read these handbooks with preconceived ideas. Jews and Christians may often use the same vocabulary, but the individual words we use frequently have completely different meanings. If I were to present these handbooks with no theological background to the ideas I am expounding, I would not achieve my goal of telling you, my reader, about some very important – and pretty amazing – biblical concepts. In a sense, you first have to *unlearn* your preconceptions, before you can go on to learn about some new and wonderful things.

---

[a] The Israelite teaching in contrast, is that sin is not passed on from generation to generation – see Ezek ch 18

[b] Yeshua` prayed to God: Mk 1:35, Lk 6:12, 22:41 – if Yeshua` were God, why would God even need pray to himself to ask for things? Yeshua` did not have knowledge that only God possessed: Mt 24:36; and Yeshua` considered himself separate from God: Jn 20:17; Also, no one can see God: Ex 33:20. In the Israelite religion, 'the Holy Spirit' is a euphemism for 'the power and presence of Yahveh', not a separate person of a trinity.

[c] The biblical Israelite teaching, in contrast, is that no one can die for another person's sin (see Dt 24:16, Ezek 18:4, 20).

For too long we have only had one of two choices – either the trinitarian Christian view, or the Talmudic Rabbinic view of religious history; the original, biblical Yahwist[a] view never gets a look in. There are pitifully few champions of the Yahwist view of history – if any at all.[b] I came to the conclusion that, if we are to have any chance of understanding a fully *Jewish* Yeshua` in the context of all the biblical prophets who came before him, it would be essential to build up for you a Yahwist Israelite understanding of the Late Second Temple period[c] of Jewish history.

Doing so opens up the bigger picture. Most people with a traditional Christian background can only see Yeshua`; most people focus on that one life, as if nothing else of any relevance or importance was going on at the time – as if the world around him had no impact on the content of his words. He is portrayed in the *New Testament* as being totally disconnected from the historical and theological world in which he and his followers lived. If we are willing to give the Yahwist view of history a fair hearing, then such an undertaking will open the lens wider than merely focussing on Yeshua`. We will begin to see that his sayings were often a response to the actions and beliefs of other Jewish sects, as well as the difficulties and pressures of the times, and that he was very much a man of his era. We will ultimately realise that he was just a small part in what Yahveh our God was trying to achieve overall – a small but captivating brushstroke in the greater portrait of human history.

The well-trodden road I am not going to take

From the outset, I need to make it clear that I am not going to examine Yeshua`'s ministry through the lens of any beliefs that only arose *after* the Babylonian Exile,[d] during the Second Temple period. This means I am not going to look at his ministry in terms of Rabbinic messianism – the belief that Elijah would come to announce the messiah at the end of world, and that the Davidic messiah would come to save the Jewish people; I will not examine his ministry in terms of apocalypticism

---

[a] In these books, the term *Yahwist* and *Yahwism* refers to the earliest form of Israelite theology that holds Yahveh alone is God, Saviour and redeemer of Israel and humanity. Yahwist thinking raises and restores the standing of God's power, and diminishes the power of such things as messiahs, superstition and Satan. In Yahwist thought, Yahveh is the sole focus of faith.
[b] in this regard, I commend the Karaite Jewish community for having kept the biblical Yahwist flame alive.
[c] a period usually defined as from about 6 BCE until 70 CE.
[d] that is, after the return of the Jewish exiles from Babylonia after about 539 BCE.

THE WAY

– the belief that the world will soon come to a final end in one great cataclysm, that the dead would be raised from their graves, that God will only then judge the living and the dead, and that the chosen few will live in an eternal kingdom of peace on this earth. I'm not going to interpret Yeshua`'s ministry through any of these Second Temple period beliefs, because *none of that has happened*. If Yeshua` told us that 'there are some of you standing here today who will not taste death, until you see the coming of God's Kingdom with power',[a] then if these aforementioned events are what he was referring to, we can only conclude that he was a failed prophet.

Instead, I am going to take you on a road no one has taken before – at least, not since the days of James the Just and Yeshua`'s first Jewish Followers. I'm going to examine Yeshua`'s ministry in the light of pre-Babylonian Exile, pre-Rabbinic, Yahwist Israelite theology – that he was a prophet of the 'Day of Yahveh' – a coming period of tribulation,[b] when Judea would be ravaged and Jerusalem and the Temple destroyed; but it would be a tribulation that most of the innocent and righteous would survive, and that wrongdoers would also survive if they repented of their wrongdoings, and returned to the ways of God's Kingdom. If we apply pre-rabbinic, Yahwist Israelite theology to Yeshua`'s ministry, then Yeshua` was a successful prophet, *because all these things came to pass*.

In short, the message of the Gentile Christian 'Jesus Christ' was this: 'I am a divine messiah, who has come to die a bloody death in order to save those who believe in me from their sins, so that only my believers can be guaranteed to get into heaven'; in contrast, the message of the Jewish Yeshua` was this: 'God has called me as a prophet, to warn the Jewish people that a terrible calamity is about to befall the Galilee and Judea; but by returning to the ethics and values of the Israelite faith, the majority of the Jewish people will survive.'

Therefore, to prepare you for my next book, which teaches the Talmidi Israelite faith through the words of the '*Our Father*', I want to take you through the Yahwist Israelite theology that produced Yeshua` the Jew, and which provided the real, spiritual and temporal motivation for his community of Jewish Followers. Reading this first book will help you, my reader, understand many of the images and concepts I allude to in the rest of these books.

---

[a] Mk 9:1; cf S.Yesh. 170:2
[b] There have been 3 such 'Day of Yahveh' tribulations in ancient Jewish history: the Assyrian Exile (began 740 BCE, technically still ongoing because the northern tribes have still not returned); the Babylonian Exile (597-539 CE); and the Roman Exile (70 – 1948 CE). Apocalypticism views any cataclysm as final, but a 'Day of Yahveh' is something sporadic that most people would survive (see Mal 3:19-20 / Christian bibles – Mal 4:1-2)

In this first chapter, I will cover:

- the purpose of the Israelite religion – 'the Way of Yahveh'
- the 'Glory' of God
- God's holiness
- the fire of Yahveh
- the 'trembling of heaven and earth'
- misfortune and blamelessness
- the endurance of the righteous
- the 'great and terrible Day of Yahveh'
- repentance
- what a prophet is for
- the prophet like Elijah

The Way of Yahveh

Most Christians will be aware that the first Followers of Yeshua` called their faith, 'The Way'. Some will think that it means, 'the Way of Jesus' – that is, the teaching of Yeshua` of Nazareth. However, most will not be aware that the term, 'the Way' has enormous weight and significance when used in reference to the Israelite faith.

The *Book of Acts*[a] uses this term of 'The Way' when speaking of the faith practised by Yeshua`'s first Followers. To the Jewish people of their time, the term would have had important, historical connotations. Just as the term 'the Land' is used as shorthand for 'the Land of Israel', 'the Day' is shorthand for 'the Day of Atonement', or 'the Festival' is shorthand for 'the festival of Sukkot/Booths', so too 'the Way' was used as shorthand for 'the Way of the Lord'[b] – or more correctly, 'the Way of Yahveh'.

In those days, most learned Jews would have been aware that 'the Way of Yahveh' was the name of the original Israelite faith.[c] By using this term to describe their own faith, I believe Yeshua`'s first Jewish Followers were making a very profound statement – one that goes right over our heads today, without any impact. The name implied that Yeshua`'s ministry was not the creation of a new religion, or the giving of a new revelation, but a return to the first, God-given faith of their ancestors.[d]

---

[a] Acts 9:2, 18:25, 19:9, 19:23, 22:4, 24:14, 24:22
[b] cf Acts 18:25
[c] see Gen 18:19, Jdgs 2:22, 2Kgs 21:22, Jer 5:4-5, Prov 10:29
[d] hence the significance of his assertion that *'the old wine is good enough'* – see S.Yesh. 14:1-2; cf Mk 2:22, Lk 5:39

THE WAY

In their day, the rich were ignoring the ideals of the Israelite faith towards the poor, the Zealots committed violence in the name of religion, and the Pharisees often overruled God's decrees in Torah with their own, man-made decisions. By referring to their faith as 'the Way', Yeshua` and his Followers were calling their fellow Jews back to the high ideals and principles of the original Israelite religion. Any interpretation of Yeshua`'s ministry has to be seen in the light of this understanding.

The purpose of the Israelite religion

As a people, we Jews often emphasise **us** – what **we** have gone through, what **we** have endured, **our** heritage, **our** ancestors, and **our** faith. We insist that Judaism is all about the Jewish people. Our sages and rabbis say that without the Jewish people, there would be no Judaism. However, this introspective view is not the *raison d'être* of the Israelite religion.

Take a look at Isaiah 43:6b-7, where Yahveh says, *'Bring **My** sons from afar, and **My** daughters from the ends of the earth – everyone who is called by **My** Name, whom **I** created for **My** glory, whom **I** formed and made.'*

And in Isaiah 43:21, Yahveh explains, *'**I** created this people for **Me**, [so that] they will speak **My** praise.'*

Do you see how the Followers of Yahveh – those who are 'called by Yahveh's Name'[a] – were created for God's glory, not ours? We, the Jewish people, exist for the sake of Yahveh. We exist to act as an eternal[b] witness to the power and presence of Yahveh, to what our God has done, and to what our God has promised to do in the future. The Israelite religion therefore exists to serve Yahveh, and Yahveh's greater purpose.

Through the prophet Isaiah,[c] Yahveh says, *'You are **My** witnesses… and **My** servant whom **I** have chosen'*. And in 1Chr 16:24, and again in Ps 96:3 it says, *'Declare **God's** Glory among the nations, **God's** marvellous deeds among all peoples.'*

You see, without Yahveh, there is no Israelite religion. Without

---

[a] In the ancient world, you would describe your religious allegiance by saying that you were the son or daughter of a particular god. So an adherent of the Israelite religion was called a *ben Yahveh* – literally, 'a son of Yahveh' (or in the case of a woman, *bat Yahveh* – a 'daughter of Yahveh').
[b] The Israelite faith was meant to exist forever. If God could ensure that the Israelite religion survived in spite of insurmountable odds, it was meant to act as proof that Yahveh is a real, living God. If Yahveh is a living God, then no human effort will cause the Israelite religion to become extinct, no matter how severe the persecution.
[c] Isa 43:10a

Yahveh, there would be no Jewish people.

In short, the primary purpose of the Israelite religion – or 'the Way of Yahveh' – is to act as an eternal witness to the holiness, the power and the presence of Yahveh, as well as Yahveh's values and ethics. The Israelite faith is not about *us*; it's about *Yahveh*; following the Israelite faith is therefore about learning to know Yahveh.[a] Let this perspective dictate the practice of your faith. Everything you do in the context of faith has to be for Yahveh. When you interact with other people, you always have to ask yourselves, 'How will what I do or say reflect on the good reputation of the God whom I serve?' When you are faced with a difficult situation, ask yourselves, 'What would Yahveh – who loves and cares about all His children – wish me to do?'

As Followers of the Way of Yahveh, we are ambassadors to the nations. As Yahveh declares in Isaiah 49:6, *'I will make you a light for the Nations, that you may bring **My** salvation to the ends of the earth.'*

Consider this: Yahveh has no physical form,[b] is invisible and cannot be touched. If people cannot see, feel or hear God, God needs to have something of Himself that people *can* see. That would be a way of life that reflects God's personality, God's values, God's principles and God's ethics. And that way of life had to be very distinctive, so that people would sit up and take notice.

So our way of life is not there to make the nations of the world look at *us*, but rather to catch their attention, so that we can redirect them to look to Yahveh our God – to our God's noble values and just principles, in the hope that they will take on board such life- and society-changing values. We were chosen, not because we were special, or because of any innate qualities we ourselves had, but because God wanted us to act as an eternal witness to God. We were chosen for a job – that is what 'chosen' refers to, being chosen for a particular mission – to bear witness to a powerful, incredible and amazing God. Let's take a look now at the power of that God.

The Glory of Yahveh

What now follows is an explanation of the central focus of the original Israelite faith. You may wonder why I have placed such a complex topic here, right at the beginning of my story. My reasoning is that, without an awareness and understanding of this central nexus of Yahwist faith, nothing I might say after this point in the book will make any sense. The extraordinary pinnacle of Israelite theology – that from

---

[a] cf Jer 31:34, 1Chron 22:19; in Yahwism, Yahveh is a knowable God.
[b] Dt 4:12-15

which all other beliefs and teachings are derived – will make little sense otherwise.

The prophet Habakkuk[a] tells us that one day, *'the earth will be full of the knowledge of the Glory of Yahveh, just as the waters cover the sea.'* In addition, the Book of Numbers[b] implies that the invisible Glory of Yahveh *already* covers the whole earth. The difference between the verses in Habakkuk and the Book of Numbers, is the word 'knowledge'. In other words, before that prophetic time of peace, security and universal co-existence in the future, every human being will come to know and understand what the Glory of God *means*.

The Hebrew word *kavodh* can mean 'glory' in the conventional English sense – that of the magnificence, splendour and majesty of Yahveh. Occasionally it can also mean 'awesome reputation'.[c] But the Hebrew Bible most often[d] uses the word in quite a different and unique way. If you only know the normal English meaning of 'glory' (that of 'magnificence' or 'splendour'), then you will miss the entire point of those biblical passages in which the word occurs. You will read them, and some really mind-blowing stuff will escape your attention.

In some passages[e] it is obvious that 'the Glory' can, in special circumstances, become a visible phenomenon that can be seen from afar with the human eye. On rare occasions it is something that 'appears', and is able to fill holy places. In Ex 24:17, we are even told that 'the Glory' looks like an all-consuming, fiery radiance. Later, when Moses first has a personal encounter with this fiery radiance, God tells him that no one can see it close up and live.[f] This would imply that this radiance is *so powerful* in nature, that it would kill ordinary mortals.[g] For the most part

---

[a] see Habakkuk 2:14; cf Isaiah 11:9
[b] Num 14:21
[c] the root *k-b-d* is used in this way in Ex 14:4
[d] In the Torah alone, out of 24 occurrences of the word 'glory', only 6 of them refer to 'awesome reputation', 'splendour' or greatness'. The majority – the remaining 18 – refer to 'glory' as the phenomenon of the fire of God's 'divine radiance' e.g. Ex 24:17, 33:22, 40:34, Lev 9:6, 14:10, and so on.
[e] e.g. Ex 16:7-10, 24:16-17, Num 16:42.
[f] Exodus chapter 33. God tells Moses that *'No one can see My face and live'*. I have a theory about what the phenomenon Moses saw might have been: I think a doorway or interface opened up into heaven, and the brilliant light from heaven shone through; this would have been the 'face' or front of the doorway. To Moses, this interface would have appeared like a small but brilliant sun. However, as it passed by, it would have become evident that this sun was flat; once it had passed, one would have been able to see its 'back', which would have appeared like a ring of light, with the sky visible inside and outside of this ring; this 'back' would have been something Moses could see and live.
[g] e.g. Ex 33:5, where God says that his actual 'Glory' cannot accompany the Israelites, because if it did, the Israelites would be destroyed.

however, the 'Glory' is completely invisible to us.

Knowledge of God's Glory is not just for the future time of universal peace; understanding the Glory – the *kavodh* – of Yahveh, is central to understanding the underlying reasoning of ancient Israelite religious ritual and spiritual belief, and how our human souls can actually derive benefit and blessing from the living presence of Yahveh, here and now. What we learn in Exodus chapter 33, is that the full power of Yahveh's *Shekhinah*[a] cannot openly move about with human beings, because Yahveh's *kavodh* is far too powerful and dangerous.[b] Moses is told how Yahveh's Glory cannot go with them, because if it did, the Israelites would be destroyed.[c] In complete contrast to pagan gods, whose followers claimed could incarnate in human or animal form at whim, these warnings were meant to impress upon us that Yahveh, the God of Israel and of all Nations, has an Essence so incredibly powerful, that no physical, earthly body can possibly contain Yahveh.

A pivotal episode in the *Miqra*[d] which helps us understand this power, is the one where David has the Ark of the Covenant brought up to Jerusalem.[e] In this story, we are told that the oxen pulling the cart stumble, and the Ark almost falls off. Uzzah the Levite touches the Ark to steady it, and he dies instantly. David is so terrified by this event, that he abandons the Ark at the house of a Philistine, Obed-Edom.

Now, the biblical writers of both *Samuel* and *Chronicles* interpreted this act as God being angry, but that is only how human beings would see the incredible event and interpret it. You could almost replace the word 'anger' with 'the burning fire of God's Divine Radiance' – as in, "Then the *burning fire of Yahveh's Divine Radiance* was kindled, and it struck Uzzah because he had put his hand out to steady the Ark, and he died because of God's Presence."[f]

Whenever the Ark was being transported, normally no one could see it, because it was always covered by three sets of coverings.[g] So when Uzzah touched the Ark, what actually happened was that a doorway to the powerful Presence of God opened up in-between the covered cherubim on the Ark;[h] so when Uzzah touched the Ark, it was far too

---

[a] that is, God's In-dwelling Presence.
[b] Ex 33:20
[c] Ex 33:3-5
[d] pronounced mick-RAA – that is, the Hebrew Bible, or what Christians call, 'the Old Testament'.
[e] 2Sam ch 6, 1Chron ch 13
[f] a rewording of 1Chr 13:10
[g] Num 4:5-6; paintings showing an *uncovered* Ark being carried from place to place are therefore not historically accurate.
[h] cf Ex 25:22, where the visible Glory appears above the ark between the cherubim.

powerful for any mortal human to endure, and he sadly died. Uzzah's death was not a deliberate act or punishment of God, but an accidental result of a mortal man touching God's Divine Radiance. It would be like someone putting their hand into a nuclear furnace and touching the uranium rods; death inevitably ensues, but that doesn't mean that the furnace is angry, just incredibly powerful. In the same way, God was not 'angry' at Uzzah; the poor Levite unfortunately touched something that was dangerous and fatal for mortals to touch.

The 'Glory' or 'Divine Radiance' is an aspect of God's power. It is an intrinsic part of the very nature of Yahveh. It would not normally be visible. However, God's full presence has a powerful effect on the fabric of our own universe. If God were ever to break through from heaven into our world at full strength, the effect of God's full-blown Presence on our realm would cause a brilliant, fiery light to be produced.[a] That radiant light is not God Himself, but one of the physical effects on our world of Yahveh's Glory – the light that exists everywhere in heaven.

If the Glory of Yahveh – or rather, the 'Divine Radiance' – already fills the whole earth, then as I said earlier, it is invisible. It is an unseen force that, when properly approached, brings blessing, not destruction. David realised this when, instead of misfortune, the presence of the Ark in the Philistine's house brought blessing to Obed-Edom.[b] This realisation of the power of God, prompted David to bring up the Ark with great joy into the city of Jerusalem.

In my second book, I will explain the purpose of the Tabernacle and the Temple more fully, but basically, the Sanctuary forms a protective barrier, allowing the Glory of Yahveh to enter this world at full strength, and remain among us without harming anyone. The holiness of the Temple therefore had to be maintained, *so that* the Glory of Yahveh could enter our world, to bless and protect Israel, and thereby the whole of humanity.

The Glory of God's Divine Radiance is like a fire that cleanses us.[c] The altar of burnt-offering symbolised the fire of God's Glory, and the blood[d] dashed against it represented the human soul approaching God's Glory for purification from sin. In the Israelite religion therefore, *it is the*

---

[a] see Ex 16:7, 16:10, 24:16-17; also cf Isaiah 4:5
[b] the presence of the Ark brought blessing to the Gittite called Obed-Edom after David left it at his house (2Sam 6:10-11). David finally understood the power of Yahveh, and so continued with the Ark's journey to Jerusalem.
[c] Zech 13:9, Mal 3:3 – the life-changing thing to realise, is that the purifying power of God's fire is not metaphorical but real and actual.
[d] As the blood is the life-force of the body, so the *néfesh* is the 'life-force' of the soul (cf Dt 12:23). The blood of the sacrifice symbolises the soul of the offerer approaching the Glory of God to be cleansed and made whole.

fire of God's Glory that cleanses the human soul of sin, not blood. This is the crucial and central understanding of the Israelite faith that has been lost. Today, we read about the rituals in Torah, but we don't understand the symbolism behind the rituals. This understanding – the 'knowledge of God's Glory' of which Habakkuk spoke – will change your life, and enable you to experience the living Presence of Yahveh every day!

When we repent of our wrongdoings, in prayer we bring our souls before the living radiance of God's Glory, to be cleansed and wiped clean of our sins. Even without a Temple, this still happens – a belief that the wise King Solomon understood when he dedicated the First Temple:

> *"When they sin against you .... and their captors carry them off to a country be it far away or near .... if they come to their senses in that country ... saying, 'We have sinned ....' and turn back to you with all their heart and soul ... then listen to their prayer from heaven .... and **forgive your people**."*[a]

Solomon understood that blood sacrifices were not required for the forgiveness of sin, as did the Prophets.[b] It is by the loving mercy of Yahveh that we are forgiven, and it is by the fire of God's Glory that our souls are cleansed and made whole.

The holiness of God

When an English-speaker mentions the word 'holiness', we immediately think of goodness, sinlessness, kindness, piety and compassion. However, although these are indeed innate qualities of a holy God, this is not the primary meaning of 'holiness' in the Israelite tradition.

Even in Pharisaic and Rabbinic thought, holiness is merely 'apartness' and 'separateness'. But even this doesn't come close to the profound and life-altering original meaning of the word. If you want to feel the full impact of this word on ancient Hebrew thought, you have to go beyond the Christian meaning, and even beyond the Rabbinic meaning of the word, and understand it instead from a completely Yahwist Israelite perspective.

There are four basic meanings of the Hebrew word $q^e dushah$ – holiness. The first is shown by the example of how a man is holy to his

---

[a] extracts from 2Chr 6:36-39
[b] see Jer 36:3, Isa 55:7, Hos 14:2-3. In the Book of Jonah, the people of Nineveh were forgiven by God without the need for animal sacrifices, and in 2Sam 12:13, God forgave David his sin without sacrifice.

wife, and vice versa. This means that in marriage, husband and wife have given themselves *exclusively* to each other – that's what marriage is. Holiness in this sense means 'mono-loyalty', whereby allegiance, faithfulness and duty is only to one person. Holiness of a person or people to Yahveh implies this exclusive allegiance and loyalty. If I declare that I am 'holy to Yahveh', it means that I worship *only* Yahveh, and follow only Yahveh's ways.

The second meaning of holiness is 'exclusive use', and applies mostly to things and places. For example, there are certain ritual objects that were intended only for use within the Tabernacle or the Temple. They belonged to God, and were only to be used in a religious context. There was a profound psychological purpose to this, in that positive cognitive association with certain objects reminds us of the special and powerful nature of God.

Also, one of the implications of saying that Yahveh's Name is 'holy' – apart from the implied power of the Name – is that the Name can *only* be used by Yahveh, applied *only* to Yahveh, and *to no other being, person or entity*. When you become aware of this side of holiness, you realise that to say 'Jesus is Yahveh' is a tautology; giving the Holy Name to another person or being means it is no longer 'holy'. Most non-Jews are not aware of this aspect of the meaning of holiness. When Yahveh says, *"I, and I alone, am Yahveh"*,[a] God is referring to this aspect of the holiness of God's exclusive Name; only Yahveh can be called Yahveh – no one and nothing else can share that name.

The third aspect of holiness is 'distinctiveness'. Our way of life is to be holy. It has to be culturally and ethically distinctive. Culturally distinctive on the one hand, so that it would be representative of an otherwise invisible God; and ethically distinctive on the other, so that such a way of life would enable the in-dwelling Presence of Yahveh to live among us without harming us. And this leads us onto the fourth, most important meaning of holiness – the one which all the other meanings are subordinate to and dependent on.

I would venture to guess that to most of us – even to those of us who firmly believe in God – that God remains a purely theological concept, whose existence can only be taken as a matter of faith. However, there is one group of people for whom God becomes very real – prophets.

For prophets, God is not just a voice one hears in one's head. God is an extremely powerful force that seizes hold of their very lives. Yahveh is a living, sentient Being who is so overwhelming in nature, that these men and women shudder in trembling awe at what they experience,

---

[a] Isaiah 43:11

and are never the same ever again. For example, Isaiah feared for his life[a] when he had his visions from God; thereafter, the driving force behind his message was the tremendously powerful, unassailable, incorruptible and unconquerable holiness of Yahveh. So to understand holiness in the ancient Israelite way of thinking, you have to come to terms with the awesomely powerful nature of the God of Israel.

Yahveh's holiness is inextricably linked to God's physical unapproachableness, because of the incredible power of the 'Divine Radiance' (or 'Glory'). Now, I want to affirm here that the God of Israel is *absolutely* spiritually approachable – our God is closer to us than our own breathing. But if we were to experience God the same way that, for example, the *serafim* in heaven experience God – the fiery angels that dwell in the immediate presence of God – then we would all be burnt to a crisp!

Now, some people will have difficulty believing any of this, even though the story of the Israelites' wandering in the Sinai desert,[b] and the experiences of the prophets mention the awesome power of God's holiness at every turn. So to you I say: my friends, you already believe in a God you cannot see or touch. Is it easier for you to believe in a God who has no effect on you *at all*? One that you can define on your own terms, one that you can control – a safe God you can turn on and off whenever you wish? Is it so uncomfortable to believe in a strong, mighty and awesomely powerful God? One who is distinctive in personality and nature? And One whose power and majesty cannot be equalled or exceeded by anyone or anything?

When Moses went up Mount Horeb the second time,[c] what he experienced there was an opening between heaven and earth – a kind of doorway. This doorway allowed him to see through to heaven, and to the light of God's Glory that suffuses all things there. What he saw was the 'face' (or 'front') and 'back' of this opening.[d] God would have been able to open this doorway anywhere, at any time.

Now, Moses had asked God to travel with his people,[e] but God warned Moses that if God were to travel with the Israelites, they would

---

[a] Isaiah 6:5
[b] e.g. in the story of the Qorach rebellion (especially Num 16:46-50), Aaron desperately rushes about to try and close the doorway to God's Glory, which is causing something like a plague amongst the people.
[c] Ex 34:4-7
[d] this opening would have appeared like a flat circle of light. The front would look like a brilliant circle of light, and the back would look like a ring of light, inside which and around which the sky was visible (which is why Moses could look at the back, but not the front of this opening) – see also (c) on page 6.
[e] Ex 33:16

be destroyed by the raw power of God's Glory.[a] If God's Glory opened up right amongst the Israelites, they would have all been incinerated by it. So the Tabernacle[b] was built, to allow a doorway to God's Glory in heaven to open up above the Ark,[c] anywhere the Israelites went. Such a Tabernacle would also protect the Israelites from the harmful effects of God's Glory. That was the main purpose of the tent of the Tabernacle (and later of the Temple) – to protect the Israelites from the harmful effects of God's Glory, but also to allow its positive effects to filter through and bless them; its place as a focus of worship, and as a symbol of God's Presence among God's people, was secondary.

Now I have shown you something of the physical unapproachableness of God – that we cannot encounter Yahveh's Glory without endangering our physical bodies – I want to tell you about a secondary aspect of holiness: moral purity, or how Yahveh is incorruptible, and incapable of sin or wrong. When prophets such as Malachi speak against injustice, oppression and corruption, their speech is full of metaphors about God's justice being like a consuming fire – that it would consume the wicked, but purify the good. Wickedness and injustice cannot stand before God, because the fire of God's holiness will utterly destroy it.[d]

In Yahwist theology, it wasn't the blood of sacrifices that brought about a cleansing of the soul from sin, because if an unrepentant person offered a sacrificial sin-offering, then *there was no forgiveness or atonement.*[e] The primary purpose of the sin-offering was symbolic – to show what would happen to our physical bodies if we were to approach God's Glory;[f] the fire of the altar in the Temple was therefore a physical metaphor for God's Glory in heaven.

Although our bodies cannot approach God physically, repentance

---

[a] Ex 33:3, 5
[b] The great tent that stood in the middle of the camp of the Israelites wherever they went in the Sinai desert.
[c] Ex 25:22
[d] e.g. Habakkuk 1:13
[e] hence Yeshua''s parable about making up with one's brother before making a sin-offering, S.Yesh 125; cf Mt 5:23-24.
[f] The secondary purpose of the sin-offering was to show how God's Glory removed the stain of sin and the burden of guilt, and so purified the soul to restore the wholeness of one's being (all of which is what atonement means). It was believed that when you sinned, or when you became ill, your being or life-essence (*néfesh*) was diminished. The blood of the sacrifice was supposed to symbolise the approach of the soul to God's Glory, and the restoration of the soul thereby to wholeness. However, in practical terms, the ideal way to restore the wholeness of one's being was to apologise or make reparation to the one whom you wronged. If this is not possible, alternatively one can do good or charitable works.

does allow a soul to approach God spiritually. It is the purity and power of God's Glory *alone*, and not blood, which cleanses us of our sin. That is the primary effect of God's holiness – a divine, moral purity that is able to obliterate wickedness and injustice, and cleanse us of the stain and injury of sin. At Yom Kippur, with sincere prayer we bring our souls into the Presence of God's fiery Glory, and it is that fiery Glory which cleanses us of our sin – even today, without the sacrifices of the Temple.

So this is what we have learned so far: that God's holiness is inextricably linked to God's physical unapproachableness – that our bodies cannot physically approach God's Glory. The second is the fact that we can approach God *spiritually*, and that a repentant soul can thus be cleansed by the fire of God's Glory.

There is a line in the Psalms that says, *'Cleanse me with hyssop, and I shall be clean; but wash me* [that is, in Your Glory], *and I shall become whiter than snow.'*[a]

Whenever Moses went into the Tabernacle to speak with God directly,[b] and whenever he thereby encountered the effect of God's Glory, the Miqra[c] tells us that when he came out again, his face was radiant. This implies that whenever Moses entered into the presence of Yahveh, he was temporarily cleansed of the spiritual stain of all his wrongdoings. As a result, his own human soul glowed within him. The psalmist understood this when he told us how washing with natural soap would make us clean, but being cleansed by the Glory of God will make our souls whiter than snow.[d]

Once you let the implications of this sink in, you realise that it is not the blood of sacrifices that cleanses us of sin, nor the death of a godman, **but the very holiness of Yahveh itself**. Saying that Yahveh is holy, in and of itself implies that Yahveh – by God's very nature – is able to cleanse us and free us of sin; to counter-claim that it *can't* (as Paullist theology teaches), implies that the God one believes in is weak, and not all-powerful. The Israelite faith teaches that we are purified and restored to spiritual health by the simple fact of God's holiness, once we have

---

[a] Ps 51:7

[b] Ex 34:29-35

[c] This is the oldest short appellation for the Hebrew Bible; a longer ancient term was 'the Torah and the Prophets', to which was later added, 'and the other writings' (see the Book of ben Sirach 1:1). In the rabbinic era this became, 'the Torah, the Prophets and the Writings'. In accordance with standard rabbinic practice, this was given an abbreviation in the Talmud, the T.N.K. This rabbinic abbreviation for the Hebrew Bible eventually became a word, Tanakh. This is how the Hebrew Bible is referred to in the Rabbinic Jewish community.

[d] Ps 51:7

repented. It is the fire of God's Glory – the very holiness of Yahveh – that cleanses and purifies us of sin; not blood, and not the death of 'Jesus'.

When we live a holy way of life, the in-dwelling Presence of Yahveh can dwell amongst us without harming us. The ongoing effect of God's holiness in the midst of such a community is to guide it, strengthen it, sustain it and make it secure and safe. The purpose of a holy way of life, is to enable the cleansing and protective Glory of Yahveh to come through from heaven to earth, and thereby enable God's Presence to dwell among us; ***that*** is the central focus and understanding of the Israelite religion.

The follow-on teaching from this, is that when we reject an ethical (and therefore, holy) way of life, God's Presence can no longer remain among us without doing us harm. A holy people is protected, but a people that allows injustice, corruption, cruelty and oppression in its midst will be harmed and disrupted by the raw power of a holy God.

The effects in this world of the 'fire' of Yahveh

In the preceding section, I explained about the Glory or 'Divine Radiance' of Yahveh which cleanses our souls, and how before the holiness of Yahveh, evil, wickedness and sin cannot endure. Before the awesome and powerful Glory of Yahveh, they are wiped out and obliterated. Nothing evil can possibly harm God or even come close to God; the mere power of God's Presence will wipe it out. God's goodness and Glory are unassailable. This is why in Israelite theology, it is simply not possible to have disobedient or 'fallen' angels, or to have wars or conflicts in heaven; heaven is eternal and unbreachable peace, precisely *because* of the holiness of God.

Now, the Miqra often speaks of a metaphorical 'fire' or 'flame' that punishes the wicked.[a] Most Christians naturally think that this fire refers to hell,[b] but the fire is actually from God – or at least, from the all-consuming *effect* of God's Glory. In the Miqra, the power of God is often described as an all-consuming flame.[c] This fire is God's Glory, before which evil, sin and wrongdoing cannot stand. This fire is described as a

---

[a] Num 11:1, Dt 32:22, Ps 21:9, Isa 30:27-30, 66:15, Nah 1:6, Zeph 3:8
[b] The Israelite religion has no belief in hell. There was a belief in a place called Azza Zeil or 'the Outer Darkness' (or 'Sheol'), a cold unpleasant place where, according to ancient Talmidi belief, the deceased soul works through their unrepented sins before being cleansed to enter heaven.
[c] Deut 4:24

flame that sweeps across the land in judgment.[a] The Prophet Micah[b] saw a vision of God melting mountains like wax – an allegorical allusion to this unstoppable fire of God.

As I have already said, the Glory of God is an intrinsic part of the nature of God. When it touches our realm at full force, it produces a brilliant, fiery light. This light is especially visible in heaven. On earth, if we were to step into this light with our physical bodies, we would be consumed – destroyed. Only our penitent souls can withstand this fiery Glory. As I have said, this is what the metaphor of animal sacrifice was supposed to symbolise and bring home to us.[c]

Our God is so powerful, that it is by the power of God's love that God forgives, and it is by the power of God's Glory that God purifies the penitent soul of wrongdoing. The pagan gods of the ancient Middle East could only forgive through death and blood sacrifice, but Yahveh purifies us by the fiery power of God's Glory.

This Glory – this fire – is so powerful, that as it moves through the world, it consumes everything, both good and bad. God's invisible Glory is like an all-consuming fire that rages across the face of the earth.

The prophet Malachi[d] describes the effect of God's fire on both bad and good people:

> "Surely the day is coming; it will burn like a furnace. All the arrogant and every evildoer will become stubble, and the day that is coming will set them on fire, says Yahveh of the heavenly battalions. Not a root or a branch will be left to them.
> **But for you who revere My name, the sun of righteousness will rise with healing in its wings. And you will go out and leap like calves released from the stall."**

Basically, what this verse implies is that because the fire of God's Presence is so very powerful, when God rights wrongs and enacts God's divine justice, *everyone* will be affected by this divine fire. However, the effect on bad and good people will be totally different. The effect of

---

[a] Ps 50:3-4
[b] Micah 1:4
[c] According to ancient Talmidi belief (see *Ascents of James*, ch 37), God merely tolerated animal sacrifice. During the wanderings in Sinai, it became obvious that if God were to ban animal sacrifice altogether, the Israelites would simply have gone off and worshipped other gods that did allow sacrifice. So blood sacrifice was permitted, but only on Yahveh's terms. It could only be made to Yahveh, and offered in such a way that its symbolism would make people see how forgiveness really worked.
[d] Mal 3:19-20 (Christian bibles – Mal 4:1-2)

God's Glory on bad people will be to discipline and chastise them, *even in this life*. However, once the judgment-event is over, the effect on good people will have been to purify and cleanse them, just as a smelter's fire purifies precious metals.[a] The soul of a person who strives to be good is forever precious to God, like gold or silver.

The trembling of heaven and earth

Let's now look at what the justice-dealing Glory of God will feel like to us, living in this earthly realm. As I have previously mentioned, the root of our understanding of the way that God works is contained in the story of the Exodus, and of the wandering of the Israelites in the Sinai desert. For example, when God's Presence came to rest on Mount Horeb, it says that *'the whole mountain trembled violently'*.[b] What this is meant to suggest to us, is that when God's Presence moves amongst humanity, metaphorically the earth and the sky shake, quake and tremble – that is, the very fabric of the Universe is shaken. The prophet Isaiah[c] describes God's movement to judge wrongdoers as *'rising to shake the earth'*. Whenever God judges humanity – even in this life – the prophet Haggai says that God *'will once more shake the heavens and the earth, the sea and the dry land.'*[d]

The Book of Samuel[e] says, *'The earth trembled and quaked, the foundations of the heavens shook; they trembled because [God] was incensed.'* These biblical verses are not merely poetic license; there was a belief in the ancient Israelite way of thinking that, whenever God's righteous anger was aroused to punish widespread injustice and wrongdoing, the very fabric of the universe shook – through the prophet Isaiah,[f] Yahveh says, *'Therefore I will make the heavens tremble; and the earth will shake from its place at the righteous anger of Yahveh of the heavenly battalions, in the day of God's burning anger'*. This movement of God's Presence had ramifications for ordinary people too, both good and bad. The prophet Nahum[g] says, *'The earth trembles at God's Presence – the world and **all** who live in it.'* In other words, *all* people – both good and bad – would be affected by God's movement to right wrongs in the world.

---

[a] See Mal 3:3 – *'He will act as a smelter and purifier of silver; he shall purify the Levites and refine them like gold and silver.'*
[b] Ex 19:18
[c] Isa 2:19-21
[d] Hg 2:6
[e] 2Sam 22:8
[f] Isa 13:13
[g] Nah 1:5

So whenever scripture says that when God moves to judge, how the earth, the sky and the sea shake, tremble or quake, most of the time it's not talking about geological earthquakes and tsunamis! Instead, this is the ancient Israelite way of saying that God's movement *shakes the very fabric of the Universe*. The result of this shaking, this *ra'ash ha-shamayim*,[a] is that **the misfortunes and trials of life increase**; both good and bad people appear to suffer for no apparent reason.

This would also explain why God seems to be so reticent to act, and delays acting *even when people beg God to act*. Just think a moment about the immense power of God, which I have likened to a nuclear furnace. Now, God has an immense and epic love for all of us, because we are all God's precious sons and daughters. It pains God deeply to hurt us – for God is fully aware of His own incredible power, and God knows how that power has the potential not only to bless us, but also to do us great harm. Rather than hurt us when wickedness, injustice and oppression increases, God at first withdraws God's Glory and God's Presence. God is hesitant to act and appears to do nothing, not because God is not powerful enough, but because God is just *too* powerful.

On the other hand, God does not want us to go unchecked and end up destroying ourselves, because God has some amazing and wonderful plans for the human race. So God sends us prophets to warn us, to urge us to change, so that God doesn't need to come and sort things out Himself. God would rather we sort things out for ourselves, since Yahveh doesn't want to do us harm – as God told us through the prophet Ezekiel, *"I do not get any pleasure out of the death of anyone"*,[b] not even of those who do evil.[c]

However, there comes a point at which God has no alternative but to intervene and act. In Israelite thought, when the Glory and Presence of Yahveh come upon us, it is considered *so* powerful, that it is thought of as having a purifying effect on anything and anyone it touches. Evil and sin cannot stand or endure against God's Glory. Through the power of God's Presence and Glory alone, God would punish the guilty but purify the righteous, even in this life. As God starts to act, the very fabric of the universe shakes and trembles. This 'trembling' is experienced by *everyone* as misfortune, upheaval and tribulation.

Good people would also experience this movement of God's Presence. They too would begin experiencing misfortune – an unintended consequence of God's movement to act against injustice. In

---

[a] literally, 'quaking of heaven'
[b] Ezek 18:32
[c] Ezek 18:23 – *"Do I take any pleasure in the death of wicked people? declares Sovereign Yahveh. Would I not rather that they turn from their wicked ways and live!"*

Ezek 38:20[a] it says, *'The fish of the sea, the birds of the air, the beasts of the field, every creature that moves along the ground, and **all the people on the face of the earth** will tremble at My Presence.'* But if good people endured through the hard times, they would be purified by everything that happened to them,[b] because to the ancient Hebrew mind, both blessing and misfortune were from Yahveh.

The oldest portions of the Book of Job were written in the period of the Patriarchs. Hebrew culture had not yet experienced the 'shaking' – the spiritual earthquake – caused by God's Presence at Horeb. Hebrew culture *used* to think that the trembling of heaven and earth – that which led to the misfortune of the righteous – was caused by the unpredictable movement of wild, non-existent mythological beasts,[c] such as the Behemoth,[d] the Leviathan[e] and the Zeez,[f] collectively called *eeyim*.[g] In the ancient way of thinking, they were supposedly all creations of God, and human beings could not defeat these supernatural creatures – only God, who alone created them.

Another 'incarnation' of the mythological Leviathan was Rachav[h] ('Rahab' in English). In the ancient myths it was specifically a 'sea-demon' – a giant fish which caused tumult and chaos, noise and disturbance. Again, it was a non-existent, mythological creature invented to explain what later became known in Yahwist thought as 'the trembling of heaven and earth' – in Hebrew, *ra'ash ha-shamayim*.

---

[a] In the preceding verse it mentions an earthquake. I don't think the Hebrew רעש *ra'ash* refers to a literal earthquake here, but a 'trembling' – a shaking in the fabric of the universe caused by the movement of God's presence to act in the cause of justice and righteousness. Similarly, we should re-evaluate other passages and decide if the Hebrew word means 'earthquake' or 'trembling' (of heaven and earth).

[b] *'Allow endurance to complete its work so that you may be perfect and whole, wanting for nothing.'* Ig. Yq. 2:3 – cf Ep. James 1:4

[c] or *eeyim* in Hebrew.

[d] Job 40:15-20; the behemoth was supposedly like a giant ox, and was the mythological wild beast of the land.

[e] Job 40:21-41:3, 41:22-24 (Christian bibles – 40:21-41:11, & 41:30-32; the leviathan was portrayed variously as a giant fish, hydra or crocodile (in Job it's a crocodile), and was the mythological wild beast of the seas and rivers.

[f] probably Job 41:4-21, 25-26 in its original form (Christian bibles – 41:12-29, 33-34); the ziz or simurg was like a giant griffon, with the head and wings of an eagle, and the body of a lion. It had scales and breathed fire and smoke. It was the mythological wild beast of the air.

[g] This word came to mean 'howling creatures', such as jackals or hyenas. But in Isa 34:14, *tsiyim*, *se'irim* and *iyim* all refer to supernatural, mythological creatures. The serpent in the garden of Eden is therefore not the devil, but one of these *iyim* – a supernatureal creature of disorder.

[h] Psalm 89:9-10

Now here we should bear in mind, that the Hebrew Bible contains a record of Hebrew theology at all stages of its evolution, including things we now know which are not true. We of course know now, that there are no such things as behemoths, zeezes or leviathans; they were all mythological inventions, designed to help the ancient Hebrews understand this *ra'ash ha-shamayim* – this trembling of the fabric of the universe when God acts to punish wrongdoing. The Ebionite[a] portions of the *Book of Revelation*[b] use these mythological devices to explain the suffering of the righteous, and they are an obvious poetic nod to the Book of Job.

In short, wrongdoers are chastised by the active fire of God's Glory, but good people are *purified* by God's fire. Misfortune and the trials of life are for different reasons, according to whether one has done good or bad things. If one has done good things, then you should not see the trials of life as any kind of punishment. You are blameless, and you can hold your head high, knowing that God is moving to right wrongs.

Misfortune and blamelessness

Whenever good people experience troubles and woes, we are always tempted to think that we are being punished for something, even though we cannot imagine what we could possibly have done wrong. That is only natural; we are human, and we tend to look for a reason in everything that happens to us.

When God judges wrongdoers – the unjust, the cruel, the oppressive, the selfish and the ruthless – in any given nation, unfortunately the whole nation suffers. This is **not** collective punishment; it is simply that the closest people to God suffer misfortune first, because they are closest to the epicentre of the 'earthquake'. God is so powerful, that when God moves against wrongdoers, good people get caught up in the tidal wave too. One must remain strong and endure at these times, because God is intervening in human history; good people are purified by God's Presence at those crucial times of life's trials.

There is a concept in ancient Hebrew thought referred to as 'blamelessness'. God commands us to be blameless,[c] and we are told that Job, before he began experiencing all his woes, was 'blameless'.[d]

What blamelessness means, is that if you as a good person

---

[a] a major ancient Talmidi (=Jewish-Christian) sect.
[b] particularly Revelation chapters 12-13; the beast of Rev 13:1-10 is the leviathan, the red dragon of Rev 12 is the ziz (pronounced *zeez*), and the beast in Rev 13:11-18 that comes up out of the ground is the behemoth.
[c] Deut 18:13
[d] Job 1:1

experience misfortune, you have the knowledge and assurance that what is happening to you is not because of any wrong you have done. Knowing that you have done your best, and that you have tried to live a good, decent and honest life, you can walk graciously and with dignity through the trials of life, because you know that you are not being punished for anything. You are blameless, and it will give you the strength to endure and overcome your misfortune.

God is aware that God's power causes suffering to the righteous. Ps 75:2-3 says, *'I choose the appointed time; it is I who judge uprightly. When the earth and all its people tremble, it is I who hold its pillars firm.'* Although both the righteous and the unrighteous suffer misfortune when God acts, God holds the fabric of the universe firm, and does not allow the suffering of good people to be in vain. God compensates good people for the suffering we endure from God's Glory, by enabling us to learn great and profound things when we experience hardship and strife – that is God's great reward to us *in this life* for what we have gone through! The wisdom and knowledge God gives us in times of trouble, is compensation for the unintentional hardship that good people experience when God moves against injustice and wrongdoing.

The endurance of the righteous

In times of trouble, it is important for good people to remain good, to enable the holiness of God's Glory to complete its work. Good people have to remain good in spite of what happens to us, and not give up in the face of trial and tribulation. To hasten the purifying work of this fire, we have to encourage others by our example to join the ranks of those who stand for justice, compassion and righteousness.[a] If the righteous lose faith in goodness itself, and instead turn to bitterness and despair, then the ranks of those who work for righteousness are not increased. The fire of Yahveh's purifying Glory cannot complete its work, and the suffering of good, decent people will have been for nothing. However, if we remain good people, and endure the trials and tribulations that befall us, we will survive and be purified by what happens to us; we will thus grow in wisdom and spiritual stature, instead of being dragged down by our problems and woes.

Jacob the Pious ('St. James the Just') encouraged the Jewish followers of Yeshua` to stand firm, and to allow the purifying power of

---

[a] This does not mean converting everyone to the same religion, but rather encouraging everyone – whether they follow a religion or not – to become people who live decent, compassionate, just and honest lives.

God to complete its work.[a] When we face problems in life, we are tempted to become cynical, bitter, resentful and melancholy. Good people have to resist the temptation to do this, because if we allow God's purifying force to complete its work, we become stronger and wiser for the experience. That is why Jacob the Pious wrote to his flock and advised them, *"Consider it nought but joy, my brothers and sisters, whenever you come to face unexpected trials of various kinds."*[b] Through this statement, Jacob shows that he is aware of the theology about the purifying power of God's Glory, which he must have learned from growing up in the Temple, being taught by the priests – for whom such a belief was a central foundation.

Many religious people explain away their suffering as God testing us, but in most cases this is not what is happening.[c] Our suffering is more often an opportunity for our souls to draw near to God's Divine Radiance; it's an opportunity for us to be purified by God as metal is purified by fire (hence the 'testing' is more like 'proving', just as gold or silver is 'proved' by fire); it's a precious opportunity to learn from our living relationship with God, and to be guided directly by God's wisdom. I can honestly say that during my recent years of anguish, suffering and hardship, I have learned the most ***profound*** lessons about God, and gained first-hand knowledge of God, that I could never have learned or experienced otherwise.

The suffering of good people is not always a test from God, but more often *an opportunity for what is most precious within us to become purer*. We become more sensitive to the living Presence of God; we learn from what happens to us, and if we maintain our dignity under trial and endure, our spirits are ennobled and magnified.

Signs of the times: the troubles in the Holy Land in the 1st century CE

Now, during the period of the prophet Yeshua`'s ministry, the Jewish people were suffering terribly under the cruel oppression of the Romans. It is vitally important for us to understand the problems going on during this time, because much of what Yeshua` said was against the backdrop of these contemporary troubles. Most modern Christians are not aware of the terrible burdens endured by Yeshua`'s fellow Jews, and think that generally the Romans were 'jolly nice people' – generally

---

[a] Ig. Yq. 2:3, 8 – cf Ep. James 1:4, 12
[b] Ig. Yq. 2:1 – cf James 1:2
[c] In fact, testing through suffering usually only happens to people who have an important part to play in God's great plan – such as with prophets – to see if they are worthy bearers of God's message.

benevolent to the Jewish people – when in reality, their behaviour was no better than that of the Nazis of the 20th century.

Most of that generation were decent people; the wrongdoings of the few had caused problems for the innocent majority. For example, Pontius Pilate seemed to enjoy offending Jewish religious sensibilities, and the Jewish historian Josephus reports that later Roman Governors (such as Albinus and Florus) were so cruel in their administration of Jewish affairs, that matters were inevitably bound to come to a violent head. There was, in addition, inter-communal strife between Samaritans and Jews; crime and banditry were on the increase; the authorities burdened the people with heavy taxes that many could not afford to pay; and the poor groaned under the increasing mountains of debt that they had no hope of escaping from.

There were also some major religious problems. Now, most people have heard of the Essenes. Most people know that they took themselves off into the Judean desert to live apart from mainstream Jewish society. What most people don't know is *why* they did this. Their reasoning is important to know and understand, because it will inform our understanding of subsequent events – especially the world in which Yeshua` lived.

The main reason they retreated into a desert community, was because they felt the priests who were in charge of the Jerusalem Temple had become corrupt – that they were not behaving in a holy manner expected of them as priests. The Essenes believed that the corruption of the priesthood (especially of the Sadducean priests) had desecrated the holiness of the Temple, and they felt in all conscience that they therefore could not worship there, or offer sacrifices there. For them, the *Shekhinah*[a] of God was no longer present in the Sanctuary of the Temple.

In the Israelite way of thinking, desecration of the Temple was the same as the desecration of the reputation of God's holiness – one day, there would come a terrible reckoning for this desecration, and those who were guilty would be brought to account.

You see, the Jewish priests were supposed to be visible representatives for God on earth. They, more than anyone else, had a huge responsibility to behave in a righteous and holy manner. If a man of God acted in a cruel, unjust or immoral fashion, he would be defaming the holy reputation of God. According to the Israelite way of thinking, this was a sin that could never be forgiven in this life.[b]

For example, the sons of the High Priest Eli, who were themselves priests by descent, were corrupt and treated people unfairly. Their

---

[a] the sacred, in-dwelling Presence of Yahveh.
[b] see Isaiah 22:14

actions defamed the holy reputation of God, so according to the writer of the Book of Samuel,[a] they suffered the ultimate punishment – death.

This view – of the consequences of defaming God's reputation – fixed in ordinary people's minds the belief that one day, the Sadducean priests would be punished severely by God for their corruption, their acts of injustice and their immoral behaviour. According to the Talmidi interpretation of certain parables of Yeshua`,[b] he prophesied the demise of the Sadducean party in a day of judgment, when God would come to deal out his divine justice in order to protect and save their victims.

The great and terrible Day of Yahveh

The Prophets spoke with burning urgency about the 'Day of Yahveh' as an approaching Day of Judgment against wrongdoers.[c] The term was used by the biblical Prophets to describe a decisive act of God in *their* near-future, but it would be a reckoning in *this* life, not in the afterlife. It was therefore not the end of the world, but a time of terrible reckoning that most people would survive.[d]

In English-language bibles, the arrival of this day is referred to as 'the coming of the LORD'. However, this 'Lord' was not Yeshua`, but rather **Yahveh**. This day would mark the coming *intervention* of Yahveh as Judge and sovereign King.[e] The 'day of the LORD's coming' that was anticipated by Yeshua`'s *Jewish* followers, was not the return of Yeshua`, but rather the coming of this day of reckoning – this 'Day of Yahveh'.

This 'day' (or rather, this period or time of trial) would have two sides to it: on the one hand, it would be a time for the manifestation of God's punitive powers of justice. It would be directed against acts of injustice and oppression, and against acts which desecrated God's holiness and provoked God's righteous anger. On the other hand, it would be a time for the vindication and liberation of righteous people. Good people would also experience troubles, and indeed go through a

---

[a] 1Sam ch 2

[b] such as the parable of the wicked steward who beats the other servants – S.Yesh 110; cf Mt 24:45-51, Lk 12:41-46

[c] Joel 1:15, Amos 5:18, Mal 3:19

[d] This day of judgment was supposed to purify priests so that they could serve God in the Temple better (Mal 3:3). To do this, they would have to be alive (i.e. they would have to have survived the Day of Yahveh)!

[e] cf Isaiah 19:1, where Yahveh is described as 'coming to Egypt' i.e. was about to intervene and act as judge over Egypt; also Isaiah 40:10, where **Yahveh** is foretold to come with might.

time of great tribulation and trial, but this time would be shortened,^a and they would be saved from these troubles if they followed Gods' ways; and if they trusted in the power of God alone to rescue them,^b the majority of the Jewish people could be saved from annihilation and the worst of the tribulation – this was Yeshua`'s 'good news'. So this is the distinction to make: that the sinful minority would be dealt with, but the righteous majority of that period would be rescued and purified by the trials to come.

There are various ills in society that bring on the Day of Yahveh. Most of us are aware of biblical warnings against worshipping idols and false gods – and this has little relevance or impact on us today. Most of us are not aware however, that a sharp decline in the fabric of society also brings on the Day of Yahveh – things such as neglecting the needs of the least in society and exploiting them,^c deliberately working against justice and righteousness,^d extolling wealth for wealth's sake,^e corrupting the integrity of knowledge and wisdom,^f rulers misleading and oppressing the ordinary people,^g and creating conditions which lead to unbearable levels of murder and violence.^h

The corruption of religion also brings on the Day of Yahveh – when ministers of religion become deceitful, unjust or oppressive, when people commit violence in the name of religion and so desecrate God's holiness,ⁱ when false men of religion deliberately stifle spiritual life and growth,^j and when false teachers dishearten or deceive good people in times of trial with false prophecy.^k When society comes up against one or two of these dangers alone, people of faith can deal with them, but all at once, and they build up to a stage where they have become insurmountable; only God's intervention can set things aright.

There are many, even today, who are unhappy with the evils in society and long for the Day of Yahveh to come. This is because they don't understand that it is not a single, 'end-time', 'end-of-the-world' event, but happens whenever society veers disastrously off-course.

---

^a S.Yesh. 162:18; cf Mk 13:20, Mt 24:22
^b *"I, and I alone, am Yahveh, and apart from me there is no other saviour."* Isa 43:11; *"Those who trust in Yahveh are like Mount Zion, which cannot be shaken but endures forever."* Ps 125:1
^c Amos 5:11-12
^d Amos 5:7
^e Zeph 1:18
^f Hos 4:6
^g Isa 3:12-15
^h Hos 4:2
ⁱ Zeph 1:9
^j Joel 1:10-12
^k Ezek 13:22

The prophet Amos cautions us that *'the Day of Yahveh shall not be light but darkness, blackest night without a glimmer'*.[a] We should therefore take note that he strongly warns people against longing for it. For Isaiah likewise, the Day of Yahveh brings fear and loss even to ordinary people[b] – definitely not something to be longed for!

The Day of Yahveh is said to come as *'a fire which refines silver'*;[c] compare this with the words of Isaiah,[d] where the righteous are described as those who can withstand the fire. The righteous will be given the strength from God to endure; Jacob the Pious[e] speaks of this endurance making them whole.[f] They are able to endure because they trust in Yahveh as a just Judge and King; they have listened to God's prophets, they have taken their advice; they have, in humility, tried to keep faith with the good and sacred heart of God's teaching, in spite of what angry religious people have told them.

God promised that before this great and terrible Day of Yahveh, He would pour out the spirit of prophecy on the people of the Land,[g] so that prophets would arise to warn the people of what was to come. The message of these prophets was that there was only one way of avoiding this terrible Day of Yahveh – and that was for the guilty to repent (and it goes without saying, for the good to remain good).

Repentance as a way of avoiding the Day of Yahveh

In the Israelite way of thinking, the worst consequences of the Day of Yahveh would mean exile for the tribes of Israel.[h] In Yeshua``'s time, that meant potential exile for the Jewish people – yet again. Anything that threatens to suggest to the world that Yahwist values and principles are not working – and by extension, that the God of Israel is ineffective – will result in the expulsion of the Jewish people from the Land. The terms of the Covenant[i] gave the land of Canaan to the descendants of

---

[a] Amos 5:18-20
[b] Isa. 2:12, 10:3, 22:5; comp. Micah 1:3
[c] Mal. 3:2-3
[d] Isa. 33:14-16
[e] that is, St James the Just, author of the 'letter of James' in the New Testament.
[f] Igg. Yaq. 2:1-4 – cf Ep. James 1:2-5
[g] see Joel 3:1-5 (Xtian bibles Joel 2:28-32); this prophecy does not refer to the end of time, but to the last days before any 'Day of Yahveh' event – Joel 3:4 (Xtian 2:31). Before every 'Day of Yahveh', God will send prophets to warn us.
[h] e.g. 2Kgs 17:23
[i] A covenant is an agreement between two parties, with responsibilities on both sides. 'The Covenant' mentioned in the Hebrew Bible is basically this: 'If

Jacob – the Israelites. Therefore according to Torah,[a] the most fitting punishment for breaking that Covenant would be to be removed from that land.

The Hebrew concept of 'national repentance' contains within it the idea of return (to God), and sorrow (for what one has done). Traditionally, the outward manifestation of this was fasting and dressing in black sackcloth, as if in mourning. In order to avoid the Day of Yahveh, it was necessary for the whole nation to get involved in this national repentance.

There is an Israelite principle that, if one does not point out the wrongdoing of one's neighbour when one has the opportunity and ability to do so, then one shares in their guilt.[b] When someone does wrong, and you deliberately turn a blind eye when you could have done something about it, then you share in the consequences. As I have said, Yahveh is a very powerful God. When Yahveh moves to punish injustice and wrongdoing, God is so powerful that everyone is affected, not just the wicked. It is therefore important that good people do not allow bad things to reach such a terrible level that everything falls apart.

Because God's actions to punish the unjust also hurt the innocent, and because Yahveh is a compassionate God, Yahveh would rather not have to cause devastation in order to punish wrongs. Perhaps this is why God seems to delay acting, and why God has to rely on good people to do God's job on God's behalf. Perhaps this is why, in the Miqra, God only seems to take action after a long period of troubles (such as the long-suffering of the Hebrew slaves in Egypt, when God finally acts to redeem them only after generations of misery).[c] Ultimately, Yahveh would rather that wicked people turn from their evil ways and live:

'Do I take any pleasure in the death of wicked people?'
declares Sovereign Yahveh. 'Would I not rather that they turn
from their wicked ways and live?'[d]

Take the case of the prophet Jonah's mission. Jonah was called to deliver a message to the people of Nineveh, the capital of Assyria (now East Mosul in modern Iraq). They had become an unjust and oppressive

---

you will worship Me alone and follow My teachings, then I will give your descendants the Land of Canaan forever, and preserve you as a people forever.' Everything else is terms and conditions.
[a] Dt 29:22-28. Conversely, God also promises that the exiles would be returned to the Land, Dt 30:1-5.
[b] Lev 19:17b; see also Prov 17:15
[c] Ex 3:7
[d] Ezek 18:23

people. God sent Jonah to tell them that if they did not repent, and turn from their evil ways, their own actions would result in their destruction.

Jonah did not want to go. He knew that if they *did* repent, then God would rescind God's threat and they would live in peace.*ᵃ* And that is exactly what happened – the entire city decided to turn from their evil ways, they fasted and dressed in sackcloth, and so God cancelled the punishment that God had prepared for the city and its people.*ᵇ*

The calamity of the Day of Yahveh could be avoided if the nation repented, and if the wicked among them turned from their evil ways and returned to God, with a genuine sorrow for what they had done. Putting out the call for national repentance is where the prophet comes in, and so next, we need to understand what a prophet means in the Israelite tradition.

The role of the prophet in the Israelite tradition

In both mainstream Christianity and Islam, a prophet is someone who gives a *new* revelation from God. If you, as my reader, wish to understand the Prophet Yeshua`'s mission from a completely Jewish perspective, and realise why Talmidis view him solely as a prophet of God, then you need to fully comprehend what a prophet means in the *Israelite* tradition.

A prophet is called to deliver a message directly from God, word for word. A prophet believes that he/she has had a personal communication from God – either directly by hearing a voice, or by receiving a vision – and whether one believes or doubts that such things can happen, this is the absolute quintessence of what an Israelite prophet is. The prophet becomes the mouthpiece of God. Rather than delivering a new revelation or a new message, Hebrew prophets instead reiterate and reinforce the *original* message; that is a vitally important point to understand. Remember how Yeshua` told his followers, *'the old wine is good enough'?ᶜ* The old wine referred to the original message of our Israelite faith.

God makes God's will known to individual men and women, who receive it, and are driven by the power of that message to impart it. They are filled, or rather, *intoxicated* by that message. The power of God's Presence so fills their soul, that it feels as if something inside them is

---

ᵃ Jonah 4:2; Jonah also feared that because this would mean there would be no calamity for the Assyrians, he could be accused of being a false prophet – because, after all, what he prophesied did not come to pass.
ᵇ Jonah 3:10
ᶜ S. Yesh 14:2; cf Lk 5:39 – see also Mk 2:22, Mt 9:17, Gosp. Thomas 47:3-4

clawing – bursting – to get out, and the power driving it will not stop until the message is delivered.

Unlike other religious teachers, a prophet does not choose his/her vocation; the man or woman in question is plucked from life by God, often against their will (the prophet Jonah is the prime example of this). A sage or a preacher can learn their art; a prophet cannot. There is no school you can go to in order to learn how to become a prophet; there are no books to read, no qualifications to be gained. Preachers, sages and rabbis can learn how to become these things,[a] but a prophet delivers a message, just as a river delivers its flood of water after heavy rain.

The prophet has not necessarily striven previously for oneness with God; they may not even formerly have been a very religious person, and they may not necessarily have even been a learned person (the prophet Amos for example, was a simple farmer,[b] not a man of religion). However, God seizes their mind and soul, and they become so full and bursting with God's message, that they are compelled to impart it, regardless of the consequences to themselves, and even though in some cases, they might even disagree with it.

The prophetic office is a difficult one to endure. The sage or preacher can amend their message to make it more palatable to their audience, so that their personal lives will be easier; a prophet cannot do this. They cannot escape or run away from their calling. A prophet has to deliver an often uncompromising, sometimes distasteful message that people would rather not hear. As a result, the prophet faces constant opposition and rejection. As a prophet of Yahveh, it would naturally be expected that you would suffer hardship, trials and even face death. Yeshua` was therefore not unique in this respect. The suffering he endured, and what he went through – even his death – was to be fully expected in his role as a Hebrew prophet.[c] No ulterior meaning for his suffering and death has to be sought; no theological justification for why he died has to be found.

A prophet often has a lonely life as a result of his calling from God: *"I sat alone because Your Hand was upon me"* laments the prophet Jeremiah.[d] A prophet's life is often one of anguish and fear. Such is the

---

[a] The prophet Samuel put together a guild (some translations 'school') of prophets. This guild was not to teach people how to be prophets, but rather to bring together people whom God had already called to be prophets.
[b] Amos 7:14
[c] In the Letter of Jacob (Epistle of James), in addition to the biblical test that predictions come true in the lifetime of the prophet, Jacob cites a further test of a true prophet – that a true prophet also endures suffering for the sake of the message God has given them to deliver (Ig. Yq. 2:12 – cf Ep. James 5:10).
[d] Jer 15:17

life that prophets face, that some cry out to God, *"Why are you doing this to me!"*[a] Yeshua` was not unique in having a lonely, single life; Jeremiah also never married, in accordance with God's actual command.[b] No one in their right mind therefore would deliberately seek to become a prophet. A true prophet has no fame or glory, only trial and anguish.

In Yeshua`'s day, in addition to the corruption of the priests, the rich were ignoring their financial responsibility to the poor. Debt was mounted upon debt, and the sacred religious laws that were intended to relieve poverty were being ignored by the wealthy. The Zealots also faced God's judgment, because they were committing violence by falsely using God's authority. Eventually, they committed violence and shed human blood inside the Temple compound itself, which was the ultimate desecration. All these injustices invited God to act decisively – for 'God's kingship'[c] to intervene. It was therefore the job of the prophet to warn people that if these wrongs continued unchallenged and unchecked, there would be terrible consequences. The only way to avoid those calamitous consequences, would be for the guilty to repent and change their behaviour and thinking.

The prophet like Elijah

According to the Oral Law of rabbinic tradition, the prophet like Elijah is supposed to announce the coming of the messiah. As a consequence, most Jewish people today eagerly yearn for the coming of the prophet like Elijah (some even believe that Elijah himself will literally return). This rabbinic belief that the Elijah-like prophet will precede the messiah has passed into Christianity (so that the sole purpose of 'John the Baptist' is to presage 'Christ the messiah'). However, this belief comes from the Oral Law, and is not found in the Hebrew Bible, which has a very different picture of this type of prophet.

The prophet Malachi spoke about the corruption of priests in his day,[d] and that there would come a prophet like Elijah who would purify the priests through his fiery words.[e] Such a prophet would also warn of 'a great and terrible day of Yahveh' – a day of judgment or reckoning if

---

[a] compare the cries of Jeremiah, 14:9, 15:18.
[b] Jer 16:2
[c] cf Yeshua`'s call for people to repent, because 'The Kingdom of God is upon us', which actually means, 'God's Kingship – i.e. God's judgment as King – is almost upon us.'
[d] Mal 1:6, 2:8, 2:11
[e] Mal 3:2-3

the good and just reputation of God's holiness was not restored.ᵃ If the guilty priests did not listen, then there would be a day of reckoning for such priests.ᵇ

In Talmidi theology, Yochanan the Immerserᶜ was such a prophet like Elijah. *However*, he is not seen by us as someone who would presage the messiah, but rather someone who would warn the nation of a coming 'Day of Yahveh' – exactly as it says in the Book of Malachi. His ministry of immersion was primarily directed towards the priests of that time, warning them to amend their ways. Yochanan was also called by God to purify those priests who still remained faithful to God's ways and principles, and so prepare them for holy service in the Temple. As a secondary ministry, Yochanan called ordinary people to a righteous way of life through his ministry of immersion.

In the Christian tradition, immersion (or 'baptism') is about being accepted into the community of Christian Believers, and is therefore only carried out once by most Christian denominations. However, to understand the nature of Yochanan's ministry and its impact, you have to understand the purpose of immersion in the *Jewish* tradition.

You see, before anyone went to the Temple, they had to immerse themselves in a *miqveh*.ᵈ If someone went to the Temple to make an offering to atone their souls of sin, then they had to immerse first. As I have mentioned previously, if there was no repentance beforehand, then the sin-offering did nothing – there was no forgiveness or atonement.ᵉ

Repentance had to be there before the sin-offering. What Yochanan's ministry of immersion did, was to impress upon people that repentance had to be there *even before the immersion*ᶠ – remember, people immersed *before* going to Temple to make offerings.

You see, people erroneously thought that it was the blood of the sin-offeringᵍ that brought about forgiveness. They would think to themselves, 'Right, I've made the sin-offering, so that means that God has forgiven me'. However, by insisting that repentance had to be there

---

ᵃ Mal 3:23
ᵇ Mal 2:1-3
ᶜ 'John the Baptist'.
ᵈ an immersion pool – usually a square pool with steps leading into and out of it, filled with water from a natural source of water.
ᵉ cf Prov 15:8, 21:27 – the sacrifices offered by a wicked person are unacceptable before God i.e. a sacrifice offered without repentance is an abomination.
ᶠ cf Josephus, 'Antiquities of the Jews', Book XVIII, chap 5:2 *"Yochanan taught that the heart had to be purified by repentance before the body could be purified by water.'*
ᵍ Torah allows for the poor to offer up a tenth of an eifah of fine semolina-flour as a sacrificial sin-offering (Lev 5:11-12)

even before immersion, Yochanan made people see that the intent of the heart[a] was more important than insincere ritual. And if insincere people came to Yochanan for immersion before repentance, then **neither did the immersion cleanse them of their sins.**

I am increasingly of the opinion that Yochanan may have been brought up in an Essene community. The Essenes practised celibacy to keep themselves ritually pure,[b] and therefore adopted children as their heirs, in order to increase their community's numbers. The Essenes had originally taken themselves off into the desert to distance themselves from what they saw as a corrupt Temple hierarchy. They *never* attended the Temple, instead maintaining a way of life that kept themselves in a permanent state of ritual holiness and purity (which consequently meant they could never have sexual relations). As Essenes, they already had an inherent disdain for the Sadducean priests, and this shows in Yochanan's castigation of the priests who come to him for immersion. Yochanan is also recorded as having first appeared in the desert.

Summary

To understand Yeshua`, you have to understand the world he lived in. You have to understand why he did what he did within a *Jewish* context – not only the historical but also the *theological* context. You have to understand the Yahwist theological milieu that produced him.

The primary purpose of the Israelite religion is to act as an eternal witness to the power, presence and holiness of Yahveh. A follower of Yahveh therefore has a responsibility to consider the result of his or her own actions on the good reputation of Yahveh.

It must never be that the people of Israel – who are meant to act as representatives of Yahveh to the world – become an unjust, corrupt and wicked people, because that would impugn the good and holy reputation of God. For this reason, as Jews we will always be judged with greater strictness than non-Jews, who do not have this responsibility. So when the corrupt Sadducean priests and the war-hungry Zealots threatened the reputation of God's holiness, and when the threat of social inequality and oppression of the poor by the wealthy elite became so great, God had to act.

Yahveh is a holy God, before whom evil and wrongdoing cannot

---

[a] Better than blood sacrifices is to do good things – see Isa 1:13-17, Ps 51:19
[b] After sexual intimacy, a person required immersion before they could attend Temple to make purification offerings, just as a woman did after childbirth. Since Essenes could not attend Temple to make these offerings, they had to keep themselves in a permanent state of ritual purity.

endure. God's power is described as a fire that sweeps the land, consuming wrong but purifying good. When God moves to act against bad people, the misfortune of good people increases, because they are closest to the epicentre of this quaking of heaven and earth. It is important that good people take comfort in the fact that what is happening is not any kind of punishment against them – that they are blameless. It is important that they gain strength and wisdom from their troubles.

The 'Day of Yahveh' was the term for a decisive yet calamitous act in Israel's history – a finite period of judgment or reckoning – when God would punish the unjust, the corrupt, the oppressive and the cruel, but vindicate and purify the righteous. For Israel and the Jewish people, 'the Day of Yahveh' usually results in exile – the Assyrian, Babylonian and Roman exiles were therefore all 'Days of Yahveh'.

The only way to avoid these 'Days of Reckoning' was for the guilty parties to repent, to turn from a wicked and unjust way of life – and so return to God and God's values. To this end, God sent prophets to warn God's people of the consequences of injustice, violence and oppression. God sent Yochanan the Immerser, and then Yeshua` to call the guilty to repent. In addition, it was Yeshua`'s job to encourage good people – the majority – to remain good, so that they would in a way be sheltered in the days to come.

Knowing about the fire of God's Glory changes the whole focus of religious faith. It is not enough to carry out the rituals and customs of our ancestors; it has to be accompanied by a change of heart, a change in the inner soul that enables the human spirit to come into direct contact with the living Presence of Yahveh. And knowing the power of that Presence changes the very essence of our being. It is the living Presence of Yahveh, and the fire of God's Glory, that cleanses and transforms the human soul into a new being – one closer to what Yahveh our Creator originally intended us to be.

Chapter Two: The Forgotten History of the Way: the Talmidi Israelite view of the Prophet Yeshua`, and the community of his earliest Jewish Followers

Introduction

In one famous ancient Indian parable, a group of blind men are asked to describe an elephant. You've heard the one – where the man who felt its trunk said it was like a snake; the one who felt its legs, said it was like a tree; and the one who felt its tusk said it was like a bone. When trying to understand Yeshua` of Nazareth, most people examine just one part of the story, and nothing else. They look at his three years of ministry, and then focus on Paul of Tarsus almost as a second 'Christ'. They are not interested in anything or anyone else. They can therefore contort and deform history to fit their beliefs, because they only see either the trunk, the leg, or the tusk.

When I wiped the slate of my faith clean in order to start anew, not only did I want to start at the beginning, I wanted the *whole* picture from God – I wanted to see 'the whole elephant', so to speak. I didn't say to myself, 'This is what I believe, now I'll make what I learn fit my beliefs.' That's like starting at the end, and moving backwards; it's like starting with a conclusion, and then making all the evidence one finds fit neatly with that conclusion. Instead, I started with Abrahamic faith and Yahwist beliefs, moving forward in time, and interpreting what came next through the lens of what had come before. Often, I took a different fork in the road to the one taken by mainstream religion.

Most writers examine the motives of the people around Yeshua`, or the motives of Yeshua` himself. No one *ever* looks at God's motives in all this. That is what I have been trying to do so far – look at what **God** was thinking, and what **God** was trying to do.

Most writers in search of the historical Yeshua` also have an agenda – they need to prove him as a Zealot, a Pharisee, an Essene, or merely a strolling wonder-worker. As for me, I had no such agenda. My only agenda was to exalt and magnify the living God of Israel – no one and nothing else. Therefore in my previous chapter, I deliberately avoided post-Babylonian Exile theology – things such as messianism and apocalypticism; and instead, I stuck to pre-Exile, biblical Yahwist Israelite concepts about God – those specific ideas that turned out to be most relevant in my search for the historical prophet of Nazareth, and for the authenticity of the Jewish community that came after him. If I was ever going to connect Yeshua` to the faith of Abraham and Moses, this was the only logical path of investigation to take, because neither Abraham nor Moses longed for a messiah to save them, nor did they wait expectantly for the end of the world.

In this chapter, I'm going to present you with a history that the mainstream would rather that you not look at or know about. The fundamentalist insistence on, "Stick to the Bible, stick to the Bible!" means sticking to the sanitised, official view of history – which in turn means that the true and real story of Yeshua`'s Jewish followers never gets looked at. History always gets to be written by the victors, and in the New Testament, what we have is the edited propaganda of the victors' view.

In this chapter, I'm going to take a look at:

- the place of Yeshua` in the overall prophetic scheme
- the ancient community of the Way itself
- Jacob the Pious ('St James the Just')
- the actual crisis that led James to write his famous letter
- the real issues that led to the Council of Jerusalem[a]
- why Peter parted ways with the Jerusalem community
- the lead-up to the destruction of Jerusalem
- Shimon bar Qlofas,[b] the man who took over from James
- and the 'curse' that led to the expulsion of Jewish Followers from synagogues, and the split from mainstream Judaism

The prophet Yeshua`

Yochanan the Immerser ('St. John the Baptist') called people to repent, so that the Day of Yahveh could be avoided. Unfortunately, Yochanan's warnings went unheeded and he was put to death by King Herod Antipas. Now, Yahveh is not a belligerent or violent God; Yahveh is a just God who gives people a second chance. So after Yochanan, God

---

[a] which is what it is called in the Catholic and Orthodox Churches; in our community it is known as the Convention of Jerusalem, and took place in the summer of 49CE.
[b] also known as St. Symeon of Jerusalem – a paternal cousin of Yeshua`, full brother of James the Just, and the second leader of the community of Yeshua`'s Jewish followers.

called Yeshua` of Nazareth to act as a prophet so that he could continue with God's warnings.

Yeshua` continued to speak against the corruption of the Sadducean priests, as well as the lack of action on the part of rich people to play their part in relieving the misery of the poor – to remind them of God's concern for the least in society, and of the laws in Torah that God instituted to protect the least in society. Yeshua`'s job was also to encourage good people to endure the problems they were having by not falling prey to bitterness and violence, and so remain faithful to God's ways of justice and compassion. He prophesied that God would deal with all that was happening in God's own way; that the final days before the terrible day of Yahveh would see frightening events and disturbing problems for the good and the innocent, but that there would metaphorically be a great harvest.[a] During this 'harvest', the righteous would be gathered to God like ripe and precious wheat into a barn, but the wrongdoers would be judged in the purifying fire of God's Glory, and burnt off like stubble in the field.[b]

One part of Yeshua`'s mission was to ensure that the number of those who would be judged as blameless and righteous would be increased. Most religious groups at that time, such as the Essenes, were only concerned with the chosen 'remnant' or 'elect' (this is, incidentally, one of several reasons why Yeshua` cannot have been an Essene).[c] However, God was concerned to protect *everyone* who was innocent and penitent, and so called Yeshua` to minister even to the outcasts of society, so that their number could be added to those 'sheltered on the day of God's righteous anger'.[d]

One group of people that don't get a mention at all in the New Testament, but who were a big part of Jewish political life at that time, were the Zealots. They were the anti-Roman religious terrorists of the day. Now, there are quite a few arguments recorded in the New Testament which are purportedly with the Pharisees, but which in fact would make much more sense if the polemics described had been with the Zealots. For example, the argument about whether the people should

---

[a] On a number of occasions, Yeshua` refers to the coming tribulation as a harvest (S. Yesh 93, 167 – cf Mt 9:37-38, 13:24-30).
[b] Mal 3:19 (4:1 in Christian bibles)
[c] because Yeshua` believed his message was for everyone: 'Whatever I tell you privately in the darkness, go say openly in the daylight. And whatever you hear whispered in your ear in private rooms, go proclaim publicly upon the housetops!'. S.Yesh. 65:2-3; cf Mk 10:27
[d] Zephaniah 2:3 – *'Seek Yahveh, all you humble of the Land, you who do what he commands. Seek righteousness, and seek humility; perhaps you will be sheltered on the day of Yahveh's wrath.'*

pay taxes to Caesar[a] would make much more sense if it had been with a nationalist Zealot; consider also the statement, 'Let the Dead bury their own dead'[b] – perhaps 'the Dead' was Yeshua`'s nickname for the fundamentalist Zealots.

In Jeremiah's time, God gave a warning that the Jewish people were not to resist the Babylonians,[c] since they were not a threat to the Israelite religion itself. Eventually God would deal with them in God's own way. I propose that this was also the line God took with the Romans; the Jewish people were not to engage in proactive violence against the Romans, because they were not a direct threat to the Jewish religion, and because God would deal with them in God's own way and in God's own time.

Unfortunately, the Zealots were so incensed and fired up by the injustice and cruelty of the Romans, that they took up arms against them. They assassinated not only Romans, but also those of our own people whom they saw as collaborators with the Romans. But zeal for God is not enough; one must also have reverence and knowledge.[d]

Yeshua`'s mission was to warn the Jewish people about the coming destruction and exile, and to teach people that by national repentance, this calamity could be avoided. As a secondary part of that mission, if the guilty parties did not repent – corrupt priests, rich people who ignored their responsibilities to the poor, and Zealots who by their violence desecrated God's name – Yeshua` was to warn people that a destructive tribulation would come. But Yeshua` also taught good people how they might survive this calamity: by being just, merciful, compassionate and forgiving – by being true to God's ways, principles and laws.

The ancient community of the Way

Having listened to the words of Yeshua` as a prophet, the Jewish followers of Yeshua` would have been intensely aware of this terrible, calamitous event that was shortly going to take place – that even the Temple would be destroyed, and that *'not one stone would be left standing on another'*.[e] In the Israelite tradition, the test of a true prophet was that warnings of bad things would take place **within the same**

---

[a] S.Yesh. 82 – cf Mk 12:13-17
[b] S.Yesh. 7:7 – cf Mt 8:21-22, Lk 9:59-60. Traditionally, those who followed God's ways and followed the way of life were 'the Living', and those who went against God and followed the way of death were 'the Dead' (cf Deut 30:15-19).
[c] Jer 21:9
[d] Prov 19:2
[e] S.Yesh. 133:5 – cf Mk 13:2

generation as the people who heard the warnings,[a] not in the far distant future, as most people nowadays think.[b]

Therefore, Yeshua`'s Jewish followers would have spent their days waiting for this 'coming'[c] of Yahveh – primarily by continuing the prophet's work in calling for national repentance in order to avoid such a catastrophe, as well as adding to the number of those who would be sheltered from God's righteous anger, if and when the calamity eventually did come.

In the Israelite tradition, warnings of doom and tribulation were supposed to keep ruthless, greedy and cruel people in check; they were also intended to give hope to good and decent people, by assuring them that oppression and injustice would be dealt with by God. Unfortunately, even as today, unscrupulous people would hijack religion and use it for their own nefarious ends. Doom-mongers would use biblical warnings of apocalypse and tribulation to keep good and decent people cowed and under their thumbs, making them too afraid and preoccupied to object to the actions of oppressive and unjust people. With good people too fearful to say anything, unscrupulous people are thereby free to go about their regular business.

Because of the power of religion, charlatans can take over a religion and turn it into a hollow travesty of what God designed it to be – a bulwark against injustice, the cement that binds society, the link between the young and the old, so that generations don't become isolated, and a vehicle by which spiritual knowledge and wisdom can be passed on from generation to generation. Unscrupulous deceivers can turn a message of peace and hope into a message of violence.

True religion is a protection for the weak against the strong, a voice for the least in society against the repression and exploitation of the powerful. This is the eternal relevance of the Israelite faith; anyone who says that religion has no place in modern society does not know Yahveh, and those who say that religion should not poke its nose into matters of social justice, most certainly do not know Yahveh![d]

---

[a] Ezek 12:25

[b] The 'end of the age' that Yeshua` spoke of is therefore not something that is yet to come – it has already happened. When the Temple and Jerusalem were destroyed, and the Jewish people exiled in 70 CE, that *was* the end of their world. The Greek *aiōnos* means an era or epoch; the Aramaic `iddana` refers to a portion of time, an era where one period of time ends and another begins. The destruction of Jerusalem marked the end or completion of one age and the beginning of another.

[c] i.e. the *arrival* of Yahveh's divine judgment; the 'Lord' they awaited was not Yeshua`, but rather Yahveh.

[d] Instruction in the Israelite faith involves, among other things, teaching others to know Yahveh – cf Jer 31:34. Cf also the advice of David at 1Chron 22:19

THE WAY

So this is why prophets are so essential in the overall framework of Israelite religion. The office of the prophet has to be ongoing, so that God's goals and long-term plans can be kept on track, and so that God's protection for the least in society can be maintained. For the Israelite religion, staying on that track meant maintaining a holy and ethical way of life, so that God's Glory and blessing could continue to come through from heaven to earth – to the benefit not just of Israel, but of all the human race.

God told the Israelites, *'Be holy, just as I, Yahveh your God, am holy'.*[a] As I have said before, there are different aspects to holiness in human beings – such as preserving oneself only for Yahveh, living a way of life which is culturally and ethically distinctive, and so on. However, the sum effect of this is that, just as God is holy, and therefore no evil or wrongdoing can endure before God, so also a people that strives to be morally and ethically holy, will become a people before whom evil and injustice cannot endure among them. This is why religious people who oppress others, and engage in hatred and violence are a desecration of God's holiness – they work against what God has planned for us.

God said that if we maintained our holiness, then God would be able to dwell among us.[b] The prophet Jeremiah[c] also implied that God's great and powerful Presence would dwell with those people who were ethically and morally holy – God dwells with people who do their best to live God's goodness. The true quality of holiness is that inner holiness of the heart; the Sadducees maintained perfect *external*, ritual holiness, but their inner hearts were corrupt and decadent – they lacked this inner holiness of spirit.[d]

The effect of God's holiness, as I have previously mentioned, was that evil and injustice could not endure before it. If a people – or in this case – a community – lived this way of inner holiness, they would rightly foster the hope to become a force and influence for good in the Holy Land and throughout the world; a community before whom evil and injustice could not endure.

It is God's presence among a group of people which makes them holy – which magnifies the effect of their efforts, and enables them to achieve far more than what mere human effort alone can achieve; as God

---

to seek Yahveh, because Yahveh is a God who can be found and known; and Hosea 6:3, where people who have been rebuked by God, repent and seek to know Yahveh once more.
[a] Lev 19:2
[b] Num 35:34
[c] Jer 3:16-17
[d] They are criticised for being like whitewashed tombs, which look fine on the outside, but inside are full of dead people's bones (S. Yoch. 4:2 – cf Mt 23:27).

said, *'I am Yahveh, who makes you holy'*.[a] I propose that this ancient community of Jewish Followers hoped that, if they lived a way of life which was ethically and morally holy – living a life that eschewed greed and material concerns, was humble, compassionate, just and forgiving – that God's Presence would dwell with them. I propose that they hoped that God's indwelling Presence among them would help them encourage others to repent, change their ways, and so survive the destructive calamity that the prophet Yeshua` had warned them about.

Consider this also: if we leave it to God to act against the evils in society, and do nothing ourselves, then the consequences for our society are dire. It is not enough for people to wait for God to act. As I have described previously, when God moves against evil, *everyone* suffers, because God is just too powerful. Is it not better for human beings to live and teach this way of goodness, so that good people do not have to become collateral damage while enduring the tribulation of *God's* punitive actions? And does this not impress upon us that we cannot just sit back and wait for God to act against the wrongs in society – that *we* have to do something *ourselves*? I firmly believe that the ancient Jewish followers of Yeshua` were intensely aware that they had a responsibility to work on God's behalf, and live a way of life that reflected their heavenly Father's principles and values. In this way, I believe they hoped to become a light for God – a source for good and for positive change in their troubled society.

Jacob the Pious ('St James the Just') – the real first leader of the Community of the Way

After Yeshua`'s death, his cousin[b] Jacob the Pious became leader of the Jewish community of Yeshua`'s followers. This means that even Simon Peter was subordinate to him. Jacob guided the community from the years 30 – 62 CE of the first century. He was greatly admired by many in the wider Jewish community, as being a just and a pious man.

He is better known to Christians as 'St. James the Just',[c] the author of 'The Letter of James' – the twentieth book of the New Testament. Within our community, Jacob the Pious and Yeshua` ('Jesus of Nazareth') are both admired and respected as holy men of God - Jacob as a *Tsaddiq* (a 'Pious One'), and Yeshua` as a prophet.

Let me quickly explain what a *Tsaddiq* is in Jewish terms. There are two terms used to describe what a modern westerner would

---

[a] Lev 20:8
[b] as the son of Joseph's brother, Cleophas (Qlofas).
[c] 'Ya`aqov ha-Tsaddiq' in Hebrew

understand as 'saintly' individuals: a *tsaddiq* (a 'Pious One') and a *chasid* (a 'Devoted One'). The difference of these in Judaism compared to Christian saints, is that we don't pray to them, or expect miracles from them, and we definitely don't ask them to intercede on our behalf in order to obtain favours from God. They are mortal men and women who live lives of piety, humility and simple devotion to God. In the manner of their lives, it becomes evident to those around them that God is supremely present with them, and their souls overflow with the sanctity of God's Presence. In Talmidaism, instead of praying to these holy men and women, we study their lives and try to learn from them, or even emulate them.

Both *chasidim* and *tsaddiqim* are, in a sense, Jewish 'saints' or more properly, 'holy people'. The difference between *chasidim* and *tsaddiqim* is that, according to ancient Jewish belief, a *tsaddiq* is also able to gain forgiveness for the sins of others through the elevated quality of their prayer – this is a really important point to take in. In Chasidic Judaism, they say that *tsaddiqim* are not aware of who they are while they live, or what they are capable of doing. Considering that Jacob was only crowned 'a Pious One' (a *tsaddiq*) after he died, he most likely was unaware himself of his status in God's sight while he lived.

When comparing Jacob and Yeshua`, the odd thing is, Yeshua`'s ministry lasted for only about 3 years, and yet the world has an almost infinite amount of literature on him. In total contrast, Jacob's ministry lasted an incredible 32 years, and yet what has been written about him would barely fill one bookshelf – even given that we have more proof of his existence than we do of Yeshua`![a] In mainstream Christianity, 'St James' is little more than a minor saint, and within the Catholic Church especially, there is an almost deliberate, intentional confusion over who 'St. James' was.

From what our community has found out, we have come to the conclusion that this sorry state of affairs is down to two things: first, that Jacob was the *real* leader of the Jewish community of Yeshua`'s followers, and that Shimon Keyfa (the apostle 'Simon Peter') was in fact subordinate to him. This fact alone is an uncomfortable one for those who believe that 'Jesus put Peter at the head of the Church'.

The second is the more stunning fact – and potentially, the more subversive. Now as I have already mentioned, there is a Jewish folk belief that, "for the sake of the Pious Ones, the world is not destroyed". It was the belief of the Jewish community of Yeshua`'s Followers that, through Jacob's ministry of prayer on behalf of the Jewish people,

---

[a] Jacob the Pious is mentioned in contemporary sources outside of the New Testament, such as the works of Josephus.

Jerusalem was spared destruction for as long as he was alive to continue his ministry of prayer. Jacob's ministry was viewed by Jewish Followers of the time as one of prayerful intercession for forgiveness on behalf of the sins of the people.[a] Because Jacob was such a pious and holy man, his prayers were able to gain forgiveness for the sins of the many. And this is the extraordinary thing to take note of: He didn't have to suffer, or die, or shed any blood – **his prayer alone as a man of piety gained forgiveness for the nation.**

In terms of theology, this early Talmidi belief about Jacob is an earthquake. No one had to suffer and die, no blood had to be shed, and no animal sacrifices were necessary to effect forgiveness of sin. Instead, he prayed constantly in the Temple every day for most of his life;[b] God heard him, and the misery of exile was held back. The nation was saved from the tribulation by Jacob's prayer. Shortly after Jacob's death however, the situation in Galilee and Judea went from bad to worse; within four years, there was war, and eight years after his death the Temple was destroyed.

These two things – that Jacob was the head of the community, not Peter; and that Jacob's ministry of prayer gained the forgiveness of sins – are uncomfortable for adherents of Paullist theology, who believe that only 'the death of Christ' can achieve this. It is better therefore for the mainstream that Jacob's existence remain a confused blur.

Another interesting little point that has come up in our community's collective research: there is a possibility that the reason why we have so little about Jacob, is that the details of his life – his deeds and his words – were hijacked, and used to write the backgrounds of other historical and quasi-historical characters.

The best case in point is the martyrdom of Stephen in the NT *Book of Acts*. There is an ancient Ebionite work called the *'Ascents of James'*, now found within a larger work called *The Clementine Recognitions*. After we remove the few Christian interpolations from the work, we come to realise how strikingly similar Paul's assault on Jacob the Pious is to the story of the martyrdom of Stephen. I have no doubt that the story of Paul's attack on Jacob in the 'Ascents of James' (and in other historical works), and the story of the martyrdom of Stephen in Acts, are actually one and the same story. The only difference in the *Ascents of*

---

[a] Jerome/Eusebius (quoting the Jewish-Christian Hegesippus) Ecc Hist. 2.23.5-6 – that he *"was often found upon his bended knees interceding for the forgiveness of the people"*.

[b] same quote from Hegesippus: *"and he used to enter the Temple alone, and was often found upon his bended knees ......, so that his knees became as calloused as a camel's, because of the constant importuning he did and kneeling before God......"*.

James is that Jacob was not killed when Paul physically assaulted him; he was merely left for dead.

The second example is that Jacob the Pious, when he was being stoned to death in 62 CE, was famously credited as saying, *"I beseech you, Lord and Father, forgive them, for they know not what they do"* (a quote from Hegesippus,[a] a Jewish-Christian writer of the early 2nd century CE). The tale is also told that people would vie to touch the hem of his clothing,[b] in the hope of being blessed by some of the holiness God had endowed Jacob with.

He was also dedicated as a Nazirite from the time of his mother's womb;[c] it is therefore possible, like the prophet Samuel (who was also a Nazirite from the time of his mother's womb), that he was brought up from early childhood as an attendant in the Temple,[d] and so spent most of his life there in service and prayer. Even knowing that Jerusalem and the Temple were going to be destroyed, he decided to stay in Jerusalem, praying for the sins of the people, serving the poor, and encouraging the people to endure through the troubles and resist violence. His life growing up in the Temple (and therefore his learning) would explain his knowledge of priestly theology,[e] as well as the excellent Greek[f] of his epistle; presumably he would have spoken excellent Hebrew and Aramaic too as a result of his Temple education.

From what little our community has gleaned from the scant sources, and from the opinions of Jacob voiced in the *Ascents of James* in the *Clementine Literature*, it is possible that a lot of what Jacob the Pious was, actually got overlaid onto Yeshua`. For example, the traditional image of Yeshua` as a man dressed in white, with a long beard and long hair, was probably actually Jacob, since HE was a life-long Nazirite; Yeshua` could not have been a life-long Nazirite, since he drank wine[g] –

---

[a] In Eusebius's *Ecclesiae Historia* 2:23

[b] Eusebius, *Ecclesiae Historia* 2:23, quoting Hegesippus

[c] *Ecclesiae Historia* 2:23

[d] This would not have been an unusual thing to do; in fact, if a woman vowed her male child to God as a Nazirite, then it would be *expected* that the child would serve out his youth in the Temple. A previously barren woman could dedicate her firstborn in service to God as a votary offering in thanks to God for giving her a child (see Lev 27:1-8).

[e] James 1:2-4 seems to suggest an awareness of the theology related to the power of the Glory of Yahveh.

[f] Some writers contend that 'the Letter of James' cannot have been written by James because of its excellent Greek; being unaware of the tradition that he was brought up in the Temple, they cannot account for his erudite language, assuming that he was, like his cousin Yeshua`, a mere peasant from the Galilee.

[g] cf the (somewhat hyperbolic) accusation in Mt 11:19 that he was a glutton and a drunkard.

which is something expressly forbidden to a Nazirite during the time of their vow. The only Jewish men in that time period to have had long, uncut hair and a long beard were Nazirites.

This brings up some tantalising questions: Could it be that, in the attempt to wipe out the memory of a man whose ministry is so theologically dangerous to Paullist belief, that Paul's early Gentile Believers took apart Jacob's words and put some of them into Yeshua`'s mouth? Is it possible that some of Yeshua`'s deeds in the *New Testament*, were actually the deeds of Jacob the Pious? Did the sacred reputation of Jacob become the reputation of Yeshua` instead? Could the story of the 12-year-old Jesus in the Temple actually have been taken from an incident of Jacob as a child? Sadly, these are questions which will never be answered with any degree of certainty.

We are left instead with the words of Robert Eisenmann. In his book, 'James, the Brother of Jesus', he wrote: "Whatever James was, Jesus was also."

The new, updated image we get of Yeshua` is one of an ordinary, rustic Jewish man, a true man of the people, who was able to put the Jewish religion into terms that the ordinary man and woman in the street could relate to – someone who was charismatic and inspired people. He was a true prophet, plucked from his rural, country life, called by God to speak as a prophet, and placed on a path which would eventually lead to his death.

Then we have Jacob the Pious – 'St. James the Just'. He was a very religious, learned man, pious and faithful to Torah in all his ways, who attended Temple every day. He was considered extremely wise, and was approached often by both the learned and the simple for his opinions. He was a true *Tsaddiq*, whose ministry was one of constant intercession to God for the city and people of Jerusalem.

Furthermore, the picture that forms in our minds of Jacob is of an intensely holy and prayerful man, a man of justice and selfless kindness. He seems to have been a man so filled with God's love that, despite his humble demeanour, he was able to disarm others with his words. He was loved and respected by the people of all Jewish religious parties of the time – even the Pharisees, who actually tried to defend him against the High Priest who sentenced him to death. And when that failed, it was their protests that got the High Priest deposed, for carrying out a sentence which was normally reserved for the Roman governor to pronounce and carry out.[a]

Jacob and Yeshua` were two different people; their ministries were each distinct but complementary. Jacob carried on where Yeshua` left

---

[a] Eusebius, *Ecclesiae Historia*, 2:23

off.

We, as Followers of the Way, are incredibly privileged to have had such a wonderful, saintly man of simple piety as Jacob in our faith's history. On the whole, mainstream Christianity does not want him; it would rather he remain obscure. Actually, we're glad they don't want him. He was ours. And his life is ours today to inspire us towards the same humble and compassionate service of God.

The Gaius Crisis and the 'Letter of St James'

It is possible that as the troubles in the Galilee and Judea became progressively worse, those who had originally turned a deaf ear to Yeshua`'s warnings, began to realise that there had in fact been some substance to his message – that his prophecies concerning the destruction of the Temple and of Jerusalem were coming dangerously close to fulfilment. This might also account for the widespread respect in which Jacob was held across most Jewish religious parties.

For most Christians today, Jacob the Pious is better known as 'St. James', the author of 'the Letter of James' in the *New Testament*. However, even though the letter itself is unambiguously addressed to 'the twelve tribes in the Diaspora', very few commentaries on *The Letter of St James* mention anything about what was happening in the Jewish world to the Jewish people at that time.

Most people only ever take notice of the 3 years of Yeshua`'s ministry, and ignore everything either side of it as irrelevant. Ancient Talmidi Jewish history, however, continues on for a further one hundred years after that! Ignoring that *enormous* chunk of history, enabled early Gentile Christianity to remove Yeshua` completely from his Jewish context, and helped Paullist theology to turn him from a Jewish prophet into a 'son of god', not that dissimilar from the saviour god-men of the pagan Mediterranean world. It has also helped Christian fundamentalists to fervently insist, every year over the course of the last two thousand years, that the end of the world is only just around the corner!

Ignoring this huge swathe of history is just like as if you were to write a drama set in 1915, and never once mentioned the First World War; or a Jewish drama set during the Second World War, and never once mentioned the Holocaust. Even when discussing how Jacob the Pious wrote about enduring trials,[a] and how *'the Judge stands at the very gates'*,[b] very few commentaries mention the turbulent events suffocating the whole Jewish population of Galilee and Judea; the majority tend to

---

[a] Ig. Yq. 2:2-3, 13; cf Letter of James 1:3-4, 5:11
[b] Ig. Yq. 2:16 – cf Letter of James 5:9

centre instead on the persecution of early Gentile Christians in Asia Minor and Rome. Few have any kind of awareness regarding the impending destruction of Jerusalem, and the subsequent exile of Jews from Judea. It has to be remembered that Jacob the Pious was a Jew, writing to Jews; I have to say again that the letter was explicitly addressed to the Jewish Diaspora of the Mediterranean, not Gentile Christians.

Furthermore, because of its lack of Christology[a] – that is, of any discussion of 'Jesus' as a messiah-saviour – *The Letter of St James* almost got left out of the Christian canon of scripture. What it does focus on, is to exhort the Jewish world to endure a crisis which is never actually described; the letter seems to assume that its Jewish readers around the Mediterranean would know exactly what this crisis was. Even though most modern Christians are completely unaware of this crisis, it is an important one for modern Talmidis to know about and understand.

Some writers[b] think the crisis is the one which has come to be known as 'the Gaius Crisis', which heightened tensions between Rome and the Jewish world between the years 39-40 CE. For this reason, I personally would date *'The Epistle of St James'* (or *'The Letter of Jacob the Pious'* as it is called in Talmidaism), to this period. This would make it the earliest document written by a follower of Yeshua` – even earlier than Paul's letters.

The Roman Emperor Gaius is better known to us today as the psychopathic Caligula. His mentally unstable cruelty must be borne in mind when recalling all these events. The crisis was initially centred in Alexandria in Egypt, which had a sizable Jewish community at the time. Under the Roman governor Flaccus, anti-Jewish sentiment increased. Flaccus was so scared of Caligula, that he regularly gave in to the anti-Jewish demands of his local Greco-Egyptian subjects. For example, the visit of the Jewish King Agrippa I in August of the year 38 CE, was publicly mocked by the Egyptian citizens of Alexandria; subsequently, as a result of the demands of the local populace, the status of Jews in Egypt was redefined as that of aliens. The Jews of Alexandria were herded into a single ghetto and confined there, synagogues were desecrated, and Jewish elders were arrested without cause and flogged.

At the end of the year 40 CE, the Emperor Caligula won a significant military campaign in what is now Germany. So the Gentile population of Jamnia in Judea itself, set up an altar in honour of the

---

[a] Notably, James does not make *any* attempt to back up his arguments by trying to prove that Yeshua` was a messiah. This in itself suggests that he did not believe Yeshua` to have been a messiah. The words 'servant of the Lord Jesus Christ' are likely to be an early Christian interpolation.

[b] e.g. 'New Testament History', by FF Bruce, chapter 19: 'Crisis under Gaius'.

Emperor's victory, hailing him as a god. However, the Jewish population felt this was idolatry, and pulled the altar down. Tensions increased significantly thereafter between the Gentile and Jewish populations of Judea (it's important to realise here that at this time, the coastal population of the Holy Land was mostly Gentile and pagan). Caligula's angry response to the pulling down of his altar in Jamnia, was to order that a legionary force be sent to Judea, and that a giant statue of himself be installed in the Jerusalem Temple.

This of course brought back memories of how the Syrian ruler, Antiochus Epiphanes, had set up a giant statue of Zeus in the Jerusalem Temple nearly 200 years previously. In fact, Caligula saw himself as *Zeus Epiphanes Neos* ('the young Zeus made manifest').

During this crisis, the words of the prophet Yeshua` would have had greater meaning: *"But when you see abominations of desolation standing in the Holy Place – where they have no right to be – then you will know that the end is almost upon you."*[a]

This crisis was only averted at the intervention of Herod Agrippa, who would shortly after[b] become the king (or 'messiah')[c] of Judea[d] at that time. He had grown up with Caligula in Rome, and so wrote to his childhood friend to persuade him to draw back from his plans for this gigantic statue in the Temple. Despite his many faults and wrongdoings, at this dangerous moment in Judea's history, Agrippa proved himself to be God's 'Appointed One'. This is the alternative, metaphorical meaning of 'anointed one' or 'messiah'; consider how the non-Jewish, Persian Emperor Cyrus was also called a 'messiah' in Isaiah 45:1 – meaning not 'Anointed One', but rather 'Appointed One' – someone chosen by God to fulfil a specific purpose in God's plans for the Jewish people.

If for nothing else, I personally feel that God specifically 'appointed' Agrippa for this one task; in spite of his many errors and failings, God put Agrippa in place so that he could avert this crisis. This is the crisis about which Jacob the Pious wrote in his famous letter to the Jewish communities of the Mediterranean. Most Christians today are unaware of these events, but I feel it is important for us as Followers of the Way to remember that time, those dark and fearful days, and understand them and Jacob the Pious's letter in their true historical

---

[a] S.Yesh. 162:14 – cf Mk 13:14, Mt 24:15
[b] His short reign over the whole of Judea lasted from c. Jan 41 to 6th Aug 44 CE.
[c] Whether or not Agrippa was literally anointed with oil in a ceremony to consecrate him king is not known, but nevertheless, 'anointed one' was an automatic title of all the reigning kings of Israel and Judah.
[d] At the height of Agrippa's reign, Judea covered most of what was David and Solomon's kingdom of ancient Israel.

context.

Subsequent to these events, it was widely believed that his ministry of prayer as a *Tsaddiq*[a] atoned the priests of their sins,[b] as well as those of the Zealots and the rich, who all desecrated God's holy reputation with their immoral actions. According to ancient Talmidi belief, Jacob's ministry of prayer delayed the calamitous events which culminated in the destruction of the Temple in 70 CE.

Some in our community even think that, had Jacob not been killed, the fall of Jerusalem might have been delayed even longer. When Jacob spoke against the cruelty of the High Priest Hananiah[c] in the year 62 CE, the High Priest took advantage of the absence of a Roman governor[d] over the province. Normally, only a Roman governor would have had the power to execute the death sentence, so when Jacob stood up to the High Priest, Hananiah had him stoned to death without a trial.[e] According to tradition, his body was taken and buried in a tomb to the south-east of Jerusalem. The location of this tomb is now lost to us.

In summary, the *Letter of St James* in the *New Testament* was addressed to the Jewish communities around the Mediterranean and in the Galilee and Judea, at a time of impending crisis. Most Christians are entirely unaware of this crisis, but it is important for us, as Followers of the Way, and as inheritors of the James-tradition, to remember these events. It's vital we recall what led up to them, and how this chapter of Jewish history was resolved.

The Convention of Jerusalem

I now come to write about the most significant event during Jacob the Pious's long term of office. Long before his death, a convention (or 'council') was convened in Jerusalem in the summer of the year 49 CE, in order to discuss Paul's activities in Antioch in Syria. In the Catholic and Eastern Orthodox Churches, this convention is considered as the Church's first ecumenical council. Now, because of the way in which the

---

[a] A *Tsaddiq* is someone who is especially favoured by God because of the piety and devotion of their life. Their prayer is considered so powerful, that it is able to atone for the many sins of others. Ancient Followers of the Way used to believe that Jacob's prayers delayed the day of judgment.

[b] Eusebius, *Ecclesiae Historia*, 2:23

[c] Ḥanan ben Ḥanan, High Priest for only 3 months in 62 CE. He would send his men to seize tithes as grain was being threshed, so that poorer priests got nothing, and their families starved to death (recorded in Josephus, *The Antiquities of the Jews*, bk 20, ch 9).

[d] between the governorships of Festus and Albinus

[e] Josephus, *The Antiquities of the Jews*, 20.9.1

episode is described by Luke in Acts chapter 15, we are made to think that the big issue was about circumcision. However, considering Paul's own account of the incident in Galatians chapter 2, circumcision seems to have merely been a side issue.

Mainstream Christianity tells us that the outcome of the gathering was that Gentile Christians were reconciled with Jewish Followers, and were all integrated to become part of the same, single community of faith. However, when you finally understand all the issues from a completely Jewish perspective, you come to realise that the actual outcome was that Paul's Gentile Believers were formally defined as non-Jewish, and Paul's ministry is given freedom to teach and minister to non-Jews. Far from bringing Jewish Followers and Gentile Believers into one united community, the convention marks the formal break between Paul's ministry and the Jerusalem elders – the break between Paullist Christianity and Judaism.

In Acts 15:1, we are led to believe that certain Followers from Judea came down to Antioch and told Paul's non-Jewish Believers, *'Unless you are circumcised according to the custom of Moses, you cannot be saved.'* Now, as a Jew I can immediately say that this statement *cannot* have come from the mouth of a Jewish Follower of the Way, because it shows a blatant lack of understanding over what circumcision is for (a physical sign of the Covenant between God and Israel, binding you and your descendants to the land and people of Israel). The statement in the *Book of Acts* is false, anti-Jewish propaganda from Luke, because **circumcision is nothing whatsoever to do with salvation from sin or going to heaven.** If this is false, what else in Luke's selective history of Christian origins are false inventions?[a]

If you read Paul's own account in Galatians chapter 2, it appears that Peter had been happily sharing meal-times with Paul's non-Jewish Believers. When some people arrived from Jerusalem and told Peter that the food he was eating might not be kosher, he stopped eating their food. Subsequently Paul, instead of explaining the issue of *kashrut* to his non-Jewish Believers, and instead of working to find some accommodation – for example, by making sure Peter's food was kosher, so that he *could*

---

[a] Luke also gets the time period of the messianic prophet Theudas wrong, as he does that of Quirinius's census. In Acts 5:36-37, Luke has Gamaliel place Theudas's ministry *before* the non-existent census in 6 BCE (it was actually in 6 CE, a full 12 years after Yeshua` was born)! The Jewish historian Josephus places Theudas 50 years after Luke's date, during the procuratorship of Cuspius Fadus (44–46 CE). The *Book of Acts* is therefore pro-Paullist propaganda, rather than a reliable account of history. Luke claims to be following historical sources (Lk 1:2-4), but never actually says what those sources are (which, even for ancient times, makes him a bad historian).

important

Shmuel ben Naftali *+ explaining*

continue eating with non-Jews – <u>instead of being a good Jew,</u> Paul takes issue and makes out that this is nothing but typical Jewish condescension towards non-Jews. It is a prime example of Paul's manipulative nature – twisting the facts of a situation for his own ends.

In effect, Paul seems to have seized on the incident in order to raise his own standing in the eyes of his non-Jewish, ex-polytheist converts. He appears to use the episode to make it appear as if he is standing up for their rights – in effect, he paints himself as their champion. In his own letter to the Galatians, and in the *Book of Acts* (written by his devoted follower Luke), <u>Paul's stand makes it look as if we Jews think that only Jews can be 'saved'</u>,[a] and that salvation and eternal life is obtained through circumcision. Both these points are **completely** fictitious and untrue, but the important point to realise is this: that none of Paul's Believers – who knew nothing of the Jewish religion – would have known that these things are untrue. Apparently, <u>neither do most modern Christians,</u> and so the dishonest myth is perpetuated.

There are some people today who say that the issue was this: do you have to be circumcised and convert to Judaism in order to be a follower of Jesus?

To Jewish Followers, this would have been as odd a question as, 'Do you have to convert to Judaism in order to be a follower of Moses? Or Isaiah? Or Jeremiah? Or Habakkuk?' When it becomes clear that 'being a follower of Jesus' in Christian parlance *actually* means 'following God's moral and ethical teachings', then for someone with a Jewish mind-set, it becomes clearer that in practical terms, this effectively means being a follower of the ways of God's Kingdom – a follower of the God of all Nations. So, rephrased in Jewish terms, the question becomes: <u>do you have to convert to Judaism in order to be a follower of the good ways of God's Kingdom? The Jewish answer, and our answer, would be: no.</u>

To Jewish Followers, it was *Yahveh's* message of salvation which is open to all humanity, and you don't have to be Jewish – or even a Follower of Yeshua` – to be 'saved' (to put it in Christian terms; for us as Jews, salvation is, and always has been, open to the whole human race through Yahveh). If Paul wanted his Gentile Believers only to follow the ethics of 'Jesus Christ' – then fine, but they are not just his ethics, they

---

[a] I put the word 'saved' in inverted commas, because I am using the word here (and subsequently in this section) in its Paullist Christian sense, not in its Jewish sense. To a Christian, it means being given a cast-iron guarantee that you will go to heaven. In the Israelite religion it means being miraculously rescued by God from real-world peril (eg Gen 19:19-20, Ex 14:13, Dt 33:29, 2Sam 3:18, Ps 34:6), or from a dangerous emotional or spiritual state of mind (eg Jer 17:14).

are *Yahveh's* ethics. They did not enter the world for the very first time with 'Jesus Christ'; they were a part of the faith of Abraham and of all the prophets from the very beginning – an intrinsic part of the Way of Yahveh.

In contrast, Yeshua`'s job was very specific – he was a prophet sent to the Jewish people to call the sinful among us to repent, to call us back to a good and righteous way of life according to God's ways, so that the prophesied destruction of Jerusalem could be averted. If it could not be averted, then he would call the lost sheep of Israel, so that they could be saved (in the Jewish sense of the word), along with the innocent when the tribulation came. Before Paul, Jewish Followers *would* have considered the kingdom of God open to all humanity, but would not have even thought about the relevance to non-Jews of Yeshua`'s warnings of destruction in the Holy Land and of Jewish exile – after all, at the time of Yeshua`'s ministry, all non-Jews were polytheistic pagans.[a]

I also think that, because we today are looking from the outside in – encumbered by the baggage of everything that has happened in the last two thousand years – we cannot see what the problem truly was. In order to understand what was really happening, we have to approach the issue from the inside – with the awareness *only* of that time period. Only then can we figure out where the two sides were coming from, and what the real point of contention actually was.

As I said previously, circumcision was merely a side issue. It was used by Paul purely as a symbol of full conversion to Judaism and full adherence to Torah.[b] Unlike today, where you are either Jewish or you are not, in those days, there were also Godfearers[c] – non-Jews who lived according to Jewish law, but who did not fully convert. In the case of men, significantly this meant that they remained uncircumcised.

The ancient community of Followers, like any Jewish sect of the time, would have had its own Godfearers. ***You could therefore quite happily follow the teachings of Yeshua` without going through full conversion – without being circumcised.***

The issue at hand therefore, had to be about non-Jews who *did not follow any aspect of the Jewish religion whatsoever.* So just what was the issue with them?

For an answer to this, we turn again to Paul's letter to the Galatians. In Gal 2:11-13, Paul describes the initial spark for the argument. As I've

---

[a] apart from 'Godfearers' – non-Jews who followed Torah and worshipped the God of Israel without fully converting.
[b] Gal 5:3
[c] in Hebrew a Godfearer is called *yireh elohim* (female: *yirat elohim*). A Godfearer can also be called a *nilveh* (female: *nilvah*), meaning, 'one who attaches him/herself' i.e. to Yahveh (Isa 56:6).

already said, before certain people arrived from Jerusalem, Peter had been eating alongside Gentiles – remember, these were <u>*not*</u> Godfearers who followed Jewish kosher law, but regular Gentiles. After these visitors speak to Peter, he and other Jewish Followers (and presumably also Godfearers) withdraw from table-fellowship with them.

Now, someone today would think, 'Peter is being told to withdraw just because these Gentiles are not Jewish,' but that isn't the problem at all – we would be looking at this from a 21st century perspective, with 21st century prejudices and baggage. You have to remember that up until that time, 'Gentile' automatically meant 'pagan' – pagan culture and pagan values. You see, in those days, Jewish people had to be *very* careful about social contact with pagans, especially with respect to food. Jewish law <u>forbids</u> the consumption of blood, the meat of animals that have been strangled, and food that has been dedicated to pagan gods – which it often was. When eating with Gentiles, Jews could never be sure exactly what they were eating. So as a result, social contact at meal times was limited.

Peter had obviously been eating everything that had been put before him; but after the visitors had words with him, he and other Jewish Followers withdrew from table-fellowship with Paul's Gentile Believers. Not knowing anything of Jewish sensibilities regarding food, you can understand that Paul's Gentile Believers would naturally have been very offended. However, instead of explaining the Jewish problems about non-kosher food – *which he should have done if he were a good Jew* – Paul seizes this opportunity to set himself up as the champion of Gentile Believers against the central authorities in Jerusalem.

This episode created the following question: 'What minimum would Gentile Believers have to do to enable social contact at meal-times with Jewish Followers (and indeed, with Gentile Godfearers who *did* follow Jewish dietary laws)?' This, and not circumcision, is the main question that would have been taken to Jerusalem for discussion and resolution.

However, once in Jerusalem, another question seems to have cropped up – a much more important one. The Jewish purists in the community might have tried to resolve the first question – that of social contact – by insisting on full conversion, and full adherence to Jewish law, *including* circumcision for men. Even at that time, such a radical solution would have been asking way too much, and in any case was entirely unnecessary, given <u>the existence of *un*circumcised, yet Torah-observant Godfearers in the community</u>.

Logically, the ensuing debate would have examined to what extent a non-Torah-observant Gentile would have to make compromises with regard to Jewish law – which was not just concerned with ritual purity, *but with moral and ethical righteousness as well.* So this would inevitably have brought up the issue of moral righteousness among non-Jews. If Jewish Followers were to mix socially with Paul's Gentile Believers, then what minimum *ethical* code should Paul's Believers adhere to? After all, Paul seemed to be insisting that all that was needed, was 'faith in Christ'.

Because of this, the second question to arise would have been: 'What is the minimum code of ethics that Paul's Gentile Believers would have had to follow, in order to be considered righteous before the God of Israel?'

At this point, you have to forget about the Noachide laws regarding 'righteous Gentiles'. If you have not heard of these Noachide laws before, I'll quickly explain. In the Israelite religion, any good and righteous person is acceptable to God – *regardless of religion or ethnicity*. So the question arises, what makes a non-Jew a righteous person? The Pharisees came up with 7 qualifiers that marked a non-Jew as righteous, and named them after Noah – hence the Noachide laws.

Now, at that time, these 'laws of the Righteous Gentile' were neither fully formulated, nor widely accepted by all Jewish sects. Each Jewish sect had its own ideas about what constituted a 'righteous Gentile' – that is, a non-Jew whose behaviour and ethics were acceptable in the sight of God. The seven Noachide laws that mainstream Judaism has now, were only accepted at that time by the Pharisees. Some sects listed more laws, some less.

Paul's teaching was that his Gentile Believers were considered righteous by God simply because of their faith in 'Jesus Christ'. So, Paul becomes the champion of his offended Gentile Believers; the debate seems to strengthen his resolve that his Believers should not in any way, shape or form, follow Jewish custom or law. It makes him even more determined to insist on his view that 'Believers are justified before God through their faith in Christ.'

The issues over which the Convention of Jerusalem was called, had little to do with circumcision. As head of the Jewish community of Followers, Jacob the Pious had to resolve firstly: what was the minimum that Paul's Believers had to do to facilitate social contact with Jewish Followers of the Way, especially at meal-times? His answer was this: *'You are to abstain from food offered to idols, from blood, and from the meat of strangled animals'.*[a] As to the ethical righteousness of those Gentiles, he only considers the one thing that would directly affect immediate social contact with Jews, and so adds, *'and keep yourselves from sexual immorality.'*

---

[a] Acts 15:20, 29

In Acts 21:17-18, Jacob the Pious mentions the letter he sent with Paul that contained the Convention's decision. He makes it clear that those who upset Paul's church in Antioch did not speak for the elders in Jerusalem.[a] Jacob the Pious's words also imply that the decision was only meant to apply to Gentiles who didn't follow the Jewish religion in any way.

The debate was therefore *never* about circumcision. It was never even about whether you had to be Jewish to be a follower of 'Jesus'. It was *always* about facilitating social contact – especially at meal-times – between non-Yahwist Gentiles on the one hand, who followed not one single iota of Jewish law or belief, and on the other hand, Jews and Yahwist Godfearers who did.

One last thing. There is something that was not overtly discussed, but which was implied, and that was the relationship between the Jews and Godfearers who allied themselves to Jacob the Pious, and on the other hand, those non-Yahwist Gentiles who followed Paul's teaching. The Jerusalem Convention concluded that Paul's teaching was a way of extending a code of righteous moral conduct among the Gentile pagan nations – of spreading Yahveh's values and principles among Gentiles; they would *not* have viewed Paul's teaching as a way of extending the Jewish religion among non-Jews.

The natural, definitive – and binding – conclusion of this, was that Paul's Gentile Believers were not Jews – remember, they did not follow any cultural aspect of the Jewish faith. This facilitated the start of a break between Paul's Gentile Christian Believers and the Jewish religion. Thereafter, according to the *Book of Acts*, Paul's evangelical zeal to convert Gentiles takes off. The practical effect of the Jerusalem Convention was to make a cultural and spiritual break between Paul's Gentile Christianity, and Jacob the Pious's still very much *Jewish* sect of the Way.

It would seem that for a while at least, the elders in Jerusalem tolerated Paul. My personal opinion is that with Paul, the Jerusalem elders were dealing with a completely new phenomenon. Never before had they encountered a philosophy that was built solely on the ethics and morals of Judaism, but without *any other link* to the Jewish religion – neither with regards to cultural practice, nor to theological belief.

Of course, there had been previous attempts to marry Hellenist philosophy with Jewish culture, but never the other way round – Jewish philosophy on its own with Hellenist culture. We have to remember that at the time, no other culture in the Mediterranean world regarded kindness, compassion, social justice and forgiveness very highly at all;

---

[a] Acts 15:24

they were seen as weaknesses by most peoples.

It may have been that initially, the elders in Jerusalem saw Paul's mission as a good thing – that it was an effective way of spreading Yahveh's *values* among the pagan peoples of the Mediterranean, without the need to convert to Judaism. Perhaps in the beginning, the elders would have thought that Paul's philosophy and ministry could bring benefits for the international standing of the Jewish religion and people. It may even have been seen as a way of spreading the Kingdom of God among pagan peoples; such would have been well within the goals and ideals of the Israelite faith.

I get the impression that the decision of the Jerusalem Convention restricted Paul's activities[a] to non-Torah-observing Gentiles – Gentiles who did not follow any aspect of the Jewish religion. I think that initially, the Jerusalem elders supported his work and sanctioned his activities, and Paul took full advantage of that approval; according to Acts,[b] following the meeting in Jerusalem his missionising activity moved forward with added momentum and vigour.

However, they then begin to get reports that Paul was indeed going around various synagogues (i.e. thus exceeding his remit), telling Jews that they should abandon Torah.[c] I think at that point they began to get suspicious and concerned about his activities. I think it was at *that* point that they withdrew their support for him.

Jacob the Pious was now concerned that Paul was also teaching Jewish converts, as well as Godfearers and fully-Jewish Followers of the Way, not to follow Torah either (i.e. going far beyond his remit under the decision reached by the Jerusalem Convention). This further emphasises that the debate at the Convention of Jerusalem was really *only* about Paul's Gentile Believers who did not follow Jewish custom or practice in any way.

As long as Paul's work left Jews and synagogues alone, his activity was not covered by the authority of the Jerusalem Council of Elders. However, once he started teaching Jews to abandon Torah, and began causing disruption in synagogues, then it very much became the concern of Jacob the Pious and the Jerusalem Elders.

I would surmise that Paul's disruptive action in synagogues was the

---

[a] see Gal 2:7-9
[b] ch 16 onwards
[c] Acts 13:14-52, and 21:21. Luke makes it appear as if by rejecting Paul, Jews have rejected 'Christ' out of jealousy (Acts 13:46-47). In fact, the reason why Jews rejected Paul, was because he wasn't teaching anything Jewish (Acts 13:39) – such as teaching that following Torah was pointless (2Cor 3:6-7 – the letter of the Law kills, and is a ministry of death), and that following God's ways did not bring anyone salvation.

practical cause of the effective break between Paul's teaching and Jacob the Pious's teaching. Thereafter, while Jacob the Pious remained the authority and leader for Yeshua`'s Jewish Followers, Paul became the sole authority for his Gentile Christian Believers. One might even wonder if his insistence on visiting the synagogues of every town he visited and so causing disruption, was actually designed to *provoke* this break in authority. Even today, his letters in the New Testament – not that of James – are the foundation stones of mainstream Christian belief.

Varieties of belief: The ancient schools of the Way

After the destruction of the Jerusalem Temple in 70 CE, the Jewish Followers of Yeshua` of Nazareth coalesced into one main sect – the Ebionites. However, before the fall of Jerusalem, there is evidence to suggest that the Community of the Way was much more diverse.

Luke, in his writing of *The Acts of the Apostles* in the *New Testament*, is keen to portray the early 'church' as a united one under the sole leadership of Peter. The historical reality is that the Jewish community of the Way was a very diverse one under the leadership of Jacob the Pious. And I need to say for the record, this was no bad thing.

I would like to conjecture that after Yeshua`'s death, there were two main centres of the Community of the Way. The first were the Galileans,*[a]* originating from Yeshua`'s original ministry in the Galilee, and probably centred in Capernaum. The second were a group referred to by modern Talmidis as the 'Emissarians', who evolved from the ministry of Yeshua`'s Apostles ('Emissaries')*[b]* in Judea, and centred in Jerusalem.

The leader of the Galileans was probably Yochanan bar Zavdi (John son of Zebedee); in Gal 2:9, he is named as one of the 'pillars' of the early community. Since a major part of Yeshua`'s ministry was spent in the Galilee, it seems logical to assume that he would have had a considerable number of followers there. And since for most of that time he was headquartered in Capernaum – again, logically it is safe to assume that the main seat of the Galilean school would be that town. In fact, in writings where Yavnean rabbis criticise heretics (or '*minim*' in Hebrew), the main hotbeds of 'heresy' were Capernaum and Sepphoris, Galilee's capital.

It is therefore odd and suspicious, that in all the activities which Luke writes about in the *Book of Acts*, he rarely mentions the seminal

---

[a] Acts 9:31
[b] This is the word Hugh Schonfield uses for the Apostles in "The Original New Testament".

community of Followers in Galilee – they do not seem to be that important to him. He seems to concentrate on the community in Judea; in the Holy Land, Judea and Samaria[a] are mentioned numerous times by Luke, and various Gentile towns and cities are mentioned around the eastern Mediterranean, but the founding communities in the Galilee are only mentioned in passing.[b]

There is one very odd passage in the Gospel of Matthew, 11:21-23, where 'Jesus' castigates Chorazin, Bethsaida and Capernaum for their lack of faith, and predicts that *"Capernaum, which art exalted unto heaven, shalt be brought down to hell"* (KJV). This would have been a completely false prophecy, because Capernaum and other Galilean towns are recorded in history as actually having ***prospered*** after the fall of Jerusalem. I would surmise that the gospel writers were irritated at the fervent Jewish faith of Yeshua`'s Galilean Followers, and at their refusal to take on board Paullist beliefs. The more likely wording of the original prophecy would have been castigation of places like Jericho, Hebron and Jerusalem – places which all fell before the Roman onslaught.

My own theory is that because Galilee is where it all started, we can safely assume that the Galilee kept faith with Yeshua`'s original and earliest teachings – Galileans, more than anyone else, were familiar with Yeshua` the man, the human prophet. I would suggest that Luke was uncomfortably aware of this, and in his view, Galileans were awkwardly lacking in any kind of messianic christology to warrant mentioning them to his intended Gentile audience. The easiest way around the problem was not to mention the Galilean communities at all.

So what was the Galilean school like? If we are being logical, then we have to assume that Galilean teaching was a reflection of the Galilean regional identity and character. Galileans were ordinary country and farming folk. They practised a form of Common Judaism[c] which was simple and down to earth, yet replete with all the essential elements of Jewish piety and devotion.

It is well-known that Judeans regularly criticised Galileans for their lack of observance in the minutiae of Torah. An overriding feature of Galilean life was poverty and the daily struggle, so it would only be natural to assume that Galileans should place especial emphasis and value on the books of the Prophets, with their powerful message of social justice and of God's concern for the poor.

There is also evidence in the *Book of Acts* for another school of the Way in Judea and Samaria. The character of this community was

---

[a] communities in Samaria, which wasn't even Jewish, is mentioned 8 times, whereas the communities in the Galilee are only mentioned 3 times.
[b] They are only given fleeting mention in Acts 9:31, 10:37 & 13:31.
[c] that is, a non-sectarian form of Judaism practised by ordinary people.

markedly different to that in the Galilee. In Acts 2:44, Luke writes that Followers in Judea were devout in following the teaching of the Emissaries ('Apostles'). By common consent, they were regular in attendance at prayers in the Temple.*a* These particular Followers held everything in common.*b* They would sell their goods and possessions and distribute the proceeds to all, according to individual need. They did not hold any of their possessions as their own, but held everything as common property.*c* None were in want, as all those who owned lands or houses sold them, and brought the price they realised and laid it at the feet of the Emissaries.*d* It seems that money poured in, as they managed to gain some influential, wealthy women as converts.*e* It appears that they also carried out a healing ministry. The sick were often brought into the street for the Emissaries to minister to them.*f* Simon Peter and John son of Zebadee would go up to the Temple to pray at the afternoon service at 3 o'clock each day,*g* and Philip became the leader of the Emissarian communities in Samaria.*h*

There then arose a conflict with the Greek-speaking Followers of the Way. In Acts 6:1-5, Luke writes that Greek-speaking Followers felt that their widows were being discriminated against in the daily distribution of alms. A full council of the community's elders was convened, and it was decided to select seven lay members of the Greek-speaking community to oversee the distribution of alms to their own members. The seven members mentioned in Acts 6:7 (Stephen, Philip, Prochoros, Nicanor, Timon, Parmenas and Nicolaos) all have Greek names. What happened in effect, was that Greek-speaking Followers (or 'Hellenicists') were given permission to form their own group or 'school'.*i*

Whereas the Emissarians were devout and attended Temple, it seems that the Hellenicists held to a strong rejection of the Temple and all it stood for, as evidenced in Stephen's speech before he was stoned to death.*j* As a result, the Hellenicists alone were sought out by the High Priest's police under a general persecution (i.e. other sects of Followers

---

[a] Acts 1:14, Acts 2:46
[b] Acts 2:45
[c] Acts 4:32
[d] Acts 4:34
[e] Acts 13:5, Acts 17:4
[f] Acts 5:15
[g] Acts 3:1
[h] suggested by Acts 8:4-8, although I don't know who they would have been – perhaps Jews living among Samaritans? Yeshua` told his apostles not to go anywhere among the Samaritans.
[i] in the sense of 'school of thought or tradition'.
[j] Acts 7

were not sought out). Hellenicist Followers first dispersed around Judea and Samaria,[a] and then further afield[b] to Phoenicia, Cyprus and Antioch in Syria.

What this diversity of Galileans, Emissarians and Hellenicists can teach us, is that diversity is important within a community – the modern Talmidi community is equally diverse. Different people have different spiritual needs in worship, and enjoy different forms of cultural expression in their daily lives. It would therefore be unhelpful to impose spiritual communism on everyone, as was the hallmark of the Emissarians, or for everyone to have either a relaxed form of worship, or a highly ritualised one.

Paul's bogeymen: the 'Judaisers', and those who clung stubbornly to God's Torah

We Jews do not think we have a better chance of getting into heaven just because we are Jewish. God's salvation, God's love, God's forgiveness and God's atonement are all open to the whole human race, and are not the exclusive preserve of born-Jews, or of those who come to follow God's Torah out of choice. Paul's teachings give Christians today the false impression that we think otherwise.[c] In his pastoral letters, Paul puts out the false propaganda that all of us believe that simply by 'doing Torah' – that is, by simply following the rituals and customs of Judaism by rote – that we therefore become righteous people.[d]

Paul's teaching also gives the fallacious impression that we Jews want all non-Jews to become Jewish, and put everyone under the 'unbearable yoke'[e] of the Mosaic Law – this is also a false premise. The fullness of God's Torah is an obligation only to Jews, and is a free choice for Godfearers who wish to attach themselves to the people of Israel. The full Mosaic Torah is not applicable to non-Jews who aren't interested in Jewish culture or spirituality, *and never has been*. If it weren't for Paul's erroneous teaching that Gentiles have to be grafted onto the Covenant between God and Israel, NO JEW WOULD EVER HAVE INSISTED THAT PAUL'S BELIEVERS CONVERT TO JUDAISM.

---

[a] Acts 8:1
[b] Acts 11:19
[c] Phil 3:7, Gal 3:28 (also Eph 3:12-13, but Ephesians may not have been written by Paul)
[d] so Paul implies in Phil 3:9
[e] Acts 15:10; also Gal 2:4, 5:1, where the Torah is considered a form of slavery or bondage, and 2Cor 3:6-7, where Torah is seen as a ministry of death.

James's ruling[a] at the Council of Jerusalem proves to the Jewish mind that the issue being debated was never about whether you have to be Jewish to be a Follower of Yeshua`, but rather, *what minimum food standards did non-Jews have to follow in order for us to be able to share meals together with them?* Remember that at that time, Jews could never be quite sure what they were eating – whether their food might have been previously offered to pagan gods, or if their food still contained blood in it. Instead of explaining this sensitivity over kashrut, Paul seized upon it as a golden opportunity to set himself up as champion of his Gentile Believers, and show them that this was just another sign of the stupid, spirit-stifling Law making an unjust distinction between Jew and Gentile – which it wasn't.

In Philippians 3:2, Paul calls people like us 'dogs' – people who cling to God's Torah. All native-born Jews – those who reject his version of 'Christ' – are nothing but fallen branches,[b] and those non-Jews who are attracted to Torah are stupid and foolish.[c] In his writings, 'the Law' is made out to be this fearsome bogeyman lurking in the shadows, waiting to drag non-Jews down into hellish darkness and backward ignorance. In order to capitalise on the Gentile fear of Torah, he bases his arguments on a number of false premises:

- Gentiles have to become part of the Covenant between God and Israel in order to be 'saved' (i.e. in order go to heaven);
- This means that Gentiles have to be grafted onto the Covenant[d]
- This does not however mean following any aspect of the Torah whatsoever.

This is the fundamental point of Jewish bewilderment and incomprehension over Paul's teaching. As often as Paul says that Gentiles need to be part of the Covenant, Jews will then say, 'If you want to be part of the Covenant, then surely you have to follow Torah at the least, and at the most, undergo full conversion.' The rudimentary flaw in Paul's logic, is that **Gentiles do not have to be part of the Covenant between God and Israel in order to be 'saved'** (in the Christian sense of the word); Jews do not believe, and have *never* believed, that you have

---

[a] *'You are to abstain from food offered to idols, from blood, and from the meat of strangled animals'* - Acts 15:20, 29. The guidance to abstain from sexual immorality facilitates social contact between Jews and non-Jews.
[b] Rom 11:17a
[c] Gal 3:1
[d] Rom 11:17-24

THE WAY

to become Jewish in order to get into heaven. Luke's fictitious statement in Acts 15:1, which has a Jewish Follower asserting that Gentiles have to be circumcised in order to be saved, is utterly mendacious, anti-Torah propaganda, and not something that a Jewish Follower of Yeshua` would ever have said – because in essence, it is factually not true; Luke has Paul fighting a fight which doesn't exist!   *Luke's account*

The Covenant[a] between God and Israel is this: *"If you will worship Me alone forever, and follow My Laws and principles forever, then I will give you the Land of Canaan forever, and preserve you as a people forever."* The bit that has Jewish people utterly flummoxed and scratching our heads, is this: What part of that Covenant did Paul think Gentiles needed to be a part of? Especially if they have no interest in Jewish culture, beliefs or traditions? If Paul had never insisted that Gentiles be a part of God's Covenant with Israel, then Jewish people would never insist that non-Jews – especially those who don't follow any aspect of the Mosaic Torah – go through full conversion. Any Jewish insistence on full conversion would only have been a response to Paul's unnecessary notion that non-Jews have to become part of the Covenant in order to be 'saved' – in order to go to heaven.

Then there is the false propaganda that our supposed insistence on conversion is because we teach that, in order to be followers of Yeshua`, you have to become Jewish. As I've explained previously, this is also untrue. If a Christian Believer only wishes to follow the ethical and moral teachings of the Jewish faith – which are presumably what Paul wants to restrict his Believers to – then ancient Judaism already had its teachings on the path of faith for a righteous Gentile. The different Jewish sects of the time had various ideas of what ethics a righteous Gentile had to follow, but nevertheless, a righteous non-Jew would have been naturally understood as one who does not have to follow the whole of the Mosaic Torah – once again, Paul's argument is founded upon a conflict that doesn't exist.

What becoming part of the Covenant does, is it enables a non-Jew to become part of Israel's mission to be a light to the Nations, and become representative of God's values and ideals before the eyes of the world. For someone who feels that special calling from the God of Israel to come out from among the nations and join Israel, it enables us to stand under the visible banner of ethical principles and a distinctive culture, which God has given us to unfurl as a rallying sign to all peoples who

---

[a] The text of this Covenant (with the Patriarchs) is found at: Gen 12:2-3, 13:14-17, 15:1, 15:4-5, 15:7, 15:13-14, 15:18-21, 17:1-2, 17:4-16, 17:19-21, 22:16-18, 26:3-5, 28:13-15; (with Israel at Sinai and Moab) Ex 19:3b-6, 31:16-17a, Ex 34:10-27, Lev 26:1-45, Deut 29:1 – 30:20.

seek Yahveh's truth.[a] Israel has a special job and a mission that is not asked of any Gentile nations, because we will be judged with greater strictness than other nations. One other thing I will say: as a consequence of following God's way of holiness, never before have I felt this close to the raw power of our heavenly Father! Each day I feel the warmth and Presence of our living God pulsating around me!

The next piece of false propaganda is that God's Torah is nothing more than following a series of ritual actions – that we believe that simply by following these ritual actions by rote, we will get into heaven. If you go by the teachings of the original Israelite faith – and therefore by what we as Talmidis teach – this premise is also completely false. Modern Christians seem to judge the whole of ancient Judaism on the ethos of ancient Pharisaism and the modern Orthodox Jewish faith – which are indeed very legalistic and ritualistic. But that way of thinking is not what God's Torah is ultimately about.

Paullists state that simply by 'doing Torah' in and of itself will not make you a better person. Now, God's Torah – God's Teaching and Instruction – is not just about the commandments laid down in the five books of Torah, but the whole of God's ethical and moral principles contained throughout the whole Hebrew Bible. So if you look at the declarations of the biblical prophets, you can see how they themselves castigated people for simply following God's laws mechanically by rote – just look at how Isaiah[b] criticised those who fasted, and yet continued to ill-treat others and ignore God's ethical teachings. The Hebrew prophets also rebuked people for neglecting the needs of the lowest in society.[c] Torah's concern is also for justice and fairness,[d] and not siding with the majority when they do wrong[e] – Hosea even criticised the corruption of knowledge and wisdom.[f]

Then there are the secular laws. Torah is God's protection of the weak against the strong – the rule of law, when some people would rather follow their own selfish desires, and disregard the needs of others. This is why historically, the poorest in Jewish society were often the most faithful to its social ideals. God's Torah (i.e. God's Teaching) – that is, the ***whole*** of it – gives the powerless a legal voice, and prevents them from being exploited by the rich and powerful. We can see today that those who ignore God's ideals in Western society, now treat the least in

---

[a] Ps 60:4 – *"You have given a banner to those who revere You in awe – that it might be displayed in the presence of Truth".*
[b] Isaiah 58:3-4
[c] eg Amos 5:11-12, Isa 3:14-15
[d] Dt 16:20
[e] Ex 23:2
[f] Hos 4:6

their countries with the most deplorable disdain, often regarding them as mere commodities or capital, to be treated like chattel in the pursuit of greater power and wealth.

Paul's final false accusation is that the Jewish soul, in following Torah, can never attain any kind of righteousness, because we are all untransformed beings. He taught that Jewish people, in following God's Torah, were under a curse,[a] and would never experience the living Presence of God[b] – even those who followed the ethical and moral principles of God. What he never allowed his Gentile Believers to know, was that biblical, prophetic Judaism taught that practising religion by rote is never enough – it wasn't a new principle that Yeshua` dreamed up himself. It was God's original intent all along, that in order to follow God's teachings fully, you have to allow yourself to change and become a new person.[c] It is the very essence of God's Being and Glory that transforms the human soul from within. Following the spiritual guidelines of God's Torah allows the penitent soul to approach the fire of God's Divine Radiance, and *be completely transformed by it.*

Some people are born with a soul that yearns for Yahveh. More often than not, that soul is born into a community that does not know Yahveh. Yahveh will call that soul out from among the nations, and that soul will feel a yearning to follow God's Torah – Yahveh's values, principles and ideals. This yearning is a special calling from God – not everyone is called to follow Torah, only those souls who have the courage and strength to answer such a calling. So when Paul calls such people stupid, foolish dogs[d] for longing for Yahveh and Yahveh's Torah, his teaching stands as a wall of angry condemnation between God and those whom God has chosen and called from among the Nations – and woe betide such a man who stands between God and those whom God has called! No one demands that the whole human race follow Torah; why then do Paul and his Believers consistently condemn those who freely choose to do so?

---

[a] Gal 3:10, 3:13 – we are under a curse because we can never fulfil Torah perfectly. Paul's false premise is that God only has severe punishment for good people who fail in trying to be good. The truth is that God is like a shepherd who guides us when we stumble upon rocky paths.
[b] Gal 3:2
[c] In biblical language, the inner transformation of the heart and soul is called *'being circumcised of heart'* – see Dt 10:16, 30:6, Jer 4:4, 9:25-26, 38:33, Ezek 44:7. It is an ancient Israelite ideal that it is not enough to be circumcised in the body i.e to live out the externals of God's law, one also has to be circumcised of heart i.e. there has to be an inner transformation – the heart, mind and soul have to belong to God, not just the body.
[d] Phil 3:2, Gal 3:1

Jacob the Pious's edict against false teachers, and the fate of Peter

The Clementine Literature records an interesting warning from Jacob the Pious, that Followers of the Way were to *"observe the greatest caution, that you believe no teacher unless he also brings from Jerusalem a testimonial from me, or from whomsoever may come after me. For no one is by any means to be received, unless he has come up to Jerusalem, and has been approved as a fit and faithful teacher."*[a]

Similar warnings are found elsewhere in the Clementine literature. The image one therefore gets of the time, is that there were teachers going about the Holy Land and elsewhere, proclaiming a message which was at variance with the one authorised by the Jerusalem leadership – the one that they had received directly from Yeshua` while he lived – the Yeshua` they had personally known.

There is also the question of Peter's fate. Mainstream Christian history tells us that Paul and Peter became firm friends. Peter then left his homeland, never to return to it ever again.

The *Book of Acts* has no place for Jacob the Pious, whom Paul himself only grudgingly acknowledges as being the leader of the community.[b] There is an apocryphal book in the Clementine Homilies called *The Letter of Peter to James*. In it, Peter defends his preaching to Jacob the Pious, even sending Jacob the Pious copies of all his writings for scrutiny. What became of such scrutiny, is never recorded.

At this point I would like to put forward a theory. After his arrest and escape under King Agrippa I,[c] it's possible that Peter avoided recapture by leaving for Antioch in Syria,[d] where he could have stayed until well after Agrippa died.[e] During his long sojourn in Antioch (as long as five years), he would have had several periods of interaction with Paul, so becoming increasingly influenced by his teaching. Then when Paul rebuked him,[f] Peter more and more inclined towards Paul's teachings and beliefs. When the Jerusalem leadership comes to hear of

---

[a] Clem Rec, Bk 4, Ch 35
[b] Gal 2:9-12.
[c] see Acts 12:3-19; this occurred just after the Festival of Unleavened Bread in the year 44CE.
[d] Acts 12:17b – *"Then he departed, and went to another place."* This 'other place' is not specified, but could have been Antioch. By this time, the whole of what is now modern Israel and the West Bank was under Agrippa's control, and so the only natural safe places would have been outside of the Holy Land.
[e] Agrippa died in August 44CE, but Peter appears to have remained in Antioch a good while longer - until the dispute with Paul in early 49CE, after which he returned to Jerusalem.
[f] Gal 2:11-14, Acts 15:1-2; this most likely happened about the beginning of the year 49CE.

this, Peter is asked to explain himself. This he does, but I would surmise that he is found to have taken on many Paullist ideas, which contradict those of the Jerusalem elders.

The result is that he is stripped of his leadership of the communities of Judea (or at least, is put on some kind of probation, and has his preaching activities restricted).[a] Consequently, to avoid these restrictions, Peter decides to leave his homeland and travel first to Antioch, then to Rome, where he is reconciled with Paul. In Rome, Peter becomes a strong supporter of Paul, and is acknowledged as the leader of the Gentile church of Rome.

There is often the point put forward by Christian apologists, that mainstream Christian beliefs – such as the trinity – must be true, otherwise the apostles would not have died for them. However, at that stage of Gentile Christianity's development, the doctrine of the trinity was not yet fully formed, and historically we don't know what specific beliefs the other apostles died for. As for Peter, what Paul had convinced him of, was that Yeshua` had been the messiah, and that he had died to save humanity from their sins – Paul was the sole reference-point for this set of beliefs, not the apostles.[b] Having been convinced of this by Paul, *this* is what Peter died believing, but I am convinced it was not what the other apostles believed – the remaining apostles who remained faithful to Jacob the Pious and the Jerusalem leadership. Being disconnected from Jerusalem's authority, for Gentile Christians there was no referencing back to the teaching of the Jewish community in Jerusalem, nor any fact-checking of events or beliefs with Jerusalem. Being uninterested in the details of Yeshua`'s life, Paul's theology focussed entirely on Yeshua`'s death, and all theology surrounding Yeshua`'s death depends solely on Paul's teaching; Paul is the sole point of origin for mainstream Christian belief.

In Talmidi theology, regardless of what may have been the actual sequence of events, Simon Peter is basically understood to have gone over to Paul's side; further than this is speculation – we do not have enough historical evidence to say with any conviction what actually happened. He may have originally been the chief apostle of the communities in Judea,[c] but like Philip of Samaria, and John[d] of the Galilee, he was under the ultimate authority of Jacob the Pious. Then at some point, Peter loses his authority, and plays no further part in the story

---

[a] Clementine Literature, 'Letter of Peter to James', ch 4.1
[b] Paul does not consult with anyone who personally knew Yeshua` to verify his teachings or beliefs – see Gal 1:16-17. He actually takes pride in the fact that the apostles had **nothing** to contribute to him (Gal 2:6).
[c] surmised from Acts 8:14
[d] that is, the son of Zebedee.

of the Jewish community of Yeshua`'s followers; his story shifts completely to Rome.

Considering Jacob the Pious's warning about not listening to teachers unless they carry with them the proper authority from Jerusalem,[a] we can infer that a dishonest, alien message was being passed off as being the authentic Jerusalem one, and that this was becoming a serious problem – things that Yeshua` never said were being passed off as his authentic words. Documents that were written by the original apostles and disciples of Yeshua` could well have been doctored, so that what we have now in the *New Testament* may well contain material that the apostles never said or wrote, even though modern apologists vehemently claim that they did. To guard against this problem, the Clementine Writings suggest that it became the obligatory practice for authorised teachers to carry with them a copy of the 'Scroll of the Preaching'[b] – which I would like to think is the famed 'Q-gospel', the earliest scroll of the authentic sayings of the prophet Yeshua`; after all, what better proof of a true teacher of Yeshua`'s ethics than a scroll of his words!

Take the *Letter of Jude* in the *New Testament*, supposedly written by the brother of Jacob the Pious. The content of their two letters could not be more different – Jacob's letter concentrating on ethical behaviour, without any kind of Paullist christology, and Jude's letter, which speaks of burning hell and wars in heaven – both un-Yahwist concepts. Perhaps the original letter was different, but we have only the word of the letter itself that it was even written by Jude – Jacob the Pious's brother, Yehudah bar Qlofas. The original letter may well have been a victim of the common practice of early Christian sects to take the writings of others, amend or add to their content, and put someone else's name to the documents in order to give them some legitimacy and false authenticity. In those days, people did not have the luxury of picking up the phone and checking sources, or making the falsehood or veracity of anything widely known.

Whatever may be the truth of the matter, we can be certain that early on, Jewish Followers of the Way faced the pernicious dangers of pro-Paullist teachers, who tried to pass off falsified sayings of Yeshua` as authentic. I strongly suspect that these falsified documents later came to be held by Paul's Gentile Christians as authentic, whereas truly genuine Jewish documents were likely destroyed when they fell into the wrong hands. It may even be, that the sources which came to Matthew and Luke when they wrote their gospels, had *already* been amended by

---

[a] Clem Rec, Bk 4, Ch 35
[b] Letter of Peter to James, 4.1-4.3

pro-Paullist groups. Luke was, after all, a loyal propagandist for Paul and his teachings; the 'winners' of history got to write the authorised version of Yeshua`'s sayings, and they could put whatever words into his mouth they saw fit, in order to 'prove' their beliefs.

The fateful result of Peter's Paullist ministry – the Nazarenes

Having been influenced by Paul's messianic beliefs in Antioch, Peter returned to Jerusalem. While his new beliefs remained unknown to the Jerusalem leadership – that Yeshua` was the messiah, and had died to save us from our sins – Peter was free to spread his version of Paullist teaching around Judea. I tend at this point to agree with Ray Pritz's theory,[a] that the end result of this ministry was the formation of the sect of the Nazarenes (Hebrew *Notsrim*).

Historians are aware of a Jewish-Christian community in the Holy Land, different and distinct from the original Ebionites, and from those Followers who held Yeshua` to have been a human prophet of normal birth. By the year 57 CE, when Paul was arrested and brought to trial before the Roman governor Felix in Caesarea, Acts 24:5 relates that Paul was a ringleader among the sect of the Nazarenes. This term should not be confused with the 'Nazorayyans',[b] the sect of those who followed Yochanan the Immerser (John the Baptist). Neither should it be confused with those non-messianic Jewish Followers still loyal to Jacob the Pious.

Peter's Paullist ministry in Judea would explain the existence of the two groups of 'Jewish-Christians' in Judea – one non-messianic, promoting the human Yeshua` and his prophetic message of warnings about the coming tribulation which took place in 70CE; and the other a messianic one, promoting Paul's gospel that 'Christ' died to save us from our sins, and who would come in glory at the end of the world. The authentic Jerusalem community eventually left to go to Pella in Jordan, and in the 2nd century CE evolved to become the Ebionites; and the Nazarenes fled with other Jews to the Galilee upon the outbreak of war, to become the *Notsrim* so vilified in the Talmud. They would have been at some variance with the Galilean Followers already in the Galilee, still loyal to the former Jerusalem leadership, now in exile in Pella. However, it seems that the Pharisaic community made no distinction between genuine non-messianic Followers of the Way, and Paul's messianic

---

[a] *"Nazarene Jewish Christianity, From the End of the New Testament Period Until Its Disappearance in the Fourth Century"*, by Ray Pritz, Magnes Press, Hebrew University of Jerusalem, 1988

[b] *'The Mandeans of Iraq & Iran,'* ES Drower; see also *'An Aramaic Approach to the Gospels & Acts'*, Matthew Black, 1967 (p. 198)

Notsrim.
This Nazarene community had a gospel distinct from that of the Ebionites. I believe that the likeliest sequence of events was that after Peter was banned from preaching in the Holy Land, the Nazarenes got hold of a copy of the 'Scroll of the Preaching' (also known as 'the Q-Gospel'); it might even have been Peter's own copy before his teaching authority was stripped from him. They amended it to better accord with their Paullist understanding of Yeshua`'s ministry, and this then became the proto-Christian copy of the Q-Gospel that both Matthew and Luke used to write their gospels – Matthew[a] in Egypt, and Luke in Syria.

While those who followed the Way in the Galilee and Pella remained faithful to Shimon bar Qlofas – now in exile, the Nazarenes who escaped to the Galilee owed their allegiance to Peter and Paul in Rome, and to their proto-Christian beliefs.

The lead-up to the destruction of the Temple

After Jacob the Pious's death, things went from bad to worse in the Holy Land. Alongside the Saducean priests, the Zealots would become the second group whose actions desecrated the Temple, and therefore God's reputation of holiness. During the siege of Jerusalem, they set up engines of war in the Temple (the 'abominations of desolation set up where they have no right to be').[b] They also shed human blood in the Temple – they not only fought the Romans, but they also fought amongst themselves, with rival gangs setting up camp in different areas of the Temple compound. The shedding of human blood in such a sacred place as the Jewish Temple was the ultimate desecration.[c]

In the Talmidi view of religious history, God could not allow a symbol of God's holiness that had been desecrated in such a heinous way by the Saducean priests and the Zealots to remain standing, and so its fate was sealed. If the Temple had remained, so would the Saducees and the Zealots, along with their profane actions; they would have continued in their desecration. The only way to remove the sin of the Saducees and the Zealots, was to remove the Temple itself. In the year 70 CE, the Temple was destroyed by the Romans, ending the Jewish war

---

[a] Although this gospel has the name of Matthew attached to it, the author could not have been the apostle Matthew, since he demonstrates a lack of understanding of the Aramaic language, and copies Mark's gospel verbatim (which he would not need to do if he had been an eye-witness), and never speaks in the 1st person (which an eye-witness would; the apostle Matthew is referred to as 'him', and not 'me' – cf Mt 9:9).
[b] S. Yesh 162:14 – cf Mk 13:14, Mt 24:15
[c] human blood is not kosher.

against the Roman Empire. Occupying Roman forces ensured that not one stone was left standing on another – just as Yeshua` had prophesied.[a]

As Jews we mourn the loss of the Temple, that great place of reverence and holiness, that inspiring sanctuary of beauty and awe. It is a tremendous sadness to the collective Jewish soul, that we no longer have the place where Yahveh chose to 'put God's name',[b] and indeed we pray that it will one day be restored. However, I think we have to realise that in the 1st century CE, God had no other option. I think we have to come to terms with the understanding that it was God's will to take the Temple away from us in those days, in such troubled times. Perhaps it points to another understanding too – that God will not give it back to us unless peace reigns in Jerusalem.

Shimon bar Qlofas ('St. Symeon of Jerusalem')

There were 15 Nasis[c] in total, the last being Yehudah Nasi who held office for just one year. He was martyred in the year 135 CE when he was killed, probably by bar Kochba rebels for refusing to support them and their messianic aspirations.

Now, the Nasi who held office the longest was a little known prophet call Shimon bar Qlofas ('Symeon son of Cleophas'). In the Eastern Orthodox Church he is known as 'St. Symeon of Jerusalem', venerated as 'bishop' of the Holy City until he was martyred in about the year 107 CE.

He held office for no less than 45 years (the term of Jacob the Pious was 32 years by comparison). He is credited in the Talmidi Jewish community with having had visions, which prompted him to lead most of the Talmidi community in Jerusalem to seek safety in Pella[d] in Perea across the Jordan river, just before the outbreak of war in 66 CE. Shimon's prophetic visions were added to those of the Christian seer John, to form what is now known as the *Book of Revelation*.

Modern Talmidis believe that, as a result of these visions (and because of Yeshua`'s own prophetic warnings), many Followers of the Way left Judea and settled around Pella. Those who remained in Judea either perished or were taken away as slaves, sharing the cruel and unfortunate fate of their fellow Jews.

---

[a] S.Yesh. 133:5 – cf Mk 13:2, Mt 24:2, Lk 19:44, 21:6
[b] A Hebrew idiom which designated the place of central worship in the Israelite religion.
[c] religious presidents of the ancient Talmidi community; singular Nasi, pronounced naa-SEE. In modern Hebrew the word denotes a secular president.
[d] Modern Kirbet Fahil, in the present kingdom of Jordan.

Shimon bar Qlofas was actually the full brother of Jacob the Pious, and therefore likewise a cousin of Yeshua`. He was chosen because, like Jacob the Pious, he had known Yeshua` in life, and could therefore vouch for his teachings personally – or at least, knew his character sufficiently to be able to discern if something was or was not likely to have been said by him.

Even though he was the longest serving Nasi, very little is known about his life. This lack of interest shown by most of the early Church fathers in his life, has resulted in hardly anything being left to us of his work. What little we do know pertains only to the beginning and end of his term, contained in book 3 of *Historia Ecclesiae*, a history of the early Christian church by Eusebius:

- he was elected unanimously by those who had known Yeshua` personally
- as a result of several visions, he led Followers living in Jerusalem and Judea to safety in Pella, Jordan
- he was handed over to the Roman authorities in 107 CE by a local group of Gentile Christians, who accused him of being a Christian and a descendant of David
- he was tortured for several days for denying the charges, and then crucified

Here's what the Christian writer Eusebius says of Shimon's election:

> "*After the martyrdom of James and the conquest of Jerusalem which immediately followed, it is said that those of the apostles and disciples of the Lord that were still living, came together from all directions with those that were related to the Lord according to the flesh (for the majority of them also were still alive) to take counsel as to who was worthy to succeed James. They all with one consent pronounced Symeon, the son of Cleophas, of whom the Gospel also makes mention, to be worthy of the episcopal throne of that parish. He was a cousin, as they say, of the Saviour. For Hegesippus records that Cleophas was a brother of Joseph.*"[a]

In this passage, Eusebius places Symeon's election after the conquest of Jerusalem, but then he says that he and other Followers

---

[a] Eusebius, Historia Ecclesiae, Bk 3, ch 11:1-2

escaped Jerusalem *before* the conquest. I think what Eusebius is implying is that the fall of Jerusalem happened directly after the martyrdom of Jacob the Pious (which it didn't).

> *"The members of the Jerusalem church by means of an oracle, given by revelation **to acceptable persons there**, were ordered to leave the city before the war began and settle in a town in Peraea called Pella."*[a]

The passage in *Revelation* 12:1-17 about a woman (Israel) giving birth and fleeing into the desert, may have been a coded message for the community (who was the son of the woman, rather than Yeshua`) to flee into the Syrian desert.

Nothing further is recorded of his life until 45 years later. In the meantime, because Gentile Christians persistently claimed that Yeshua` was descended from David, this put all the lives of Yeshua`'s large, extended family at risk. During several persecutions, Yeshua`'s extended family was hunted down, and hundreds of them were executed by the Romans. I suspect that they were falsely accused of being descended from David precisely *in order to kill them all off* – in order to kill off anyone who had authentic knowledge of Yeshua` the human prophet. Shimon managed to survive all of these pogroms, until the time of the Emperor Trajan. During the last persecution by Trajan:

> *"Certain of these* [Gentile Christians][b] *brought accusation against Symeon, the son of Cleophas, accusing him of being a descendant of David and a Christian; and thus he suffered martyrdom, at the age of one hundred and twenty years, while Trajan was emperor and Atticus governor."*[c]

Eusebius makes it sound like those who handed Shimon over to the Romans were merely heretics, but going back to the earlier work by Hegesippus alone, it sounds like the bottom line is that these local Gentile Christians (whoever they may have been) were opposed to Shimon. I can only guess that, because he had personal, unassailable and

---

[a] Eusebius, Historia Ecclesiae, Bk 3, ch 5:4
[b] The text records that these were Gnostic Christians, considered heretical by what became the mainstream.
[c] Eusebius, Historia Ecclesiae, Bk 3, ch 32:3 (quoting Hegesippus)

irrefutable knowledge of his cousin Yeshua`, he was able to repudiate their form of Gentile Christianity, which was ultimately based on Paul's teaching (even Paul had a scornful disdain for those who knew Yeshua` while he lived).[a]

Shimon was obviously a thorn in their side; they probably realised that as long as he was alive, they could not prevail against his teachings and beliefs. Likely concealing the fact that they themselves were Christians, they purposefully accused Shimon of being a Christian, and deliberately accused him of being a descendant of David (because anyone descended from David was a political threat to Rome, and therefore someone to be arrested and executed). These two accusations sealed his fate. Eusebius goes on to record that his accusers were later found out to be Christians, and were themselves arrested, tried and executed.[b]

The prophet Shimon was betrayed into the hands of the Romans:

> *"the above-mentioned Symeon, son of Cleophas (a cousin of the Master), was informed against by the* [local Gentile Christians]*, and was himself in like manner accused for the same cause before the governor Atticus. And after being tortured for many days he suffered martyrdom, and all, including even the proconsul, marvelled that, at the age of one hundred and twenty years, he could endure so much. And orders were given that he should be crucified."*[c]

This elderly and pious man of God was tortured for several days. Logically, there would have been no need to torture him, unless **all the while he denied that he was a Christian or a descendant of David**. This is significant – if he admitted being a Christian and a descendant of David, he would have been executed straightaway. And if **he** was not a descendant of David, then neither was Yeshua`, since his father Qlofas, and Yeshua`'s father Yosef were brothers. Nevertheless, he was falsely crucified for being a messianic claimant – which in the eyes of Rome, was a treasonable offence.

We do not know where he was buried. The only memorial of his

---

[a] cf 2Cor 5:16 - *'Even if you were once familiar with Christ while he was alive, that is not how we know him any longer'.*
[b] Eusebius, Historia Ecclesiae, Bk 3, ch 32:4 (quoting Hegesippus)
[c] Eusebius, Historia Ecclesiae, Bk 3, ch 32:6 (quoting Hegesippus)

life are the visions[a] he had, which saved the Jerusalem community of Followers from certain death.

Blessed be the memory of Shimon son of Qlofas!

The Benediction of the Heretics

Shortly after the Temple was destroyed, the post-Temple rabbis sat in a council, in the coastal town of Yavneh (Jamnia), between the years 90 - c.130 CE. They made decisions on a vast number of different things, codifying rabbinical law – expanding and clarifying the Oral law. Many wise things came out of Yavneh; unfortunately, some of the most hateful things ever to have proceeded from the mouths of religious men also came out of Yavneh. One of these things was to extend the meaning of *mamzer*[b] to cover any Jewish sect they did not approve of.

For example, there was the rabbinic edict that marriages between non-Pharisaic Jewish men and women would not be recognised, and that our children would therefore be considered *mamzerim*. Pharisaic Jews were also forbidden to marry non-Pharisaic Jews.

The Yavnean rabbis also formulated a curse, the '*Birkat ha-minim*' (the Benediction of the Heretics),[c] to be said during the synagogue service. It effectively cursed those Jews who didn't agree with Pharisaic (or 'Rabbinic') Judaism, and those individuals who couldn't say it were thus identified as non-Pharisees. As a result, all non-Pharisees – including Followers of the Way – were effectively expelled *en masse* and excluded from Jewish synagogues. This event in about the mid-90s of the 1st century CE is viewed by Talmidi Jews as the date of the schism between Rabbinic Judaism and Talmidi Judaism – a schism not of our wanting or doing. In the Name of Yahveh I pray that one day, the mainstream will come to realise the resource they have shunned, the benefit they have cursed, and the loyal brothers and sisters they have cast out from amongst their own people. We stand therefore in the wings, ready to resume our place as dedicated sons and daughters of Israel.

Before the Second Jewish Revolt in 133-136 CE, there was a sizable community of Followers of the Way in Sepphoris, the chief city

---

[a] Now reconstructed in *The Visions of Shim`on bar Qlofas*, one of the 14 books of *The Exhortations* (the Talmidi Jewish equivalent of the New Testament).

[b] In Rabbinic Oral Law, a *mamzer* – 'bastard' – is defined as the child of a marriage forbidden by Jewish law.

[c] The wording of the original curse is: *"For the apostates let there be no hope. Let the heretics be destroyed immediately. And let them be blotted out of the Book of Life, and not be inscribed together with the righteous. Blessed art thou, O Lord, who subdues the wicked."*

of the Galilee. However, pronouncements from the rabbis of Yavneh ensured that contact with them was limited, since they were viewed as heretics (Hebrew: *minim*). Rabbinic Jews were therefore forbidden to derive any kind of benefit from *minim*,[a] or eat their food, or marry their children. The status of *minim* was considered even lower than that of non-Jews – a rabbinic ruling from the time[b] stated that a Gentile was not to be cast into a pit or helped out, but a non-rabbinic Jew was to be cast into a pit and left there.

It is logical that, faced with persecution, the Rabbinic Jewish community would close ranks, and it is understandable that such a community would want to tightly define their beliefs and teachings. However, to then treat other Israelites with such a lack of mercy, and with such a cold-hearted denial of compassion, flies in the face of one of the teachings of the Israelite faith – that *'you shall not hate your brother in your heart'*. If your fellow Jew is in trouble, you should help him or her. To circumvent this commandment, the rabbis of Yavneh redefined the meaning of 'brother', and so nullified God's law on a technicality. However, your brothers and sisters are still your brothers and sisters, and no human law can change that. Ultimately, the *Birkat ha-minim* was contrary to the spirit of Yahveh's Torah; the Council of Yavneh that formulated it was brought to an abrupt end by the Second Jewish Revolt, which culminated in the expulsion of all Jews from Jerusalem.

I have no doubt that the exclusion of all non-rabbinic Jews from synagogues – and effectively, from the House of Israel – was a body-blow to Jewish Followers of the Way. Like any other Jew, they required shelter and protection from the ravages of the times, and it was denied to them.

For our part, I feel confident that the earliest Followers of the Way would have forgiven these hateful curses and pronouncements. I hereby reiterate such forgiveness, and I urge modern Talmidis to bear no malice towards our fellow Jews on account of those hateful, Yavnean edicts and curses. The Benediction of the Heretics should always be remembered as part of our history – if anything, to remind us of what a righteous Israelite should *never* do.

Our love for the Jewish people has not diminished; although we have our disagreements, modern Talmidi services often have blessings in our services for our fellow Jews, in total contrast to the Yavnean curses. I therefore want to share with you what we pray in our modern Shabbat services, as a direct response to the Benediction of the Heretics:

"May those among the Jewish people who do not follow the Way

---

[a] Tosefta, Hullin 2:20-21
[b] Tosefta, Baba Meziyah 2:33

we follow be blessed, and may their names be enrolled in the Book of Life; may they prosper, and may their names and the names of their descendants not be blotted out; may their wise men and women be found a place among the righteous, and may their holy ones be uplifted over the wicked, and be saved by the Glory and power of Yahveh. May they find peace, may they be protected from our common enemies, and may they not become lost or extinguished."

The final demise of the community

After the death of Shimon bar Qlofas in c. 107 CE, there was a succession of Nasis (religious presidents of the community) up until about 135 CE. Yehudah Nasi was the very last Nasi of the ancient Congregation of the Way. Thereafter, without organised leadership, the authentic community of Yeshua`'s Jewish Followers went into rapid decline. I would say that there were two main reasons for this. Firstly, the vigorous animosity and belligerence of those who disagreed with them, and secondly, the phenomenon of syncretism – taking on the beliefs and teachings of other religions.

The first problem was the community's forced isolation. The edicts of the Yavnean rabbis cut them off from the root stock from which they were born. I can only guess how awful and soul-destroying this must have been – to be cursed and stigmatised by one's own people, unwanted and shunned.

Then there would have been the big problem with Paul's Believers – Gentile Christianity. Somehow, Paul and his Believers learned the insidious technique of how to pressurise people with such determined and tireless badgering, that their victims would give up and convert – a technique evangelicals use to this very day. There is little one can do in the face of someone who is wrong and uninformed, but who nevertheless believes they are right, and looks down their noses at you with an air of condescending superiority. Conversion would not have been due to the quality of the faith they converted to, but to the systematic, unmerciful and unrelenting persistence of their adherents.

From the quoted writings of Hegesippus, we know that certain Christians of the time, unable to silence those who had known Yeshua` in life, resorted to reporting Yeshua`'s relatives to the Roman authorities during the various persecutions, falsely accusing them of messianic insurrection. As long as there lived those among us who knew, from personal experience, that Yeshua` was not a god or a messiah, they were a clear and present danger to Paul's Christianity, and had to be removed. For a community like ours, which teaches that one should not do to others, anything which is hateful to oneself, they were helpless before the onslaught of Paullist evangelism.

The second problem was that of syncretism – taking on the beliefs of other religions. There is evidence to show that 'Jewish-Christianity' of some form or another survived into the 4th century CE, and maybe even into the 10 century CE. In his book, *'A History of Jewish Christianity'*, Hugh J Schonfield writes that these syncretist sects may have existed right up until the early Islamic era. He speculates that Mohammed might even have been shown hospitality by the descendants of one of these sects in the Nabatean desert, and that this was how he came into contact with those who believed in a human Yeshua`; as a result, Islam views Yeshua` as a human prophet, just as we do. Other 'Jewish-Christian' groups took on Gnostic dualist beliefs e.g. that the spirit is good, but the flesh is evil; and that Satan is an equal and opposite force to God.

Modern Talmidi groups are painfully aware of the problem of syncretism and the coercion of Christian missionisers, and as a result, we have a clearly defined theology for a good reason. This strategy was never intended as intolerance, but as a very necessary way of protecting the integrity of modern Talmidaism. Knowing clearly what you yourself believe, does not automatically mean hating others who believe differently; a good Follower of the Way has to learn to make this distinction. A decent and noble child of Yahveh has to learn how to 'love one's neighbour as oneself' – regardless of what faith (or absence of faith) that neighbour has.

As for the problem of the condescending scorn, and the unforgiving persistence of the modern disciples of Paul, there is nothing we can do, except cling to Yahveh as our high tower of strength, and live lives which show that we will not fall prey to the same abhorrent disrespect which they show towards people of other faiths. I myself have been a persistent victim of such spiritual violence; it is not pleasant, but I have never wavered in my devotion and love of Yahveh – in fact, their unrelenting and unmerciful evangelisation has made me all the more faithful to Yahveh. Any community of religious people ultimately reflects the personalities of their *true* founders; fundamentalist, evangelical Christians effectively reflect the personality of Paul of Tarsus, not Yeshua` of Nazareth. Any community of faithful Followers of the Way needs to learn how to reflect the awesome, wondrous and inspiring personality of Yahveh, who is the true founder of the faith of Israel – the faith of Abraham, Moses, David, Solomon, Isaiah, Jeremiah and Yeshua`. May the model of our devotion to Yahveh our heavenly Father be the lives of Yeshua`, Jacob the Pious and Shimon bar Qlofas.

As for the issue of being cut off from the mainstream Jewish community, we can only wait patiently for God's good time. We can show our Jewish brothers and sisters that we are not a threat; we can expound our values patiently when asked, we can reassure the mainstream that we are not their enemy – that we can, in fact, be a valuable resource for Jewish culture and heritage.

In spite of the wish of the majority that we should be killed off at birth, the only way we can assure our survival is to maintain our devotion to the awesome and holy ideals of the original Israelite faith, for this is indeed a righteous cause that God cannot fault us for. If we remain faithful to God's original ideals and teachings, in spite of the belligerent efforts of those who would wish to convince us otherwise, then we surely cannot fail in our endeavour, because God will be with us! As King Solomon himself said, *"The Name of Yahveh is a strong tower – the righteous run into it and are kept safe"*.[a]

From the 10th century onwards, there was no organised community of Followers of the Way. Over the next one thousand years, various writers, theologians and philosophers have secretly adopted positions close to first century Talmidaism (or 'Jewish-Christianity'), but individuals remained isolated, often afraid to openly express their views out of fear of both mainstream Christianity and mainstream Judaism.

What we can learn from such a new perspective on our history

There are several things that change in our perspective by knowing the 'hidden history' of Yeshua`'s first Jewish followers. Knowing their beliefs, it gives us legitimate permission to see Yeshua` as a human prophet, and reject the authority of Paul of Tarsus. It gives us permission to *refrain* from telling those who are not of our faith that they will go to hell if they don't convert; it gives us justification to focus on how we live our lives, rather than on what we believe. It empowers us to strive towards becoming better people, to become a benefit and a blessing to God and the societies in which we live. It ennobles us to get along with those who are different from us, and it enables us to honour and respect Yeshua` in exactly the same way as his first Jewish Followers honoured him.

Rejecting Paul means rejecting his beliefs. We reject the idea of an infanticidal god, who is supposedly willing to put one of his children to death to save the world – no human mother or father would be willing to do such a terrible and monstrous thing, so why would God? Through the prophet Jeremiah,[b] God told us that such a way of thinking is an

---

[a] Prov 18:10
[b] Jer 7:30-31, 32:35

abomination, and such a thing would never even enter God's mind. A loving and all-powerful God would *never* need to invent a rule that requires one of his children to die in order to save the world.

We reject the idea that God is not powerful enough to forgive humanity, unless there is blood and death to pay for sin – the death of a god-man. The God of Israel and of all the nations is so powerful, and has such a great and awesome love for us, that He is able to forgive without any blood being shed, and without any death. Yahveh cleanses us, purifies us and renews us through the power of God's Glory and holiness, not through blood.

We reject the idea of an emasculated and weak God who needs a mediator in order to deal with us. We reject Paul's idea that no human being can come to know God except through 'Christ', and that anyone who rejects that 'Christ' will go to hell. This is *not* a portrait of a loving God, and is the very antithesis of the living God of Israel. This is, in fact, a form of brainwashing – they frighten people into believing that there is no hope for them unless people accept their God on their terms. This is not the Way of the God of Israel. We reject the idea of a heartless and merciless god who turns good people away from heaven and eternal life because they were not Christians (or Jews).

From personal experience, I can truly and genuinely say that being able to go directly to God without having to go through a mediator – just like those early Jewish Followers of Yeshua` – has meant for me that I experience Yahveh as a very real, powerful and living Being, with a knowable personality, whose life-giving presence I feel all around me every hour of every day, despite the terrible hardships I have had to endure and suffer. Fundamentalists use the bible as their anchor and sole point of reference – almost as their god – but being filled with *the living Presence of Yahveh* means that you have a direct, living and immediate relationship with Yahveh. Our living relationship with Yahveh is our firm anchor, which no one can take away from us.

The second thing this new perspective means for us, is that for Yeshua`'s Jewish Followers, the tribulation which Yeshua` warned about has already happened. Fundamentalist Christians await an apocalypse at the end of time (when only 'born-again' Christians will go to heaven), whereas we understand it as having already taken place in 70 CE, with the destruction of the Temple, and the fall of Jerusalem and Judea. The tribulation was brought to its terrible conclusion in 135 CE, with the Roman edict banishing all Jews from Jerusalem.

There is something else that changes for us too. Although the tribulation of which Yeshua` spoke has already happened, we are ever mindful that the conditions which brought about that tribulation can happen in any generation. Each generation has to be vigilant. Every generation has to watch out for the violent men of religion, just like Yeshua` did with the Zealots; we have to watch out for the greedy rich and the powerful who abuse their position by exploiting the least in society; and we have to reach out to the lost, the unwanted, the rejected and the forgotten, just like Yeshua` and his first Followers were taught to do.

Thirdly, looking at how our spiritual forebears in the first and second centuries were set upon and reviled by both Christians and our fellow Jews – both of whom should have known better, having suffered dreadful persecutions themselves – there is something that we should learn from this too. Ancient Christians poured scorn on Jewish Followers, and held them in contempt for their love of Torah; and the Yavnean rabbis cursed us because of our respect for the teachings of the prophet Yeshua`. As a community, we must resolve never, ***ever*** to behave in the same unconscionable way that others behave towards us, no matter how great the provocation. Our theology is an existential threat to Paullist Christianity, and we will always be viewed with suspicion.

If we grow sufficiently for us to become more widely known, we will inevitably be called anti-Christ,[a] along with other unpleasant names that tend to pour forth from the depths of unpleasant hearts.[b] We will be verbally and spiritually pummelled and beaten, just as our spiritual forbears were in the 1st and 2nd centuries, and our reputations will be smeared and called into question. We will be challenged to sparring debates so that we can be publicly mocked, harangued and humiliated. I exhort you to endure with dignity, because you stand on the sure foundation of what Yahveh has built. We can therefore take comfort in Yeshua`'s words: *"Blessed are you when people abuse you and malign you, because our ancestors did no less to the prophets. Rejoice! Dance for joy! Because remember, your reward in heaven is great."*[c]

At this point in time, I do not yet know how the modern Jewish community will treat us. From what little I myself have experienced, when I plucked up the courage to admit to what I am to my fellow Jews, there are a lot of misconceptions about us, and about what we believe. Much of what they think about us is entirely untrue. Most likely we will still be seen as heretics to be shunned. We will be called 'fake-Jews' or 'Jewish wannabes' – I myself have already been called these things, and once it is found that I am a convert, that is sufficient reason for all my

---

[a] 1Jn 2:22

[b] cf S. Yesh 53:2-3 (Lk 6:45): *"The good person out of the storehouse of good in their heart brings forth good, and the evil person out of the storehouse of evil in their heart brings forth evil; because from the abundance of plenty in the heart, so the mouth speaks."*

[c] SY 3:7-8; cf Mt 5:11-12

views to be dismissed, nullified and ignored. I can only advise you to do everything in your power to assure the mainstream Jewish community that you are not a threat, and most of all, that you do not return any hatred that they might shower upon you. And let me assure you that you are not fake – you are genuine sons and daughters of Yahveh, true children of your heavenly Father. You can have no doubt that *that* is real.

Summary

When people go looking for the historical Yeshua`, one thing they tend to do is ignore the story of his Jewish followers, focussing entirely on the story of Paul of Tarsus and his Gentile Christian Believers. They also assume that the story of Yeshua`'s community told in the New Testament is beyond reproach – that it is wholly true and reliable, and that there is no evidence outside of the New Testament that is worth examining.

When people start asking the question, "Who was James the Just?" the established picture starts to unravel. They begin to ask, 'Why is there no christology in the Letter of James?' and, 'Who was in charge of the earliest community – Peter or James?'

Then they start looking at what the early Church Fathers wrote about the Jewish followers of Yeshua` – that they rejected the teachings of Paul, and belief in the virgin birth and original sin. A whole, hidden – and forbidden – history comes into focus.

A careful examination of the differing accounts of the Convention of Jerusalem written by Luke in Acts, and by Paul in Galatians, leads us to question the real issues separating Yeshua`'s Jewish Followers and Paul's Gentile Believers. The issue was not circumcision, but rather, what minimum standards did Paul's Believers have to follow in order to be able to share table fellowship with Jews? The answer was to abstain from meat offered to idols, and meat with blood still in it. Abstention from sexual immorality enabled general social interaction with Jewish Followers.

Knowing the history of Yeshua`'s Jewish Followers gave me the permission and confidence to disagree with Paul of Tarsus, just like *they* did. If mainstream Christianity wants to hold up Paul as a paragon of saintliness and godly virtue, and as a mirror to 'Christ', then let them do so. That is not, however, the image of him that Jacob the Pious ('St. James the Just') and Yeshua`'s Jewish followers had of him historically. To them he was a deceiver, who told one story to Jews,[a] and a completely

---

[a] 1Cor 9:20

different one to Christians.[a] His apologists today may paint him as a 'Jew's Jew' who remained faithful to Judaism, but when it came to explaining the Jewish faith at vital moments in history (like the sensitivity over kashrut in Antioch), he failed to do so, choosing instead to paint himself the hero.

The Gaius Crisis – when Caligula threatened to set up a statue of himself in the Jerusalem Temple – would have reinforced Yeshua`'s prophetic warnings among his Jewish followers. It may even have been the spark that moved Jacob the Pious to write what is known to most people as 'the Letter of James' in the *New Testament*. In his letter, he warned his readership that the crisis was an imminent one – *'the Judge stands at the very gates'*.

Jacob the Pious, the son of Qlofas and cousin of Yeshua`, had been chosen after Yeshua`'s death to lead the community of Yeshua`'s Jewish followers in Jerusalem. Through the power of his prayer, Jacob the Pious was able to atone for the sins of the guilty, and the destruction of Jerusalem was delayed.

However, when Jacob challenged the moral corruption of the High Priest of the time, the High Priest took advantage of the absence of a Roman governor, and had him arrested. Jacob was eventually executed in 62 CE;[b] thereafter, the community of Followers tried to continue the national campaign for prayer and repentance. Eventually the cruelty of the Romans clashed with the violence of the Zealots, and Jerusalem was destroyed. Most of the Jewish population of the city were either killed, or captured as slaves or exiled.

Except in the Galilee. It would appear that, despite the pro-Roman, anti-Galilean bias of the *New Testament*, Yeshua`'s Galilean mission was in part successful. During the First Jewish Revolt of 66-73 CE, Zealot strongholds in the Galilee (such as Gischala and Gamla) were completely destroyed by the Romans. However as a region, the Galilee was mostly spared the destruction that was visited on Judea in the south. Its rural population surrendered relatively quietly to the Romans – and for the preservation of Jewish life in the Galilee, theologically it was the right thing to do. Judeans fleeing the fighting in the south eventually settled in the Galilee. Over the following centuries, with Jewish settlement banned in the south, the Galilee became a flourishing haven for Jewish life in the newly created Roman province of Palestine.

Paullist theology makes Yeshua`'s ministry all about establishing his identity as messiah, to die for the sins of the world, but I believe that

---

[a] 1Cor 9:21
[b] sometime between the governorships of Porcius Festus and Lucceius Albinus – see Josephus, *The Antiquities of the Jews*, 20.9.1.

Yeshua`'s ministry was about saving as many of the Jewish people as possible from the fast approaching horrors of the tribulation of 70CE, by teaching them the ways of God's Kingdom which the world has come to admire. The Galilee, home of Yeshua`'s early ministry, survived the Day of Yahveh and the end of that age.[a] Although recorded history only writes about the results of what happened from the viewpoint of plain historical fact, I would like to think that the prophet Yeshua`'s call to repentance in the region helped to save the Galilee from Roman destruction.

---

[a] Aramaic `*iddana*, Greek αἰῶνος *aiōnos* is a span or portion of time; history is divided up into these ages; 'age' does not mean 'end of the world'.

Chapter Three: Interpreting the person of Yeshua` in the light of Israelite theology

The problem of stripping away 'Jesus' to find the historical Yeshua`

Over the generations, biblical scholars and theologians have made various attempts to reconstruct the historical figure of Jesus of Nazareth. Upon reflection, I feel that most people reconstruct Jesus into someone who justifies their own beliefs – 'This is what I believe; now I'll recreate a figure who validates my personal theology.' After all, is that not what the authors of the gospels of Mark, Matthew, Luke and John – and even Thomas[a] – did? Create a 'Jesus' in their own image? Is that not what all the now vanished, ancient forms of Christianity did? Is that not what modern movements do – create a theology surrounding a Jesus who emphasises and validates their own emphases?

In his Epistle to the Hebrews, Paul proclaimed that 'Jesus Christ is the same yesterday and today and forever!'[b] However, in the modern world, 'Jesus Christ' can be anyone that Believers want him to be. He can be presented as a rebel in Liberation theology, or he can be an appeaser of the rich for right-wing American evangelicals. Every ethnic group has at some point or another painted him as one of their own, some feminists have re-modelled him as a woman, and New Agers redefine him as someone not too dissimilar from Gautama Buddha.[c] In his book, *'Misquoting Jesus'*, Professor Bart Ehrman shows how even in ancient times, it was not uncommon for a community who got hold of copies of the Gospels, to amend the words of 'Jesus' to address the specific needs of their own communities.

The commonest attempts by modern theologians – those seeking to

---

[a] The author of the Gnostic 'Gospel of Thomas', found in December 1945 at Nag Hammadi in Egypt, containing many of the sayings of Yeshua` also found in the gospels of Matthew and Luke.
[b] Paul of Tarsus, *'Epistle to the Hebrews'* 13:8
[c] I have the vague recollection that this paragraph was inspired by something I read in a book over 30 years ago, but I cannot recall the book, so I have been unable to check. No plagiarism or breach of copyright was intended with the use of this information however; I was simply trying to point out that the Gentile 'Jesus' has become anything his Believers wanted him to be, in contradiction to what Paul asserted.

place him back into his Jewish milieu – recreate him either as a Zealot, an Essene or a Pharisee. However, those who view him as a nationalist Zealot do not take into account his condemnation of violence, nor his views on the destructive consequences of violence. Those who recreate him as a Pharisee take no account of his mistrust of the Oral Law, or of the fact that the Pharisees had declared that there were no more prophets after Malachi (so presumably if Jesus had been a Pharisee, as a prophet he would have to have told *himself* to shut up, and declare his own prophecies invalid)! Those who propose him as an Essene, cannot adequately explain his attendance in the Temple[a] at festival times, or his desire to take his message to all Jews, instead of just the chosen few.[b] And writers who see him merely as an itinerant, wonder-working preacher pottering about the Galilean countryside, isolate his words from the everyday politics of the world he lived in. As a result, they pay no heed to the troubles and tensions of the time, and do not give him any real motive for the urgency of his ministry. Then there are the New Agers, who take no account of the fact that he was a Middle Eastern Jew, preaching to Jews about thoroughly Jewish concepts.

When I started out on my journey to the Way in my early twenties, I had already read and studied widely – being familiar with almost every shade of opinion out there – and consequently, I really didn't know what to believe about Jesus of Nazareth any longer. As a result of my studies, I had reached a point in my life which had forced a painful crisis of faith. After much prayer and soul-searching, I concluded that the only reasonable starting point would have to be Abrahamic-Yahwist theology, and the socio-political environment of Jesus's time. Everything about Jesus – or Yeshua` – had to pass the tests of these two factual, historical domains. The only theory that has never been tried before, is the one that actually passes these tests – that he was a fully human, Jewish prophet sent by Yahveh God, not a messiah or son of God. His mission was to remind the wrongdoers among the Jewish people of the ethical and moral terms of the Covenant they were ignoring, and also to encourage the bulk of the Jewish people to trust in their Heavenly Father to get them through the terrible, cataclysmic events about to hit them.[c]

As a prophet of Yahveh, Yeshua` taught Yahveh's message of justice and compassion – the very same one that had been voiced so many times through all the line of Hebrew prophets that came before him. He proclaimed the immediacy of the present Kingdom of God, in

---

[a] Essenes rejected worship in the Temple.
[b] Essenes taught that only the chosen few – the Elect – would be saved by God.
[c] That is, the destruction of Jerusalem and the Temple in 70CE, and the Roman exile.

complete contrast to the violence of the future messianic kingdom sought after by the Zealots. He preached justice for the poor by reminding the rich of their obligations under Torah – of the commandments of God they were turning their backs on. He criticised religious hypocrites ('phonies' or fakers – those who pretended on the outside that they were good and religious people, but inside were spiritually and morally corrupt). He criticised those who judged and condemned others. He sought out the 'lost sheep of Israel', and encouraged the sensible application of Torah – raising mercy and kindness above mechanical ritual, and thereby internalising the principles of God's Torah.

As a prophet of God, he himself did not belong to any sect, nor did he propose a particular sectarian theology, or even set out to found a new religion. It was his Jewish followers who first formed a community around his teachings after he died, building up their theology around the emphases of his message. God has no denominational agenda, and neither do God's prophets.

Yeshua` did not seek to set up a new religious hierarchy or social structure, because he was already working within the existing Torah-ordained framework of the Jewish society in which he lived. He made no judgments or decisions on how to overcome economic or political problems, or how to resolve halakhic[a] issues – all simply because he probably expected individuals to work out such matters for themselves, by seeking advice from the elders and sages of whichever sect they belonged to.[b] There are many ethical areas that Yeshua` never made any pronouncements on, such as betting, homosexuality, and the structural government of human society – simply because it was not his remit to do so. When cornered into making judgments and decisions, he always hesitated,[c] and sometimes even hit back at those who pestered him, saying, *'Who appointed me judge or arbiter over you?'*[d]

He was instead a thoroughly Hebrew prophet. Prophets have a specific job to do. With prophets, there is always a bigger picture. After all, when God is involved, you can be sure there will always be a bigger picture! With respect to Yeshua`, the only 'bigger picture' we have had

---

[a] Halakhah is a body of custom and tradition that is laid down by any given Jewish sect, as a way of resolving inconsistencies in Torah, or dealing with things that are not covered by the written Torah – these are 'halakhic issues'.

[b] cf Mt 13:52 (S.Yesh 156), which suggests that a scribe who becomes a citizen of God's Kingdom does not have to abandon everything he learnt before, but rather treasures things both old *and* new.

[c] Such as in the case of the woman caught in adultery (S.Yesh. 139; cf Lk 21:39-50), or when asked by a Roman commander to heal his servant (S.Yesh. 109; cf Mt 8:5-10, Lk 7:1-10).

[d] S.Yesh. 95:2; cf Lk 12:13-14 – Yeshua` did not see himself as the judge of humanity; that role was left up to Yahveh.

over the last 2,000 years has been the mainstream, all-pervasive, Paullist Christian one; other versions of the historical Jesus have failed to give a convincing alternative that takes account of anything like an alternative 'bigger picture'. I think the problem that theologians have had in recreating a historical Yeshua`, is that they have focussed so much on the motives of Yeshua` himself, that they have forgotten about *God's motives*. Looking at God's motives makes things a whole lot easier. After all, the Israelites considered Yahveh to be a living God, with a discernible personality. The God of Israel was, after all, the architect of the whole plan.

I say all this because, in trying to recapture the essence of the 'historical Jesus', most non-Jewish scholars desperately try to make the person of Yeshua` remain applicable and relevant to non-Jews, when a careful reading of his teachings makes it clear that his *personal* mission as a prophet was only to the Jewish people. I will admit this statement is most unsettling for non-Jews, because on the face of it, it **seems** to take their rock of faith away from them. However, we have to come to terms with the fact that he even passed this commission on to his own apostles: '*Go nowhere among the Gentiles, nor enter any town of the Samaritans, rather hurry to the lost sheep of Israel*'.[a] His commissions to his apostles elsewhere,[b] 'to preach the gospel to all nations', can only be later additions to the story put into his mouth, in order to make his message relevant to non-Jews.

Yeshua`'s instruction only to go to Jews, was because of the immediate danger the Jewish people were in. The basic underlying motive behind his whole message was this: "A terrible tribulation is coming soon to the Galilee and Judea; Jerusalem will be utterly destroyed and our people exiled. However, God wants to save as many people as possible from its horrors; we can be sheltered from this tribulation if we eschew violence and false piety, and return instead to the ways of God's Kingdom – honesty and fairness, compassion and mercy, justice and help for the poor." Non-Jews were not in the same imminent, physical danger that the Jewish people were in. While Paullist Christianity has focussed on Yeshua`'s Jewish ethics, it has largely ignored his exile-warning for the Jewish people – dangerously transmuting it into a universal, world-ending apocalypse instead.

There is, however, a realistic alternative approach for non-Jews. If you focus on our Heavenly Father instead – if you make *Yahveh* alone your anchor – you will see that Yahveh *is* for everyone, and the Kingdom of God is for everyone; Yahveh is after all, the God of *all* nations.

---

[a] S.Yesh. 63:5 (= Mt 10:5-6)
[b] Mt 24:14, 28:19, Mk 13:10, 16:15, Lk 24:47

Yahveh's code of moral living, Yahveh's vision for a better, stable, just and peaceful society, as well as Yahveh's message of love, social justice, forgiveness, mercy and compassion are universal – applicable to people of all religions and nations. Yeshua` was but a small piece in this bigger picture. 'Jesus Christ' might transform and change, reflecting the beliefs and needs of the communities who proclaim him, but Yahveh is unchanging – a steady, constant and faithful rock for those who follow Him.

Modern Talmidaism takes this message of the universality of God's Kingdom to both Jews and non-Jews, because the Kingdom of God is open to both Jews and non-Jews. We welcome into our fellowship whomsoever God has called out from among the nations to join us.[a]

As I proceed onward with these four books, I hope that you will come to understand and feel the renewed hope that Yahveh's message brings to all people of all nations,[b] the great optimism that our heavenly Father bestows upon us for a better future.[c] Most of all, I hope that you will be given an unprecedented glimpse of the greater plan – the unimaginable wonders that Yahveh has in store not only for Israel, but for all humanity.

'But his Apostles believed he was a god!'

The usual proof that Christian apologists give in order to establish that the belief about 'Jesus' being a god existed right from the start, and that the belief he died to save us from our sins existed right from the very beginning, is 'the gospels say so'. This is itself based on the premise that what the gospels say is undeniably true. Realistically, we have only the word of the writers of the gospels that they are true. None of the gospel writers were eye-witnesses – 'Matthew' is not the apostle Matthew, because he does not refer to himself as 'I' when speaking about him; and the author of John's gospel does not even sound Jewish, but more like a pagan Greek mystic.

As I have argued earlier, Peter was the only apostle who went over to Paul's side, and the most he subsequently came to believe was that Yeshua` was the messiah who died to save us from our sins. Peter was not an educated man, and the letters in the *New Testament* that bear his name cannot realistically be attributed to him, rather to someone writing

---

[a] Isa 14:1, 56:3
[b] This is why the Talmidi Israelite community is open to non-Jews as well as Jews; the Kingdom of God is for people of all nations. We are therefore open to anyone who wishes to follow the Way.
[c] Isa 2:2-4, Jer 29:11

in his name.

Luke paints a picture of a Jewish leadership and a Gentile Christian church in harmony, but Paul's letters tell a story of tensions between the two. Paul held the authority of Jerusalem in contempt; he was proud that his teaching and beliefs owed nothing to the apostles.[a]

The idea that the Jewish community of Followers, and Paul's community of Gentile Believers interacted regularly and lived in perfect harmony, is a total fiction. Today, we are able to fact check contemporary stories by phoning round and verifying sources; back then, you had to take the word of messengers who came to you with claims that they were telling the truth, and that they were who they said they were. Anyone can make claims to be anyone or anything; that does not make their claims true.

If Yeshua` were a god, then why did he pray to himself?

There are several episodes of Yeshua`'s life where one might ask, 'If he were a god, then why would he do that?'

The first incident that comes to mind, is the testing of Yeshua` in the wilderness. Mainstream Christianity sees this as a battle between God and the devil, but the gospels clearly state that this is a test (the Greek word is the same for 'tempt' as 'test'). Yeshua` is offered all the kingdoms of the earth, but surely, *these already belong to God*. If Yeshua` were God, then why would the accuser offer him something that already belonged to him?

The three tests only have value if they were the test of a fallible human being. Is Yeshua` the type of mortal man who will set himself on high to be glorified and served? Or is he the type of prophet who will not glory in the message he has been given, but rather serve God with humility?

And besides, James 1:3 says, *"When tempted, no one should say, 'God is tempting me'.* **For God cannot be tempted by evil***, nor does He tempt."* The so-called 'Temptation of Christ in the wilderness' would be pointless (and impossible) if he were God.

In the Garden of Gethsemane, if his will and that of his Father were one,[b] then why does Yeshua` need to ask Himself for the circumstances of the future to be different?[c] Surely, this would imply that the will of the Father-person in the trinity was stronger than – and separate from – the will of the Son-person of the trinity. A god would not need to be afraid

---

[a] Gal 2:6; see also Gal 1:16-17
[b] John 10:30
[c] Mt 26:39

of what is about to happen. The standard answer is that this was his human side being afraid. Then why couldn't his own son-god-side answer him? Why did he need to beg of another person of the trinity? This implies that the Father-person is greater than the son-person, and Christian doctrine clearly states that all the persons of the trinity are equal in every respect.

The next episode is where Yeshua` goes off to an isolated place to pray.[a] If Yeshua` were God, why would God need to pray to Himself? The standard trinitarian answer, is that this is a case of one person of the trinity communicating with another person of the trinity. But surely, if the son-person and the Father-person were both equally God, and therefore equally all-powerful, all-knowing and all-seeing, why would one person of the trinity even need to go off **into seclusion** in order to pray? Was there some inadequacy in himself, that he needed to contact the Father-person? And if Yeshua` was not all-knowing, all-seeing or all-powerful, then he wasn't a god, was he?

Yeshua` says about the coming tribulation, that he does not know when it will be.[b] If he ***doesn't*** know, then he is not all-knowing, and is therefore not a god.

All these things that Yeshua` said and did, would make much more sense if he were a mortal man under God's guidance. I personally have a much greater respect now for Yeshua`, knowing and understanding his humility before God, his mortal and vulnerable humanity before God, ***than I ever had when it was drummed into me that he was a god.*** As a human being – as someone like us – he had a firm faith and hope in the plans of our heavenly Father. I think there is a good example in that for us too – as one mortal human to another.

The evolution of Christian messianism

The prophet Yeshua`, despite the force of his calling, and in spite of his urgent need to get people to listen to his prophetic message, I believe was not tempted to accept the title of messiah for the sake of convenience. The prayer he taught us was to our heavenly Father for '*Thy* kingdom' to come (i.e. God's), not '*my* Kingdom' to come (his own).

Unfortunately, there was the huge obstacle of the Pharisaic injunction against prophets and prophecy. After his death, I believe that some of Yeshua`'s followers, perhaps anxious to get people to heed their master's warnings, may even have succumbed to the Pharisaic insistence on messianic credentials before they would listen to anyone, and maybe

---

[a] Lk 11:1 (cf S.Yesh. 40:1)
[b] Mk 13:32 (cf S.Yesh. 163:4)

some of Yeshua`'s desperate followers said, "All right, so he *is* the messiah – now will you *please* listen to our warnings about what's going to happen?"

A point which is perhaps worth mentioning here, is that at this time, many men arose in Judea, claiming to be the promised Jewish messiah. It was simply the easiest way to gain a large following. Unfortunately, because of how the Romans viewed potential messianic uprisings, it was also the easiest way to get large groups of people killed – along with their leaders. This is why I believe that Yeshua` personally felt that messianism – the hope in a messiah-saviour – served the Jewish people only ill. In contrast, by hoping and waiting on Yahveh our Heavenly Father, people would not be disappointed.[a]

Because of this danger from the Romans, I do not believe Yeshua` or his Jewish Followers would have made such public spectacles of their activities as the *New Testament* portrays; out of necessity, I think Yeshua`'s public appearances would have been much more low-key. The Gospels regularly describe a mass movement of peoples from all over what is now Israel and the West Bank, western Jordan, southern Syria and southern Lebanon.[b] If this had really happened, the Romans would have become very alarmed indeed. They would have mobilised many troops, and would most certainly have put a violent stop to it, just as they did with other messianic figures who gathered large crowds.[c]

Then there is the fact that the 1st century Jewish historian Josephus does not list our community as one of the four philosophies of Judaism at the time.[d] If Yeshua`'s movement had been as public and widespread as the New Testament portrays, drawing huge crowds, surely Josephus would have mentioned it. I suspect the lack of mention is due to the more likely scenario that Yeshua` *avoided* large public crowds, and perhaps also because our movement was likely considered part of non-sectarian 'Common Judaism'[e] – a large but ill-defined group of people that included those who did not formally belong to any organised sect.

Yeshua`'s death dashed all hopes that he might have been the messiah – at least in Jewish eyes. After all, you could only be the messiah if you proved it by your actions, and the messiah was not supposed to get killed off by his enemies. The unavoidable fact of Yeshua`'s death was an uncomfortable problem. That's why Paul had to invent a whole new

---

[a] Isaiah 49:23
[b] Mt 4:25, 15:21, Mk 3:8, Lk 6:17
[c] such as the violent put-down of the Samaritan Taheb by Pontius Pilate, or that of Theudas and his otherwise peaceful followers by the procurator Fadus in c. 45 CE
[d] *Antiquities of the Jews*, Bk 18, ch 1 pt 1-2
[e] part of which survived to become Karaite Judaism

theology to explain why he died – or in Paul's mind, why he *had* to die.

Fortunately, I suspect that Jacob the Pious (Yeshua`'s cousin or 'brother') restored the view that Yeshua` was a human prophet, and not a messiah. This is, admittedly, pure conjecture, but I base it on the fact that in Jacob's letter, *'The Epistle of James'* – the earliest document[a] in the whole *New Testament* – there is no mention of any kind of messianism whatsoever, only the continuance of Yeshua`'s prophetic teachings on social justice (in language that is distinct from that of the later gospels). Ancient Christian apologists could have doctored the letter when creating *'The Epistle of St. James'* to include some hint of messianism,[b] but they didn't.

Furthermore, if Yeshua` had been a messiah – a descendent of David – then surely, when one king dies, another takes his place.[c] Ps 132:12 says that there would be a line of Davidic kings forever until the end of time. Shouldn't everyone then have been proclaiming Jacob the Pious the new messiah – the new anointed king? Why wasn't Jacob the Pious acknowledged as a son of David ***by anyone***? I can only conclude, that during Jacob's governance (c. 30 - 62 CE) as Nasi of the earliest Talmidi Jewish community, no Jewish Follower who had known Yeshua` while he lived, ever considered him to have been a Davidic messiah. Therefore, neither was his cousin – his 'brother' – Jacob the Pious, a descendent of David.

Paul and Messianism

With the death of Jacob the Pious and the destruction of Jerusalem, the Jewish Followers of Yeshua`'s teachings lost power and influence.[d]

---

[a] which I date to the Gaius Crisis of 40-41 CE; most scholars say it was not written by him at all, because it speaks of an impending crisis, and 'You can't write about a crisis that has not happened yet, can you? Because that would suggest some supernatural or heavenly knowledge, and that's not possible, is it?' Therefore, mainstream scholarship places it in the late 1st to early 2nd century CE.

[b] The only messianic Christian addition is the title given to Yeshua`, 'the Lord Jesus Christ', at the beginning of the letter.

[c] The messiah was not meant to be just one man; there is no title of '***The*** Messiah' found anywhere in the Hebrew Bible. Messiahs were meant to be an ongoing line of kings – see Ps 132:11-12.

[d] After the destruction of Jerusalem in 70CE, the community of Jewish Followers seems to have split into the Paul-influenced Nazarenes (who were active mostly in the Galilee), and the James-influenced Ebionites (who were active mostly in the Trans-Jordan and Syria, with some in the Galilee). Nazarenes held trinitarian beliefs, and Ebionites held monotheist Jewish

The stage was set for the teachings and beliefs of Paul of Tarsus to steal the scene. Paul's Gentile Believers gradually gained ascendance, and were able to completely redefine the meaning of what a Jewish messiah was, without much opposition. Their messiah was modelled more on the dying and resurrected god-men of pagan Mystery Religions around the Mediterranean, rather than on any contemporary – or biblical – views of Jewish messiahs.

Counter to this view, it has been pointed out that there is a strong similarity between the super-messiah of Essene writings from Qumran, and the type of messiah preached by Paul. Some say that the Jewish Followers of Yeshua` were therefore Essenes, but I don't think so. James's letter, written in about 40CE, is the earliest 'Jewish-Christian' text, yet it does not contain *any* messianic eschatology. If Paul did not get his idea of a Jewish super-messiah from James or the Jewish community of Yeshua`'s Followers, then he must have gotten it from the Essenes – or at least from people like them. And if so, how?

If, as early Followers believed, Paul had been a captain in the service of the Temple police,[a] then he would have had ample opportunity to listen to the fiery speeches of sectaries who came to the Temple at festival times. I firmly believe that the super-messiah of sectarian Judaism came to Paul *directly* from fringe-movement sectaries preaching in the Temple, not from the Jewish Followers of Yeshua`. And through these sectaries, Paul was already primed to take the next step – to transform the Jewish super-messiah into a personal saviour-god, of the type found in pagan Mystery Religions.

Paul also claimed that he was an apostle of 'Jesus'. Now, you probably don't know this, but the quintessential quality of an apostle (*shaliach* in Hebrew), is that the apostle has to repeat the words of his master *verbatim*, adding nothing, and taking nothing away. If you hear the apostle, then you have heard the Master. The thing about Paul, if you have ever noticed, is that he ***never*** quotes the words of Yeshua` – not even once. For someone who is so fixated and obsessed on the person of 'Jesus Christ', he never recounts any of the details of his life – apart from the Eucharist, and the fact that he died on a cross (he never even describes the events leading up to his death). Paul is simply not interested in the human Yeshua` who lived and walked the earth; the real, historical Yeshua` of Nazareth plays no part in his theology.

Paul's theology is based upon the idea that human beings cannot help sinning,[b] and therefore the natural destination of the human soul is

---

beliefs. The early Church Fathers however, were not able to discern the difference between the two sects.
[a] cf Hyam Maccoby, 'Paul and the Invention of Christianity'.
[b] Romans 7:17

'eternal death'.[a] His teaching that 'the mind is pure but the flesh is weak'[b] has its origin in pagan Gnostic religions, which teach that the spirit is otherworldly and good, but the body is of this world and evil. The only way to guarantee going to heaven is to accept 'Christ' as your lord and saviour (according to Paul's theology, there is nothing else anyone can do to get to heaven, because being a good person is irrelevant). If we follow Paul's theology to its logical conclusion, accepting 'Christ' as your lord will not stop you sinning, but it will give you a watertight guarantee that you will not go to hell or suffer the consequences of your wrongdoing.[c] This logically means that all Christians will go to heaven, regardless of how nasty they have been in life, and all non-Christians will go to hell, regardless of how good they have been in life. This does not seem to me like the rules of an intelligent, fair or loving God!

The quintessential attraction of Paullist theology, is that a wrongdoer thereby gains a powerful, emotional release from the burden and guilt of their wrongdoing. A practical consequence of this, is that a wrongdoer does not have to examine why they have done what they have done, or root out their undesirable traits to become a better person (because being good is ultimately irrelevant in the Paullist view of salvation – I have come across this stance time and time again in arguments from Evangelicals; consider also the extremely high support amongst white evangelicals for US politicians who engage in sexual immorality, racism and corruption). All a sinner has to do is believe that 'Christ Jesus is their Lord and Saviour', and they are guaranteed to get into heaven. This is the emotional relief that Paullist beliefs give to their adherents.

Romans chapter 8 is the best statement of this manifesto of Paul. In the previous chapter of the letter, Paul described his inner nature – that he had no control over the sins he committed,[d] as if they were a separate entity within him – so therefore he was not responsible for his sins.[e] As long as he accepted Christ as his lord and saviour, then whenever he

---

[a] Romans 7:24
[b] Roman 7:18-23
[c] In contrast in Israelite theology, God forgives us at once when we turn back to God in repentance. 'Atonement' is when we are then cleansed of our sin by the fire of God's Glory, through prayer and good works. Although we are imperfect, it is our reliance on the life-sustaining power we derive from the Presence of Yahveh, and our willingness to turn back to God in repentance that keeps us whole. The Israelite religion did not believe in hell – unrepented sins have to be dealt with in Azza Zeil – which Yeshua` referred to as 'the Outer Darkness'. Once the soul is purified, every soul ultimately goes to heaven (Ps 49:15; cf Ps 103:4).
[d] Rom 7:19-20
[e] Rom 7:23.

sinned, his sins no longer mattered – he no longer had to face the consequences of his wrongful actions. Imagine the emotional freedom that gives you, not having to worry about the consequences of your actions – the ultimate sense of freedom!

The other attraction, is that this belief that 'Christ' *permanently* absolves you of your sins through faith alone, is a cast-iron guarantee that you will get into heaven, *regardless of whatever wrongs and evils you might commit **after** your conversion*. My reader, does that seem right or just to you, as a decent and honest human being? The prophet Ezekiel[a] tells us that in contrast, the Yahwist teaching is that God seeks an accounting for each individual wrong we do not repent of – that the past good deeds of a good person do not excuse subsequent evil, and that past wrongdoings are not held against the subsequent good of a penitent sinner.[b]

The soul that acknowledges their wrong and repents, is cleansed and wiped clean by the Glory of Yahveh.[c] The fire of God's Glory renews the penitent soul, purifies us and breathes new life into us.[d] In contrast, the Paullist belief that you no longer have to watch what you do because you are permanently 'saved', gives the Believer a spiritual 'high', similar to the high of a drug addict on narcotics. This 'high' is the false attraction of Paul's theology.

Paul's Believers came mostly from Gentiles living outside of the Holy Land, and would not have been aware of the teaching in Ezekiel 18. For most pagan Gentiles at that time – the vast pool of potential converts which Paul drew from – what mattered in religion was not kindness and mercy, but rather what favours you could extract from your gods through ritual appeasements; the irrelevance of being a good person was therefore already part of their cultural mindset. In pagan Mystery Religions, the attraction was that a person could gain permanent salvation and eternal life through belief in the various 'lords' of those religions. In such a Gentile environment, a new saviour who could grant you salvation just by believing in him therefore held great attraction; conversely, a traditional Jewish messiah meant nothing – after all, why would they bother with someone who was supposed to save Jews from foreign oppression, and restore Israel's fortunes and independence?

Paul of Tarsus realised that he would have to jettison Yeshua`'s Jewishness, and any Jewish relevance within the concept of messianism. Torah – 'the Law'[e] – therefore became a catch-all, Jewish bogeyman for

---

[a] Ezek 18:24-26
[b] Ezek 18:21-23, 27-28
[c] Ps 51:7
[d] Mal 3:19-20 (Christian bibles – Mal 4:1-2)
[e] Torah actually means 'Teaching' or 'Instruction' i.e. from God.

his Believers. He would have to completely redefine what a messiah was, if he was ever going to make any kind of headway with his new religion in Gentile lands. *His* messiah was going to have to go head to head with the biographies of these pagan god-men, and out-claim their claims for the salvation of the human soul.

At that time, pagan Mystery Religions were very popular throughout the Mediterranean world. Paul soon came to see that he would have to compete on an equal footing with pagan saviours like Mithras, Dionysos/Bacchus, Romulus, Horus, Baal Taraz and Attis. To this end, whatever the believers of pagan gods claimed for their lords (e.g. suffering for the sake of believers, death and resurrection or ascension live into heaven, as well as instituting a sacred baptism or meal), Paul would have to at least make equal claims for *his* lord, 'Christ Jesus'.

Typically, the god-men of pagan Mystery Religions are gods incarnated in human flesh, or the sons of gods and mortal women, who die and resurrect annually around Spring-time – Tammuz and Baal Taraz are typical of this type of deity. Mithras even had his followers take part in a ritual meal – in the 2nd century CE, Justin Martyr noted the similarity between the Christian eucharist and the Mithraic sacred meal. Zardusht, the messiah-like prophet of Persian Zoroastrianism, had a divine revelation on the bank of a river, and taught the resurrection of the body and a final judgment, when the physical, earthly body would be reunited with the soul.

Christian apologists counter by saying that no single, pagan god-saviour has a story *identical* in every, minute detail to the New Testament biographies of 'Jesus Christ' – and for Christian Believers, this argument is sufficient to dismiss all these myths out of hand. It is enough for them to say that there are many details in the myths of pagan saviours that are not found at all in the story of 'Christ'. However, the similarities between the quintessential, central mysteries of pagan myths which also occur in the biography of 'Christ', is extremely suspicious, and cannot so easily be dismissed by any rational, inquiring mind.

If you remove all the ethical, Jewish sayings of Yeshua` from the Christian gospels, you are left with a story that is virtually *identical* to the sum of the salvation-stories of pagan god-men. Between the time of Paul's vision on the road to Damascus,[a] and the time when Barnabas came to fetch him from the pagan city of Tarsus[b] (about 10-14 years later), Paul would have had plenty of time in his native land to hone and

---

[a] Acts 9:3-9; Paul is sent to Tarsus soon afterwards, Acts 9:30.
[b] Acts 11:25

formulate his own brand of theology *all by himself*.[a] I would surmise that he looked at all the myths of the Mystery Religions that his neighbours in Tarsus followed, and decided that 'Jesus Christ' was just going to have to better every single one of them. The message and person of 'Jesus Christ' is dependent on him and his story being unique – that no character in history has *ever* had the same claims as 'Christ' has. But when you examine the stories of pagan lords in Mediterranean Mystery Religions, you realise that there is **nothing** unique about Paul's 'Christ'.

There was inevitably a long struggle between pagan Mystery Religions and Christianity. As long as there existed, for example, Mithraists, who could remind Christians that their 'Christ' was not unique in any way, shape or form, Christianity would remain frustrated. Pagan writers such as Celsus would often chide Christian teachers for their unrealistic claims of uniqueness for the Christian god-man 'Jesus Christ'.

There was no alternative; Christianity had to vigorously – and brutally – eradicate all traces of pagan religion from the Roman Empire, and once every paganist (and most of their literature) was gone, Christianity could then put out false propaganda about what pagan religion had been like. After the fourth or fifth century CE, Christian claims for the uniqueness of their own god-man could go unchallenged.

The mainstream Christian notion of a messiah as "a god made man, to die as a salvation for the sins of humanity" is not unique; it is completely Paul's invention,[b] without any foundation or basis in Jewish theological thinking which is genuinely based on biblical, Yahwist Israelite theology.

---

[a] In fact, in Gal 1:17-19, Paul explains that he preached *his own gospel* to the Gentiles in Arabia three full years before he had contact with the real apostles in Jerusalem (cf 1Cor 15:1). And even then, he only spoke to Simon Peter (whom he brought over to his way of thinking), and James (who *didn't* go over to Paul's thinking, as the theological tone of the 'Letter of James' in the New Testament confirms). According to Paul, the real apostles of Yeshua` never justified Paul's message, or welcomed him with open arms or agreed with him, as some Christian apologists claim. The gospel Paul preached to the Gentiles then – if we go by Paul's own words alone – was not verified or validated by anyone who knew Jesus when he was alive.

[b] He himself admits that he was not taught Yeshua`'s words or biography by anyone (eg 1Cor 11:23-25), but received his belief system and knowledge of Jesus as a direct "revelation of Jesus Christ" – see Gal 1:12. Nor did he consult with anyone who personally knew Yeshua` to verify his teachings – see Gal 1:16-17. He is proud that the apostles had nothing to contribute to him (Gal 2:6).

Re-Interpreting So-Called 'Messianic' Prophecies

The Davidic Covenant[a] is a kind of 'addendum' to the overall Covenant ('pact') between God and Israel. It basically states that Israel's kings would be descended from David, and as long as these kings were obedient to God's law, Israel would prosper. So-called 'messianic' prophecies contained in the writings of the prophets are expansions and re-interpretations of this Davidic covenant. As we go further and further away in time from when the Davidic covenant was cut (i.e. sworn and sealed) between God and David, the expectations for the Davidic king became greater – and I believe – more fanciful.

If we are to come to some kind of better understanding of how to understand these original Davidic prophecies, the first thing we have to do is rid ourselves of all beliefs that arose after the biblical period: for example, that the 'messiah' himself will inaugurate Israel's redemption (the Miqra says that God alone will save Israel,[b] and that the Davidic monarchy is just one of the things that will be re-established when *God's* kingdom is fulfilled);[c] we need to put aside the idea that the 'messiah' is just one man (the Davidic covenant actually refers to a line of kings).[d] We should not forget that the High Priest is, by the way, also 'an anointed one'.

Mainstream Judaism asks, "What can we do to bring on the coming of the messiah?" But as Followers of the Way of Yahveh, we ask ourselves, "What can we do for Yahveh, in order to bring on the fulfilment of *God's* Kingdom?" Having a descendant of David on the throne of Israel is not about the messiah, but about an intervention in human history which displays the power and Glory of God.[e] The future age of universal peace is not about the actions and renown of the messiah, but rather about the actions and greater renown of Yahveh – about what Yahveh has promised to do one day for Israel and the whole of humanity.

The second thing we have to do if we wish to understand the original meaning of 'messiah', is stick to the wording of the Davidic covenant, and not impose meaning onto the biblical text which is not

---

[a] The text of this Covenant is found in 1Kgs 8:25b, 2Sam 7:8-16, 1Chron 17:7-14, Psalm 89:4-5, 89:20b-38, 132:11-12, 2Chron 21:7, 2Sam 23:5-6.

[b] See Isa 43:25, 41:14, 47:4, 56:8, 60:16, Ps 34:22, 111:9, 130:8, Hos 13:4.

[c] The entire prophecy is Ezek 37:1 to 39:29

[d] Ps 132:11-12 – "If your **SONS** keep My covenant, and My decrees that I teach them, then their **SONS** also to the end of time, shall sit upon your throne".

[e] Isaiah 60:21 – *"Then all your people will be righteous; they shall possess the land forever, and I shall plant there the branch* [i.e. the messiah] - *the work of **My** hands – **so that I might be glorified**"*.

there. As the situation of the Jewish people got progressively more and more desperate, the ancient Israelites expected more and more from the promised Davidic king.

Now, all the kings of Israel and Judah were 'anointed ones', and for centuries, most of these 'messiahs' were big, cruel disappointments. The people therefore longed for a 'good messiah', who would be a benefactor to God's people and encourage us in faithfulness to God, instead of being a tyrant who takes us away from God. Each successive generation tried to give people hope, by bestowing ever greater and more fantastic qualities upon this future good king.

The tendency was to give fanciful interpretations to the prophecies, ascribing God's own future deeds to the messiah himself, rather than to look at the actual wording of the original covenant. We have to stop this deceptive cycle. We need to interpret messianic prophecy by going back to the original Davidic covenant, rather than interpret the original covenant by looking at the later prophecies.

The Davidic Covenant promised that Israel's kings would be descended from David. It also stipulated that, although God would never withdraw favour from David's lineage, the covenant would only work properly if David's descendants kept to the terms and conditions of all the covenants God made with Israel. This meant being faithful to the teachings and principles given to Moses, by not going after pagan gods, and by not adopting dangerous pagan ways, beliefs or practices.

God promises that as long as there is an observant, righteous and just descendant of David on Israel's throne, then Israel would dwell in safety, and not have to fear oppression or attacks from her enemies. ***This is the biblical definition of what a messiah is;*** as Followers of the Way of Yahveh, it is the *only* definition that is relevant to us.

If one reads ***all*** the texts[a] of the Davidic covenant fully, and not just selective bits and pieces of them (as messianists tend to do), one is able to see that it will be ***God*** who will save Israel,[b] and it will be ***God*** who will gather in the exiles, NOT a descendant of David. Having a descendant of David on the throne of Israel is just one of the things that God will do when God's Kingdom is fulfilled, NOT a precondition of it.

Messianism evolved over the centuries as a corruption of the Davidic covenant. After centuries of bad messiahs (i.e. bad kings), Israel longed for a *good* messiah – the true origin of the 'messianic hope'. After each blow suffered by the Jewish people, the theology of despair invested more and more hope in the 'messiah' as a physical, earthly

---

[a] 2Sam 7:8-16, and 1Chron 17:7-14, Psalm 89:20b-38; see also Psalm 89:4-5, Psalm 132:11-12, 1Kgs 8:25b, 2Chron 21:7

[b] e.g. Isa 60:22 – *"I, Yahveh, will bring these things about quickly, when the right time comes".*

saviour they could see and fixate on, and less and less in God as our One and only true Saviour.[a] Instead of placing their faith wholeheartedly and unreservedly in Yahveh, traditional Jewish messianism puts people's faith in one, mortal man.

Jewish messianism usurps God's supremacy, diverting belief away from the astounding power of God to redeem and save us from fear and oppression, and hands it over to a mere man. Messianism was not part of the original Yahwist religion; the idea of a messiah-saviour entered Judaism from Persian Zoroastrianism, and we should therefore treat it with extreme caution. After all, Abraham did not look for a messiah to save him, knowing that such a power belonged to Yahveh alone. For me, it is truly wonderful to have as the Saviour of my soul, the same Saviour that Abraham, Moses and David all turned to – Yahveh, and Yahveh alone!

Why belief in a messiah-saviour is a rejection of Yahveh

It was not God's original plan to have a human king over Israel. Through the prophet Samuel,[b] Yahveh said, *"... it is not you they have rejected, but they have rejected Me as their king. As they have done from the day I brought them up out of Egypt until this day, forsaking Me and serving other gods, so they are doing to you now."*

Therefore, to throw yourself wholeheartedly into accepting a messiah as your saviour instead of Yahveh, is to reject Yahveh. It is still 'serving other gods' (whether you believe 'Jesus' is god or not).

Yahveh also predicted that messiahs would be a political and financial burden on the people:

> *"This is what the king who will reign over you will claim as his rights: He will seize your sons and make them serve with his chariots and horses, and they will run in front of his chariots. Some he will set up as commanders of thousands and commanders of fifties, but others he will seize to plough his ground and reap his harvest, and still others to make weapons of war and equipment for his chariots. He will seize your daughters to be perfumiers and cooks and bakers. He will seize the best of your fields and*

---

[a] Isaiah 43:11 – *'I, and I alone am Yahveh, and besides Me there is no other Saviour'*. Also Isa 60:16 *"Then you will know that I, Yahveh, am your Saviour and your Redeemer"*, and Hos 13:4.
[b] 1Sam 8:7-8

vineyards and olive groves and give them to his own attendants. He will seize a tenth of your grain and of your vintage and give it to his own officials and attendants. He will seize your male and female servants and the best of your cattle and donkeys for his own use. He will seize a tenth of your flocks, and you yourselves will become his slaves. When that day comes, you will cry out for relief from the king you have chosen, but Yahveh will not answer you in that day."[a]

One also has to understand that in biblical Yahwism, 'messiah' DOES NOT MEAN SAVIOUR – 'messiah' is **not** a synonym for 'saviour'. It simply means 'an anointed king' (and in the context of the High Priests, 'an anointed High Priest'). It does not mean anything more than that. **ALL** THE KINGS OF ISRAEL AND JUDAH WERE THEREFORE MESSIAHS – even the bad, wicked, tyrannical ones. The title of messiah is an automatic title of ALL David's descendants who are kings,[b] not just of one outstandingly brilliant, super-messiah in the future.

'Messiah' can even mean 'someone chosen for God's especial purpose'. King Cyrus the Great of Persia is referred to as a messiah (an 'Anointed One'),[c] and he wasn't even Jewish! God's prophets are also called 'anointed ones'.[d] In such a context, a better translation would be 'God's appointed one(s)', rather than 'anointed one'.

The Davidic Covenant is basically God making the best out of a bad deal (which was in allowing Israel to have kings in the first place). God really did not want Israel to have human kings,[e] and only agreed to a monarchy with extreme reluctance. So in order to keep the messiahs of Israel in line – to make sure they behaved themselves – God made a covenant with David and his male descendants. If they were good kings, obedient and faithful to Yahveh, then Israel would prosper and have peace.[f] But if they were bad kings, turning their backs on Yahveh, then Israel would fall and have only strife.[g]

As Yahveh predicted, the anointed kings of Israel and Judah were mostly despots and tyrants who turned their backs on God (just read the

---

[a] 1Sam 8:11-18
[b] Ps 18:50
[c] see Isaiah 44:24, 26–45:3, 13
[d] Ps 105:15
[e] Hos 13:11
[f] 2Sam 7:8-16, Psalm 89:20b-38, and 1Chron 17:7-14
[g] 2Sam 7:14

catalogue of reigns in the Book of Kings)! In those times people did not pray, 'When messiah comes!', because they already had 'messiahs' on the throne, messiahs who caused them only pain and suffering. In those days, messiahs were not seen as saviours. A few were good and faithful servants of Yahveh – and these are the outstanding individuals who are prophesied in the books of the prophets, such as King Hezekiah or King Josiah; there is not one immortal, sinless, super-messiah at the end of time.

Any Messiah Will Be Subservient To God

Talmidaism is not a messianic movement; it does not teach salvation through a personal messiah – that the coming of a messiah means that he will bring us spiritual salvation. Instead, it teaches most emphatically that it is and will always be Yahveh, and Yahveh alone, who will save us:

> *"I – and I alone – am Yahveh; apart from me there is no other saviour."*[a]

Talmidaism does however teach – just as the Prophets did – that one day there will be a descendant of David on the throne of Israel. What the mainstream calls 'the Messianic Age', we Followers of the Way describe as 'the Age of the fulfilment of God's Kingdom'.

Messianism is basically a corrupted interpretation of the Covenant God made with David and his male descendants. One of the benefits of that covenant was that, as long as the Davidic king obeyed God's laws and precepts, then Israel would live safely and securely within her borders. If the king – the anointed one, the messiah – disobeyed God's laws and precepts, then Israel would fall into turmoil.

This is because it was not envisaged that any future messiahs would be perfect and sinless:

> *"I will be a father to him, and he shall be a son to Me. If he does wrong, I will chastise him with the rod of men, and the affliction of mortals..."*[b]

Here, the use of the words 'father' and 'son' is meant to illustrate the guiding part that God plays in the life and discipline of any anointed

---

[a] Isa 43:11
[b] 2Sam 7:14

king of Israel, not that somehow God miraculously begets a human or even semi-divine son.

Another misconception (both rabbinic and Christian) is that there would be just one messiah, which presumes that he would be immortal, but nowhere in the Miqra does it say 'the' Anointed One. In many Christian bibles, Daniel 9:25-26 has '*the* Anointed One', but this is a translation which bends the Hebrew Bible according to one's theology; the Hebrew has no definite article before the noun, implying simply 'an' anointed one. Every descendant of David who sits on the throne of Israel will be a 'messiah', a *moshiach*, an anointed one. Every time one Anointed One on the throne of Israel dies, another Anointed One will reign in his place:

> *'If your SONS* (note the plural) *keep My covenant*
> *and My decrees that I teach THEM,*
> *Then their SONS also*
> *To the end of time,*
> *Shall sit upon your throne".*[a]

Having an anointed one is a sign that Yahveh is acting in our history, not that any particular anointed one is saving us. We have to take note that in Ezekiel 37:15-28, the return of the exiles of Ephraim (the Israelites of the northern kingdom) precedes there being a renewed monarchy in Israel. The exiles of Judah, for the most part, have returned, but we will know that God is ready to give us a new line of Davidic kings when Yahveh – and Yahveh alone – causes the exiles of Ephraim to return to the Land.

Why Yeshua` was not a god-messiah: Isaiah 9:5 in context

In the next few articles, I want to examine the biblical passages most commonly put forward by evangelicals and Messianics to 'prove' that Yeshua` was a god or messiah. By carefully explaining these passages, I will show you that they prove nothing of the kind, and that they are being used dishonestly by evangelicals and missionisers.

If you understand messianism not in its Christian context, nor even in its Rabbinic context, but in its Yahwist context, you will come to realise that 'messiah' is not a synonym for 'saviour' (in Hos 13:10, God even mocks the people's hope that a messiah will save them). Originally, messiah simply meant 'an anointed king or high priest', and that is what it still means to Talmidis today.

---

[a] Psalm 132:11-12

There is one passage that many Christians use to prove once and for all that 'Jesus' is unquestionably a god. The traditional Christian translation of Isaiah 9:5 into English (from the NIV) reads:

> *"For to us a child is born,*
> *To us a son is given,*
> *And the government will be on his shoulders.*
> *And he will be called Wonderful Counsellor,*
> *Mighty God,*
> *Everlasting Father,*
> *Prince of Peace."*

The first thing one needs to know, is that ancient Hebrew was limited in its vocabulary. It only had about 3,500 or so basic words. Contrast that with someone who has received a good education today, who will have a written vocabulary of about 20-30,000 words.

To overcome this shortfall in vocabulary, ancient Hebrew overused some words by giving them many disparate meanings, or by putting two words together to form a new idea. The titles of the Messiah of David are a good example of this linguistic practice.

The first title is (apparently), "Wonderful Counsellor". Now, the Hebrew, *pele yo'eits*, is actually a compound of two nouns together, 'wonder' and 'counsellor'. Put together, they have the idea of "man of remarkable wisdom".

The second title (at least in Christian bibles) is "Mighty God". Again, the two Hebrew words are nouns, *eil* and *gibbor*. The second Hebrew word comes from the verb-root *gabar*, 'to be mighty', and means, 'mighty hero'. The first word, *eil*, which Christians here translate as 'God', actually has 3 different meanings in the Hebrew language (consider how many meanings the English word 'rose' has). It comes from the verb *'al*, 'to be strong'. The first meaning of the word *eil* is 'mighty hero'; the second is 'might'; and the third is 'god' (= mighty being).

Now, when you get two nouns together, especially ones with identical meanings, it implies a superlative. So here, *eil gibbor* literally means 'mighty hero of mighty hero', i.e. 'mightiest hero', or 'the ultimate mighty hero'.

The Hebrew word *eil* appears several times in the Hebrew Bible with the meaning of 'hero' – it even appears in the plural in Ezekiel 32:21: *eley gibborim*, meaning 'mightiest heroes'. If it were intended to be 'mighty gods' it would have been expressed as *elohey gibborim*.

The last point to make here, is that no Jew would ever have allowed a human being to be called a 'god', even in prophecy. Although god-men are commonplace in pagan religions, the very idea is entirely alien to Israelite culture; if they had ever thought that *eil* in this context had meant 'god', they would never have included it in the Hebrew canon of scripture.

The third title is 'Everlasting Father' (*avi 'ad*). Again, we have two nouns, 'father' and 'eternity'. Together as a compound noun, they give the idea of a ruler forever devoted to his people – a father who will not turn from his watchful care of the people, a king who will be devoted to the concerns of his people, for as long as he lives.

The last title is 'Prince of peace' (*śar shalom*). Again, this is a compound noun; the two nouns together imply a ruler whose reign will be characterised by peace.

So now, let's see how a biblical, Hebrew-speaking Israelite would understand the verse:

> *"For a child is born to us,*
>   *a son is given to us,*
> *And authority will be laid across his shoulders to bear.*
> *And he will be called 'Remarkable Sage',*
>   *'Mightiest Hero',*
>   *'Devoted Ruler',*
>   *'Prince of Peace."*

This passage[a] refers to an anointed king of the line of David, since it explicitly refers to David's throne in verse 9:7. Most Jewish commentators understand the boy-king being referred to in this prophecy to be, in fact, the great anointed king (or 'messiah'), King Hezekiah.

At a time when the northern kingdom were worshipping idols (which is what *'The people walking in darkness'* in Isa 9:2 and *'those living in the land of deep darkness* refers to), King Hezekiah would bring great reforms, and consolidate the sole worship of Yahveh. The northern kingdom could have taken note of what Hezekiah was doing, but they didn't. However, Hezekiah did strengthen the worship of Yahveh in Judah, and for that he is called, *'Remarkable Sage', 'Mightiest Hero', 'Devoted Ruler', 'Prince of Peace.'* Therefore, these verses do not prove that the mistranslated titles refer to Yeshua`, or that the messiah is divine.

However, what we can also say is that all that King Hezekiah was, we can also hope of any *future* anointed king of a united Israel – that he too will be called, *'Remarkable Sage', 'Mightiest Hero', 'Devoted Ruler',* and *'Prince of Peace.'*

The final point I would make, is that Christians tend to translate

---

[a] Hebrew Bibles Isaiah 8:23-9:6, Christian bibles Isaiah 9:1-7

and change Hebrew according to their own theology, with fleeting regard to what the Hebrew actually means, or the reality of biblical history. I come across this time after time, where there are deliberate mistranslations to prove that Yeshua` was a god or messiah, when the Hebrew says nothing of the kind.

Psalm 45 – God supposedly addressing the king of Israel as 'God'

There is a line in the psalms that has been used to 'prove' that Israelite kings were addressed by God as 'God'. In Hebrew bibles, it is Ps 45:7 (Christian bibles Ps 45:6). In the NIV, the translation reads:

Your throne, O God, will last for ever and ever;
a sceptre of justice will be the sceptre of your kingdom.

The Hebrew for the first part of the verse is this:

כסאך אלהים עולם ועד

Word for word, from right to left, this reads:

throne-your | God | eternal | and-forever

In Jewish bibles, this is translated differently to Christian bibles. In the JPS Tanakh, it reads, 'Your divine throne is everlasting', and in the Soncino Press translation it reads, 'Thy throne given of God is forever and ever.'

The psalm itself was written on the occasion of the marriage of an Israelite king to a foreign bride. Some say this was King Solomon (reigned c. 970-931 BCE), others say King Jehoram of Judah (reigned c. 849-842 BCE). As the first line of the psalm indicates, a Korachite poet composed the psalm, so the first thing to point out is that the speaker is not God but the poet. Hebrew-speaking Jewish translators interpret the verse to mean that the throne is *from* God, not that the king is being addressed *as* God.

There is even another possibility. It is not beyond the realm of probability that there could actually be a letter missing in the Hebrew text.[a]

At the time this psalm was originally composed, the alphabet used

---

[a] of the type of copying error known as haplography or lipography, where a repeated letter is mistakenly copied as a single letter.

would have been the Paleo-Hebrew alphabet, and in that alphabet, the initial and final forms of the letter *kaf* (כ and ך in modern square Hebrew script)[a] were not as yet differentiated. Instead of *kissakha elohim olam va'ed*, the original might actually have been *kissakha **kha**-elohim olam va'ed* – 'Your throne ***is like*** God – eternal and everlasting.' This reading would be well within how the Miqra portrays the lineage of David – an eternal lineage of kings.

Some fundamentalists maintain that no mistakes could ever have been made in the written transmission of the books of the Hebrew bible, from handwritten copy to handwritten copy, but there are some very obvious omissions in the acrostic psalms,[b] and there are indeed differences between the standard Masoretic text and other ancient versions of the Hebrew bible. In some instances, the reading in the *other* versions make more sense.[c] If a mistake was made in copying Psalm 45, at a time when the psalm was written in Paleo-Hebrew, then the hypothetical second *kaf* (which would translate as the word 'like'), could have been omitted as a scribal error very early on in the psalm's history. By the time Hebrew changed to writing in square Hebrew script, that omission would have already been established for at least 400 years.

Even if the psalm were originally written exactly as we have it today – without any copying error – the line can be read as 'your godly throne' or 'your throne from God'; the verse is not calling the Israelite king 'God'.

---

[a] the script used to write Hebrew after the Babylonian exile in the 6th century BCE.

[b] An acrostic psalm is a psalm where every new line or verse begins with a new letter of the Hebrew alphabet. Since the order of the letters in the Hebrew alphabet has always been the same since ancient times, if a letter of the alphabet is missing, then the omission is obvious. Such is the case in Ps 9, where the lines for the letter *dalet* are missing (between 9:6 & 7); in Ps 10, the lines for the letter *mem* are missing (between 10:2 & 10:3) and *samek* (somewhere in 10:5); and in Ps 34, the lines for the letter *vav* are missing (between 34:5 & 6). In Ps 145, the line for the letter *nun* is missing (between 145:13 & 14), but the DSS version of the psalm provides the missing words.

[c] e.g. Ex 12:40, the Massoretic text says, *'the time that the Israelites dwelt in the land of Egypt was 430 years.'* But the Samaritan text reads, *'the time that the Israelites dwelt **in Canaan and** Egypt was 430 years'* – which would make more sense. Also, in the final words of Moses at the end of Deuteronomy, when he says a few words about each tribe, the tribe of Simeon is not mentioned at all – in the traditional Masoretic text. However, in the Samaritan and Septuagint versions, verse Dt 33:6 reads, "May Reuben live and not die, and ***Simeon***, may his men be few."

David's 'lord' in Psalm 110

It is claimed that this psalm is a prophecy, predicting that the messiah will be divine (because this lord is greater than David – fuzzy logic; it assumes that the only one greater than David is God). However, if you look at the biography of Abraham, you will realise that it fits Abraham perfectly.

The earliest Jewish interpretations of the psalm saw it as alluding variously to Abraham, some to the Hasmoneans, others to a Davidic messiah. However, in all of this, you have to realise that the Psalms were *not originally intended to be read as prophecy* – that's something really important to know; they weren't even originally part of the Hebrew Bible. They were one of the last books to be incorporated into the canon of the Miqra. Before that, they were used as the Israelite prayer/hymn book, **not** prophecy (i.e., when events are described therefore, for the most part they are not of things to come, but of things that once were).

The psalm therefore refers to **past** events, not future ones – specifically, to Abraham's victories over the kings around the Dead Sea. Melchizedek said of Abraham,[a] *"Blessed be God Most High, who has delivered your foes into your hand"*; Compare this with Ps 110:1 which says, *"Sit at my right hand, while I make your enemies your footstool"*.

The prayerful intervention of Melchizedek[b] gives Abraham's battles a religious dimension, with Yahveh as the One fighting the battles; God also promised Abraham that He would make his name great;[c] so therefore Ps 110:2 says, *"Yahveh will stretch forth from Zion your mighty sceptre"*. Ps 110:3 also says, *"in adornments of holiness"*, meaning that the young men who volunteer freely to fight for this 'lord' (Abraham) are as priests i.e. this is a battle under God's auspices.

When Abraham went out to fight, all his men and servants willingly fought for him;[d] so Ps 110:3 says, *"Your people willingly volunteer whenever you go into battle"*. Ps 110:5-6 continues the theme that Yahveh is the One who is actually doing the fighting in Abraham's case, and Yahveh alone is the victor. Verse 110:6 ends with how the heads of his enemies shall be crushed *'across the earth far and wide'*; in Gen 14:15, Abraham's men pursue their enemies as far as Hobah in Syria.

Abraham was also a 'king', because that is what God promised to him and the patriarchs,[e] who were all 'kings' i.e. rulers or chieftains of their people, who fought in battle against their enemies. In those days, a

---

[a] Gen 14:20
[b] Gen 14:18-20
[c] Gen 12:2
[d] Gen 14:15
[e] Gen 17:7, 17:16, 35:11

king was primarily more like a general in battle,[a] and in the case of Israelite kings, they fought on behalf of Yahveh.

As for priests, there is a common misconception that any man can become an Israelite priest – that the process of anointing is what makes someone a priest. Now, from the time of Moses onwards, priests were always the male descendants of Aaron (your mother's tribe is irrelevant). You are born a priest, not made one. To be a priest, your father has to be a priest, of the tribe of Levi. So, for example, Yeshua` cannot have been a priest, because his father was not a priest, nor was he of the tribe of Levi (you always take your father's tribe; rabbinic law actually breaks this rule by saying Jewishness comes from the mother, and not the father). However, there is still no precedent in the Israelite religion for making a non-Levite into a priest.

Now, before the time of Moses, it was the firstborn male in each family who acted as a priest and minister before God. Abraham was both priest and king, not in our modern, post-Sinai understanding of these two words, but in the pre-Moses era sense of how these two words were used. He was a priest because he was a firstborn male (pre-Sinai, *all* firstborn males were priests), and he was a king in the ancient sense of the word, because he acted as a general for God's battles, leading and defending his people (kings were also leaders of armies, not just leaders or 'chieftains' of peoples).

Abraham is king and priest 'of the order of Melchizedek' – that is, in the same way that Melchizedek was ('order' doesn't mean a religious order, but rather, 'of the same type as', or 'for the same reason as'); both Abraham and Melchizedek were firstborn males (and so were pre-Sinai priests), who were also military leaders of their peoples (and so were pre-Sinai kings). After Moses's era, a priest can only be a male member of the tribe of Levi, and after David, a king can only be a direct male descendant of David (therefore a member of the tribe of Judah). This was God's way of 'separating church and state'.

The whole of psalm 110 is therefore about the victory of Abraham in the Valley of Siddim; it concentrates on how it is God who gives victory to a 'lord' of David. This 'lord' is an illustrious ancestor who preceded David, and was greater than him. The 'lord' of Psalm 110 is Abraham, not 'Jesus'. The psalm is not about proving that 'Jesus' was divine, but that Abraham was a greater man than David.

---

[a] cf Job 15:24, 18:14, 30:15

The Suffering Servant: Isaiah 53 in context

The one prophecy that is quoted more than any other in support of the messiahship of 'Jesus' and his godhood, is Isaiah chapter 53. It is indeed sad then, that this is done by deception, since the chapter is always taken completely out of context, and its wording is deliberately distorted and mistranslated. There are pronouns that are clearly plural in Hebrew that have been changed to singular to make it look like it is referring to one person ('Jesus'), words missed out, prepositions changed, etc.

Christian apologists isolate Isaiah 53, ignoring what comes before and after it, because the suffering servant *within it* is not named. However, it is actually part of a whole section on 'The Servant' (chapters 40-55), where the Servant is most definitely named – many times in fact. In the whole 'Servant' section of Isaiah, the word 'servant' appears 30 times, and in most cases Jacob (i.e. the people of Israel) is explicitly identified as the servant.

For example, 41:8-9, and again at 44:1-2 *"And now listen, Jacob My servant, Israel whom I have chosen'.... Do not be afraid, Jacob My servant, Yeshurun,*[a] *whom I have chosen"*; 44:21, *"Remember these things, O Jacob, And Israel, for you are My servant; I have formed you, you are My servant, O Israel, you will not be forgotten by Me."* 45:4, *"For the sake of Jacob My servant, And Israel My chosen one"* 48:20 *"Yahveh has redeemed His servant Jacob."* 49:3, *"You are my servant, Israel, in whom I will display my Glory"*. Also implicitly: 43:10 – *"You yourselves are my witnesses* (plural), *and the servant* (singular) *whom I have chosen"* i.e. the servant is a collective group of people, not a single person. For other references of Israel as God's servant, see Jeremiah 30:10, 46:27-28, and Psalm 136:22.

There are those who say the servant cannot be Israel (a point which I will shortly go into). Whether the suffering servant is Israel or not, there are verses which make it plain that the suffering servant cannot be 'Jesus' *either*. The main one is 53:10 – "he will get to see his offspring and live out a long life". The Hebrew word for offspring is *zera`*, literally 'seed', which is most definitely *biological* offspring, not just followers/disciples. As far as we know, Yeshua` did not have any biological descendants. Nor did he live out a long life.

Other important points to make are: if Jesus is a god, how can a god call himself 'My servant'? How can God be a servant to Himself? If Jesus is a god, why would a god reward himself (with descendants and a long life)? Why would a god redeem himself (53:1 – *"to whom has the arm of Yahveh been revealed"* i.e. whom has Yahveh redeemed)? How

---

[a] an affectionate name God uses for 'Israel'.

can a god save and redeem *himself*?

Some of the objections to interpreting Israel as the suffering servant are that the people of Israel have not collectively died or suffered from plague. As I point out below, exile is likened to death elsewhere, and disease/plague is often a metaphor for trials and tribulations. Also, it is claimed that the suffering servant is portrayed as perfectly innocent and guiltless, but this is not the case. Even though no human being is sinless, a person can still be called righteous.

The most important thing to understand about chapter 53 is, who is speaking? Verses 52:13-15 is God, 53:1 is Isaiah, but the bulk of the passage, 53:2-12 is the voice of Gentile rulers and world leaders, who are astonished at what they see and eventually realise (the gravity of the sins they have committed against Israel over the centuries). Immediately following chapter 53 is, lo and behold, chapter 54, which speaks of the redemption of Israel after what she has suffered.

Here are explanations of the passage, line by line:
53:1 *"Who would have believed our news?"* Indeed! Who would have believed that, after 2,000 years of exile, the Jewish people could have been returned to our ancestral lands? Also, *'to whom has the arm of Yahveh been revealed?'* This is a Hebrew idiom, meaning 'who has been redeemed by Yahveh?'[a] If Jesus were a god, why and even how would he redeem himself?
53:2 the image of a sapling growing in dry ground is a metaphor for the faith of Israel thriving in a pagan environment.
53:3 *'A man of pain and acquainted with disease'*: Israel's adversities are often likened to sickness e.g. Isa 1:5-6, Jer 10:19, Jer 30:12
53:4 (and Jer 30:17), the servant Israel is regarded by the nations as an outcast, abandoned by God.
53:5 – *'he was wounded from our transgressions, crushed from our iniquities'* – the nations will realise that Israel's suffering is a direct result of what the nations have done to Israel i.e. rather than because of Israel's own faults.
53:7 – the image of Israel being like sheep led to the slaughter is found elsewhere: *"You give us as sheep to be eaten and have scattered us among the nations... we are considered as sheep to be slaughtered"*.[b] The silence does not refer to any absence of protest to our persecutors for our suffering, but rather that Israel does not turn against God or curse God as a result of what we endure at the hands of other nations. Also it is worth pointing out, that throughout the history of the ill-treatment of

---
[a] cf Deut 5:15
[b] Psalms 44:12, 23

the Jewish people, we did not do violence to our host nations; and in spite of oppressive laws enacted against us, we did not terrorise or plot to destroy our host nations.

53:8 – *'He was cut off from the land of the living'* – see Ezek 37:11-14, where Israel is described as 'cut off'. Exile is likened to death, and return to Israel is bringing Israel back to the land of the living. The 'land of the Living' is therefore the Land of Israel.
'because of the transgression of my people' (i.e. a Gentile nation – remember, this is a Gentile ruler/s speaking here),
a plague befell them' (i.e. Israel, the Jewish people; note the plural *them*, not *him*; so also 53:9 *'and with the rich in his deaths'* (plural). Remember, Gentile rulers are still speaking, not God.
53:9 *'his grave was assigned with wicked men'* – see Ezek 37:11-14, this is a metaphorical death; Israel's exile is a death amongst the nations.
53:10 A guilt-offering is always symbolic of how the human soul is brought near to the Divine Radiance – the 'Glory' – of God, for purification from the stain and injury of sin. The guilt offering does not in and of itself bring about forgiveness or atonement. By understanding the atonement process from a purely Yahwist perspective, then if Israel was a 'guilt-offering', Israel was pushed towards the fiery radiance of God's Glory against her will by the sinful actions of other nations; the guilt-offering does not bring about atonement.
'He shall see his seed (i.e. biological descendants) *and live a long life'* – Yeshua` didn't live a long life, and had no biological descendants.
53:11 *'he will cause the many to be righteous'* – not as some Christian bibles translate it, 'he will justify the many' (e.g. KJV, NIV, NAS).

Overall, this is a prophecy of how the nations will one day realise the full gravity of what they have done to Israel over the centuries, and feel shame and sorrow for the evil they have done to Israel. We were sent to bring a moral way of life to the nations, and thereby be the light of Yahveh to the nations. In ancient times, the nations had serious faults, questionable ethics and violent societies, and when they saw the way of life of Israel, they were enraged and persecuted us. They saw nothing attractive in our way of life – indeed, they saw it as a weakness and despised us. But over time the just and righteous Way of our God startled many peoples, and humbled the kings of many nations to silence. The nations claimed that what we suffered at their hands was our own fault – because of our own sins, but we were suffering because of *their* sins – because of the cruelty *they* were inflicting upon us. One day the nations will realise the awful, cruel and terrible things they have done to God's suffering servant – Israel,[a] and come to us and ask to know our God.[b]

Gen 18 - The three angels who visited Abraham were not the trinity

In Gen 18:1-33, it is in the interests of Christian translations of this chapter for there to be deliberate ambiguity between the persons of the three messengers on the one hand, and the Person of Yahveh on the other. For Christian theologians, it is claimed that the three messengers are in fact the three persons or incarnations of the Christian god. However, if you read the passage in Hebrew, the Person of Yahveh and the persons of the three messengers are most distinct and separate.

When God speaks through the three messengers, God's voice is not one of the messengers' voices, but an independent fourth voice who speaks through one of the angels. They start the conversation, but God almost finishes their sentences for them.

We should always remember that in the Yahwist Israelite tradition, angels have no will of their own. They are the mouthpieces of God, the instruments God uses in order to speak audibly to human beings. What they say comes directly from God (like someone relaying a message verbatim on behalf of someone else, or like a simultaneous translator). So when you speak to an angel, you are speaking to God, albeit secondhand. And when an angel speaks to you, what they say are God's direct words, word for word.

In verse 18:1, it says that Yahveh 'appears' to Avraham. When Avraham looks up, he sees three men standing before him. The men appear on God's behalf; God is not the three men. It often says in the Miqra, 'Yahveh appeared'. If it said every time, 'an angel appeared on Yahveh's behalf', in my humble opinion, I think that too much attention would be focussed on the angels, and the One who *sent* the angels would be ignored. That is why the sender (Yahveh) is mentioned, and not the one(s) sent. On most occasions in the Miqra, when it says that 'Yahveh appeared', more often than not it means that an angel appeared on Yahveh's behalf.

Certain verses are addressed directly to Yahveh – these are indicated in Hebrew with the singular object pronoun 'you' endings. Other verses are addressed to the three men – these are indicated in Hebrew with plural 'you' endings. It is obvious in Hebrew when Avraham speaks to God, and when he speaks to the three men.

---

[a] cf Micah 7:15-16
[b] In researching this article, I found the following invaluable: 'The Soncino Books of the Bible' commentary on Isaiah; the UAHC commentary on Isaiah; and JewsforJudaism.org

Unfortunately, it is not so evident at all in English translations; the modern English language is not able to grammatically distinguish between singular 'you' and plural 'you' (unlike Middle English 'thou' and 'ye').

For example, in verses 3 to 5, Avraham says to God, "My Sovereign, if I have found favour in Your eyes, do not pass Your servant by." All this is addressing a singular 'you'.

Then Avraham addresses the three men: "Let a little water be brought; bathe your feet and recline under the tree. And let me fetch you a morsel of bread that you may refresh yourselves." All this addresses a plural 'you'.

In Hebrew, all this has a kind of surreal, twilight-zone quality about it. The three men know God is speaking; in a sense they know what God knows, they start a sentence, and God finishes it (e.g. verses 9 & 10); Avraham's words go from addressing Yahveh, to addressing the three men, and then back to addressing Yahveh, without any breaks in between. The only thing that tells you this has happened is the change in Hebrew from singular to plural 'you', and back again to singular 'you'.

So who are these three men? Although it doesn't state as much, in Israelite tradition these three men are thought to be three of the archangels of God's Presence (in Gen 19:1 and 19:15 they are called angels or messengers – *mal'akhim*; it's the same word for both in Hebrew). Some traditions say they were the archangels Mikha'el, Refa'el and Gabri'el; they were respectively the guardian archangel of Israel, the archangel of healing and purification, and the chief archangel-Messenger of God.

When Mikha'el and Refa'el leave for Sodom, Gabri'el – the Messenger of God – remains with Abraham. Through the voice and body of Gabri'el, Abraham plea-bargains for Sodom directly with God.

Reading the chapter in Hebrew does not make it look as if the angels are the persons of the Christian trinity in human form, as some claim.

Superhuman rabbi or prophet of God?

There has always been the question of where Yeshua`'s knowledge, erudite oratory and wisdom came from. To most Christian commentators, all these skills prove that he was a god, and of royal human pedigree. To a Messianic Jewish commentator, it also proves he was a learned Pharisaic rabbi. To someone like me, who accepts him neither as a god, messiah or Pharisaic rabbi, there is a third option: that he was a human prophet.

Now, we all have our heroes; we all like to have people to look up to and admire. We like to think they are perfect and faultless. We put them on a pedestal and worship them. But then we find they have faults, they make mistakes like the rest of us, and then we lose faith in them.

In Yeshua`'s day, ordinary people in the Galilee were living in poverty, struggling to make ends meet. They wanted God to deliver them from their hardship and oppression. The Pharisees had declared there were no more prophets, and that the only person who could save them was a messiah. The ultimate effect this had on people was that they came to believe the *only* person they would listen to – the only person worthy of delivering a message of hope – was a messiah. In a sense, they came to think that the deliverer of the message somehow justified the message itself. And that the messenger was more important than the message.

If the Pharisees had never declared prophecy to be extinct, and if they had never declared that they would only listen to the messiah, then there would never have been any need for *anyone* to claim that Yeshua` was the messiah (i.e. the only person whose warnings they would heed). Therefore, looking for evidence of Yeshua` prophesied in the Scriptures would have been completely unnecessary.[a] It would have been enough for Yeshua`'s followers to explain to their fellow Jews that he was a prophet of God, and let his prophecies speak for themselves as they came true. By denying the continuation of prophecy among the Jewish people, and by elevating the status of a messiah to just below that of God, the Pharisees made a fateful rod for their own backs (and sadly, for the Jewish people).

In the traditions we have about Yeshua`'s life, they are largely silent with regard to his formative years. Consequently our human minds, full of curiosity, begin to speculate. Imagine a great speaker and orator. You listen to this guy, you know he was a follower of Yochanan the Immerser ('St John the Baptist'), and you begin to think, *he must have travelled widely; he must have spent time in secluded communities in the desert, learning all kinds of esoteric knowledge. He must have studied in exclusive religious schools, debating Torah.* You follow this man around and you think, *he must have been taught by great scholars and teachers, and gained wisdom and insight from years of learning. Otherwise, where could all this wisdom have possibly come from? There are no more prophets (so say the Pharisees), so it can't be from God, can it?*

So you follow this wise and learned teacher around the Galilee, and eventually he takes a bunch of you back to his home village of Nazareth.

---

[a] therefore, Talmidis do not see details of Yeshua`'s life predicted in the Torah or the Prophets (since no other prophet is proved by his pre-existence in scripture either); it is enough that his genuine prophecies – his warnings on the tribulation – came to pass in 70CE.

On the Sabbath, you go with him to the local – well, the only – synagogue in the village, and listen to him deliver his words of exhortation after the Torah reading. You hear more of the same wise and learned words, from someone you think spent years gleaning all this from the greatest minds of the age, the result of many years of study and scholarship.

Then you hear the women gossiping in the back. Now, you know these are people who knew him growing up. You know this is a small village, where everyone knows everyone inside out, and there are few secrets if any.

'What's he on about?' says one. 'Who does he think he is?'

'Isn't he just a day labourer?' remarks another. 'Where's he getting all these big ideas from?'

'He's the son of that Mary woman,' someone scoffs.

Yet another says, *'Yes, and his brothers are no more than farmhands and fishermen, just like the rest of our menfolk.'*

Looking around, they see his sisters and mock, *'Look, even his sisters honour us with their presence!'*[a]

Previously all that we, as his followers, knew of this man was his wisdom. We took a guess at where it came from. Now we see the man on his home turf, among the people who knew him from his days in diapers . . . and we realise he is just a man. He's no one special. He's the same as the rest of these country folk.

In *'The Ascents of James'*, there is an interesting debate between Jacob the Pious and the High Priest. Caiaphas mocks Jacob the Pious and his followers, saying that they are not even learned teachers; they are mere country-folk and fishermen, and should therefore shut up and learn their place. Jacob the Pious retorts that, if they were able to stand up to the Sadducees – these wise and erudite men of learning – one might be able to put it down to human diligence and study. But if they, as mere country-folk and fishermen, were still able to speak words of wisdom and defeat men greater than they, the High Priest should realise that their words are not the work of mere human endeavour, *but a direct message from God*.

This was the stark reality faced by Yeshua`'s followers who accompanied him back to his home village.[b] Yeshua` knew his scriptures well, he was a great speaker, he was intelligent and knew how to use scripture. However, Yeshua`'s neighbours presented his followers with a picture of a man who was, after all, an ordinary man. He wasn't a graduate student of venerable academies, he wasn't a messiah, he wasn't

---

[a] scenario adapted from S.Yesh. 151; cf Mk 6:1-4, 3:20-21, 3:31-35, Mt 13:54-57, 12:46-50, Lk 4:16-17, 4:24.
[b] S.Yesh. 151:1; cf Mk 6:1

descended from kings and priests; he was just a Galilean peasant. And why should we be surprised? The prophet Amos was just a gardener who tended fig trees!

All writers are aware that you write what you know. The same goes for great orators. You speak about what you know and have experienced. Several times he mentioned his acquaintance with Yochanan the Immerser,[a] but in all his parables and stories, he notably did NOT recount any further travels to visit any other teachers around the Holy Land, let alone to any far-flung corners of the world; he didn't mention studying in any secluded desert communities, or having learned at the feet of any great rabbinic scholars.

Instead, he spoke about *everyday life in the Galilee*. His parables are about day-labourers who wait in marketplaces for someone to hire them for a denarius a day; he speaks of finding money in a field while ploughing; he speaks of finding large fish while fishing; he speaks of sowers sowing their seed, gathering grain into barns – farmers and fisherman, house-servants and money-stewards, worrying about what to eat and drink, where one's clothes and basic needs are going to come from. A good speaker doesn't just speak about the lives of his audience, but about *his own life* too. Yeshua` was able to speak with great passion, and make that connection with his rural peasant audience, *because he had lived their life as one of them*.

The followers of Yeshua` who accompanied him to Nazareth now realise his words are not the work of human diligence and study, but are from somewhere else. They are a heavenly gift, a direct message from God. They now realise that God has taken hold of the life of this Galilean day-labourer, this country peasant, and given him a message to deliver. The Pharisees had always told them there were no more prophets, but here *was* a real prophet, living and breathing, right in front of them!

It was God's will that these things should happen, so that those of his followers who were not from Nazareth would see that Yeshua` was but a man like them, and that the words he spoke were not his own, but of heavenly origin – that his words were not the work of human cleverness or study, but rather of divine gift and provenance.[b]

Good news spreads fast. Yeshua` tries to have a quiet Sabbath meal with his followers in one of the small houses in Nazareth. No such luck! Crowds gather round the house, people who want to hear more of what Yeshua`, as a prophet, has learned from God. They eagerly clamour to

---

[a] Many times, Yeshua` speaks positively about Yochanan the Immerser ('John the Baptist'): S.Yesh. passages 11 & 12, 79:3, 94:1-2, 111:4, 113:4, 137:2-6; *cf* Mk 11:27-33, Mt 11:2-18, 17:11-12, 21:32, Lk 6:40, 7:19-35, 10:23, 16:16

[b] an explanatory midrash that appears in S.Yesh 151:11-12.

hear more of God's message. They are desperate to ask Yeshua˙ what God has to say about what is going to happen to them, to their families and to their Land.

His family, on the other hand, have other ideas. His mother has heard of this commotion, and is embarrassed by it.[a] She even gathers together his brothers to help her extract Yeshua˙ from the crowds and take him home. *How can he embarrass his family like this? Doesn't he know that people in a small village gossip? What will the neighbours think? He must be out of his mind!*

His mother and brothers arrive at the house, but they can't even get near him because there are too many people, most of whom they don't recognise. Where have all these strangers come from? What do they want? They pass word through the crowd that they want to speak to him – urgently.

Eventually the terse message gets through that his mother and brothers want to have a word with him. He knows what they are thinking. He doesn't want to dishonour their call, so he uses the opportunity to further his message – that his followers are as close to him as his real family:[b]

> *'Who is my mother? And who are my brothers?'*
> *And he stretched out a hand to his followers and said,*
> *'Here are my mother and brothers! Because whoever*
> *does the will of our heavenly Father, they are my*
> *mother, and my brother, and my sister.'*[c]

In those ancient times, Gentile cultures had myths and legends whose heroes were nothing less than gods, or were descended from gods. For Gentiles it was easier to think that the deliverer of a message was someone divine or special, or of royal lineage or of a noble family, or a powerful man of great learning.

But Hebrew culture was not like Gentile culture. Our ancient stories told us our patriarchs and matriarchs had faults; like Abraham and Sarah, they made mistakes, and were not superheroes. But they were faithful and obedient to God; they served God with faith and justice, and were rewarded for it. Hebrew culture produced imperfect, *human* men and

---

[a] narrative midrash at S.Yesh. 151:15; cf Mt 12:46 (sub-text, not openly stated)
[b] i.e. he is not repudiating his family, since to renounce his mother would be to break the 5th commandment to honour one's parents. By these words, he is not dishonouring his family, he is actually *extending* the meaning of family: that those who do the will of their heavenly Father are also part of his family.
[c] S.Yesh. 151:18-20; cf Mt 12:48-49

women whom God enabled to do extraordinary things.

If Yeshua` was an ordinary man who had previously lived an ordinary life, why did God choose him? The simple answer would have been, the same reason why God chose the prophet Amos, a simple shepherd and an orchard worker: so that people would realise the message he gave them was from the mind of God, and not from the mind of the prophet.

God wanted His people to realise that the message was by far more important than the man God chose to deliver it. If you want to know why Yeshua`'s first Jewish followers left no record of his early life – well, it was just not relevant. The prophet Yeshua` wanted his followers to look to God, and not to him.

The supposed miracles of Yeshua`

Anyone familiar with the miracles recorded in the Hebrew Bible, will easily be able to see their parallels reflected in the miracles of 'Christ' in the New Testament. Anyone who is furthermore acquainted with the abundance of miracles performed by pagan gods and higher mortals in myths and legends all around the world, cannot fail to see the practical intent of miracles in the *New Testament*. In Jewish culture, any miracles performed by holy people were merely a sign that God was with that person; in pagan Gentile culture, miracles were a definitive sign that such a person was actually a divine or semi-divine being.

The *Sefer Yeshua`* – a modern collection of the de-Christianised, re-Judaised sayings and ethical teachings of the Prophet Yeshua` – is notable for the complete absence of any miracles. There are two good reasons for this. First of all, the lack of any miracles forces the faithful Follower of Yahveh to concentrate on the actual *content* of the message delivered by the Prophet Yeshua` from God. This produces a living faith full of strong substance founded on the realities of life, because a faith built on nature-defying miracles alone will fail, when faced with the scientific truths of the modern world.

Secondly, there is the principle in the Israelite religion that a message is not proved by signs and portents, even if the miracles are real, or the sign comes to pass.[a] Consider how modern religious groups try to prove their message by filling their services with showy 'miracles'.

---

[a] *"If a prophet, or one who foretells by dreams, appears among you and announces to you a miraculous sign or wonder, and even if the sign or wonder of which he has spoken takes place, and he says, 'Let us follow other gods' - gods you have not known – 'and let us worship them,' you must not listen to the words of that prophet or dreamer."* Deut 13:1-3

However, in ancient Judea, it was only people with a lack of faith who asked for a sign; those who believed in Yahveh looked rather at the strength and content of the message, and its relevance to real life.

In my humble opinion, I do not think that any of the miracles recorded in the four *New Testament* gospels ever really happened; they are purely fictionalised accounts. The '*Letter of James*' – in my opinion, the earliest work[a] in the *New Testament* – has no discussion of any miracles. Then we have the letters of Paul – as much as I dislike his writings – which also do not contain *any* account of the miracles recorded in the gospels. It is not until the gospel of Mark, written in about 70 CE, that we get any accounts of miracles. They are there for a very good reason.

I believe they began with Peter's Nazarenes,[b] who needed to prove to their fellow Jews that Yeshua` was the messiah. They felt a need to prove that Yeshua` was greater than Moses and all other Hebrew prophets, so whereas Elijah began and ended a drought,[c] Moses parted the Sea of Reeds, and Joshua, Elijah and Elisha later parted the River Jordan, 'Jesus' commands the stormy waves of the Sea of Galilee, and walks on water. Whereas Elijah was able to make a jar of flour and a flask of oil last for may days,[d] and just as Elisha fed hundreds,[e] the gospels have 'Jesus' feed *thousands*. Just as Elijah[f] and Elisha[g] restored the dead back to life, so also 'Jesus' resurrects the dead. And just as Elisha[h] miraculously healed the sick, so too the Nazarene stories could not fail to have their 'Jesus' heal the sick in an equally miraculous way; in a world with no telephones, newspapers or TV, it doesn't take much for a story to get started, and even less for a story to spread and take hold.

To the modern Christian, the miracles of 'Jesus Christ' prove that 'Christ' was God; however, to the Jewish mind, miracles would prove nothing of the sort. Neither Moses, Aaron, Elijah, Elisha or anyone else in the Hebrew tradition who performed miracles were *ever* considered gods, or even semi-divine.

By the time the Nazarene stories of the miracle-performing messiah reached Paul's Believers in Antioch and elsewhere – places suffused

---

[a] written, I believe, in about 40 CE, promoted by the so-called 'Gaius Crisis'.
[b] The Nazarenes (*Notsrim* in Hebrew) were the result, I believe, of Peter's ministry in Judea, after his theology became heavily influenced by Paul's beliefs. Whereas early Followers of the Way and the later Ebionites owed their allegiance to James, Nazarenes owed their allegiance to Peter and Paul.
[c] 1Kgs 17:1, 18:41-45
[d] 1 Kings 17:14
[e] 2Kgs 4:38-44
[f] 1 Kings 17:22
[g] 2Ki 4:34; also 2Ki 13:21
[h] 2Ki 5:14, 2Ki 6:20

with pagan culture and pagan ways of perceiving the world – the miracle stories had to become something better and more showy. In Gentile pagan culture, gods such as Asclepius performed many healing miracles and raised the dead; Dionysos-Bacchus turned water into wine; and various other gods were able to walk on water, such as Poseidon and Horus. For pagans, miracles were proof of divinity, and that exact way of thinking has passed over into Gentile Christianity. 'Christ', just like the pagan gods, had to be able to command animals, exorcise demons to cure illness, and command nature. Anything the pagan gods could do, 'Jesus Christ' had to do better, stronger, and in an incredibly more spectacular way than anything the pagan world had produced before him.[a]

My conclusion is that the stories of miracles in the 'Jesus-tradition' were not based on anything that really happened, but were developed as a response to try and prove all the claims that Peter's Nazarenes and Paul's Believers had about 'Jesus Christ'. For the original Jewish Followers of Yeshua`, there were no fictionalised claims or miracles, because their faith was based on the true substance of his actual, prophetic message.

Giving Yeshua`'s mission its proper historical and theological context

Having spent the last 40 pages refuting established claims about 'Jesus', and trying to convince you what he was *not*, I would now like to present for your consideration a picture of what he *was*.

If one's view of the ancient history of Galilee and Judea were to be based solely on the *New Testament*, one could be forgiven for thinking that those lands were at peace. One might also believe that nothing major was going on politically, and that the Romans were pretty decent guys. As a result, the real-life impetus behind the ministries of Yochanan the Immerser ('John the Baptist'), the prophet Yeshua` ('Jesus of Nazareth'), and Jacob the Pious ('St James the Just'), becomes either a mystery or an irrelevance. As a consequence, instead of interpreting Yeshua`'s message within the real life context in which he lived and preached, his words stand in isolation from his contemporary world. Without their historical context, the meaning of Yeshua`'s words can become almost anything any theologian wants them to mean.

More than anything else, in my writings I want to put Yochanan and Yeshua` back into the real world of 1st century Galilee and Judea. I want to paint a picture of those troubled times, so that modern Talmidis

---

[a] The writer and lecturer, Richard Carrier, examines this and similar themes in his books and YouTube videos – which I highly recommend.

can interpret Yeshua`'s words in their proper and true, culturally Jewish context.

I believe the key to understanding Yeshua`'s ministry is a verse from the Book of Zephaniah (2:3):

> *'Seek Yahveh, all you humble of the land, you who do what he commands. Seek righteousness, seek humility; perhaps you will be sheltered on the day of Yahveh's anger.'*

Whereas Yochanan was sent to call the guilty to repentance, Yeshua`'s ministry was also to act as a call to the innocent to maintain their righteousness, to shelter them on the coming day of calamity; and to call the sinful to repentance, so that they could also join the ranks of those who would be protected on the 'Day of Yahveh'.[a]

Talmidaism places Yeshua` of Nazareth squarely and completely within the tradition of Jewish prophets. As a Talmidi, I believe he was called by God to warn our people of the impending destruction of Jerusalem, and of the Roman exile. I believe he was called to restore the original intent of Torah, along with the principles and the ideals of the original Israelite religion. I also believe he was called to proclaim the immediacy of the Kingdom of God, in opposition to the contemporary violence of the messianic kingdom longed for by the Zealots. Finally, I believe there was a strong emphasis on the social relevance of his message to the poor and socially disadvantaged.

In Talmidaism, Yeshua` is therefore presented as a prophet who:

- prophesied the destruction of the Temple, and the imminent demise of Jerusalem and Judea;
- warned the violent in the Galilee and Judea that they were reacting to the Roman occupation of their land in a way which was man's, not God's;
- implicitly condemned the violence of the Zealots, and warned that their murderous actions would result in a Roman-imposed exile;
- predicted the extinction of the Sadducees as a religious party;[b]

---

[a] as a set, prophetic phrase, see Isaiah 13:6-9, Joel 1:15, 2:1-2, Amos 5:18; it represents a period of tribulation that will be visited upon Israel whenever Yahveh's values are cruelly abused or abandoned, or on the Nations when they bring disrepute to God's holiness or values.
[b] see SY 110, the parable of the unjust steward; cf Mt 24:45-51, Lk 12:41-46

- reminded the rich of the God-given right of the poor to social justice;
- showed ordinary people how they could survive the coming calamity by returning to the true heart of Torah, which was justice, mercy, compassion and lovingkindness;
- reminded other Jewish sects of the original ideals, attitudes and principles of the original Israelite faith – the Way – that they had forgotten or abandoned: *'the old wine is good enough'*;
- spoke out to restore the original, simple intent of the Written Torah, against the 'burden' of the Oral Law;
- promoted a simple, direct approach to Torah;
- emphasised that God was loving and merciful, and to the penitent, that God was ever-ready to forgive and forget the past;
- proclaimed the immediacy of the Kingdom of God, and exhorted people to feel – and enjoy – the living Presence of God;
- encouraged people towards an intense, personal relationship with their Heavenly Father;
- and gave Jewish people a way of internalising Torah, of 'writing it on their hearts'.

The picture of Yeshua` portrayed in Talmidaism is quite different from that of the Christian gospels. In Paullist Christianity, 'Jesus' alone is the message, and his atoning death the sole object of his message. In Talmidaism, it is Yahveh God – our Heavenly Father – and the ways of God's Kingdom which become central, and Yeshua` merely becomes the messenger. We therefore take note of what Yeshua` actually had to say on the good conduct of human life, because what God had to say on how we live our lives – doing our heavenly Father's will – actually mattered to Yeshua`,[a] whereas it did not to Paul, or to those for whom Paul's theology is central.[b]

For Yeshua`, the impending doom of the 'Day of Yahveh'[c] – and

---

[a] e.g. when the rich young man asked him what he had to do to inherit eternal life, Yeshua` told to follow God's commandments; he did **not** instruct him to believe in him as his lord and saviour in order to get into heaven.

[b] such as Evangelicals, who say that being a good person is irrelevant if you don't accept 'Christ' as your lord and saviour.

[c] Yeshua`'s oft-repeated warning for his audience to "Repent! For the Kingdom of God is upon us!" is interpreted in Talmidaism as a warning of God's coming judgment as King; the English 'kingdom' in this particular

the strong possibility that his life could be ended at any moment – gave his message incredible urgency. As a prophet of God, he would have been made intimately aware of this terrible and horrendous time in the near future, and it would have shaken him to his very core. He told people that there were signs in the events of the times[a] that made the inevitability of the coming tribulation obvious – you didn't need a prophet to see that. God tells us that prophecies come true in the lifetime[b] of one's audience, so the tribulation of which Yeshua` spoke would have been expected by his fellow Jews to occur soon.[c] Outsiders who are unfamiliar with Jewish culture are still waiting for the tribulation nineteen centuries after it actually took place.

To enable people to survive the catastrophe, Yeshua` taught people to internalise Torah, so that God's ways of justice and merciful compassion would live within them; remember, God's Torah – God's teaching or instruction – is not just the first five books of the Miqra, but rather ***the entirety of God's principles and ethics*** contained throughout the Hebrew Bible. By internalising these values, their lives would become a living witness to who their Heavenly Father was, wherever they might be exiled to in the world. He taught them a way of transforming themselves to be more in tune with God's way of thinking, and so become better servants of God's kingdom. According to Zephaniah, living God's ways with humility, justice and righteousness would help to save some people from the calamities of the Day of Yahveh.

The Zealots and nationalist messianism

The Zealots would have spoken often of their longing for the Messianic kingdom, and their ideology was inevitably accompanied by violence.[d] I think this is why the prophet Yeshua` spoke so often about

---

instance should be 'kingship' – both translated by Aramaic *malkhuta*. Another way of translating this would be, "Repent! For the Kingship of God is nearly upon us!" Yeshua` expected that the tribulation was ***imminent***, not in the far distant future.

[a] S. Yesh passages 5 & 6
[b] *"What I say shall come true without delay; for what I say, I shall perform in your own lifetime." Ezek 12:25*
[c] see S.Yesh. 170:2 (cf Mk 9:1, Mt 16:28, Lk 9:27) – *"Believe me I tell you, there are some here who will not taste death before they witness the coming of God's kingship with power!"*
[d] For example, they would assassinate political opponents even among their own people, often by secretly attacking them in a crowd, knifing their victims and then disappearing. Such assassins were known as *Sicarii* or 'Daggermen'.

the nature of the Kingdom of God – as a counterweight to the violent messianic kingdom of the Zealots. In addition, the immediacy – the 'now' – of God's kingdom was held up in opposition to the inaction and delay of the messianic kingdom. Those who awaited the messianic kingdom were waiting for something to happen at some undetermined time in the future, and so forced their way towards it with violence.[a] Those who believed in the Kingdom of God – who realised that the Kingdom of God is now – knew that in order to make that Kingdom work, they had to behave in a way that showed that the Kingdom was already present. They had to acknowledge God's ways of compassion, justice, mercy and forgiveness, and live them in their everyday lives. Yahveh their true King, their true Lord, was with them – Israel's true Bridegroom and Husband was with them now – and their lives had to visibly display that fact and become a living witness to it.

The theology of messianism is watching and waiting for a human saviour in the uncertain future, and doing little else; the theology of God's Kingdom is acting in the here and now, because Yahveh our living Saviour is here and now.

The kingdom of God as a replacement for messianism

In Yeshua`'s day, the Jewish people were under the Roman occupation. They had suffered much, and longed for release and liberty. They looked forward to a day when a messiah would come to free them, and restore the kingdom of Israel. The kingdom of God got mixed up in the Jewish mind with a messianic kingdom, and this caused the Jewish people to end up waiting for both. Zealots fought violently for the messianic kingdom, and in doing so, believed that they were also working towards bringing about the kingdom of God:

> *'From the days of Yochanan (*John the Baptist*),*
> *right to this very moment, the kingdom of God is being*
> *proclaimed, but men of violence are trying to gain the*
> *kingdom of God by violence.'*[b]

Followers of the Way do not consider Yeshua` to have been the messiah. Consider this: in all of Yeshua`'s teachings on the kingdom of God – those teachings which can genuinely and authentically be considered his – there is no mention of a messiah being at the head of this kingdom, but there are copious mentions of what the kingdom of

---

[a] cf S. Yesh 111:4b; cf Mt 11:12, Lk 16:16
[b] S. Yesh 111:4; cf Mt 11:12-13

God is like with *God* – our Heavenly Father – at its head. The real, historical Yeshua` considered God his king, not a human messiah.[a]

This is the reason why I believe that Yeshua`'s teachings on the kingdom of God, which emphasised righteous action and moral conduct, were intended to replace the contemporary violence of messianic theology.

Messianism makes people wait for something to happen in the far distant future, beyond the lifetime of one's present audience; the Kingdom of God makes people act now. You can believe in one or the other – you can act now, and live the wondrous Way of God's Kingdom in the present, or you can do nothing and wait for something to happen later, *far beyond the time of your death*; realistically, you cannot have both.

Yeshua`'s ultimate fate – Yeshua`'s death

For most of the Gospel of Mark, no one knows quite who 'Jesus' is.[b] In Mk 8:27-30 (and so in Mt 16:13-15), he asks his apostles who the public think he is, and they give various answers – basically, no one really knows. When he is in Nazareth, his family thinks he is mad – realistically, they wouldn't have thought that, if they truly were descended from King David; they would instead have thought that this is a member of the royal family re-establishing his throne – and maybe he should be a bit more careful. But that's not what Mark's gospel says they thought.

And to the other inhabitants of Nazareth – people who had grown up with him and who had known him for the greater part of his life – he is not the son of David but the son of a carpenter.[c] For most of the Gospel of Mark, no one ever publicly proclaims him a messiah – I believe this is profoundly significant. I believe that the reason for this is not because he was trying to keep it all a secret, but because he wasn't *actually* descended from King David, and he wasn't *actually* a messiah to begin

---

[a] In the synoptic gospels, it is not until Lk 22:29-30 that Luke has Yeshua` call the kingdom 'his', but I believe this to have been Paullist propaganda - an invention of Luke, who was a devoted disciple of Paullist theology. John 18:36 cannot be considered authentic – John's gospel reads more like a treatise on Greek philosophy than the sayings of a Hebrew prophet.

[b] In the entire gospel of Mark, there are only 4 mentions of the word 'Christ' in connection to Jesus: 8:29 (where Peter says that he is the Christ; 9:41 (where he calls his own followers, 'followers of Christ'); 14:61 (where the High Priest asks him if he is the Christ); and 15:32 (where Roman soldiers mock him as 'the Christ').

[c] Mk 6:3, Mt 13:55

with!

There are certain questions that are unanswered in the gospels:

- Why does Yeshua` clearly stage an entrance into Jerusalem, when he is quite likely to draw unwelcome attention from the Roman authorities?
- Why did Judas betray Yeshua`? He was an anti-Roman Zealot – so why would he give Yeshua` up to his own enemies, the Romans?
- Why was 'King of the Jews' a criminal charge in Roman eyes?

To answer these questions and others, I wrote the following article for the anniversary of Yeshua`'s death in 2015:

One only needs to view Yeshua`'s death in terms of sin and salvation if you believe that Yeshua` was a messiah; after all, a messiah was supposed to triumph over the enemies of Israel, not get killed by them. The convoluted and complex theology Paul created around the death of Yeshua`, is only there to explain how and why he ended up dying.

If you reject the notion that Yeshua` was a messiah, and if you also reject the unbiblical idea that messiahs are saviours (because Yahveh alone is Saviour),[a] then there is no need to explain Yeshua`'s death in any kind of theological language. His death becomes a matter for political historians to examine.

I have always found it extremely odd how the New Testament completely ignores the issue of Zealots during the time of Yeshua`'s ministry. If Yeshua` was a man of peace, then he would have been a **huge** problem for the Zealots. His ministry would have deprived them of membership, and his teachings would have been a direct attack on their very reason for being. I believe that Yeshua`'s success against them ensured the survival of the people of the Galilee when Judea fell.

Consider those countries today which have terrorist organisations ingrained into the fabric of their society. Al-Qaeda in Pakistan, ISIS in Iraq and Syria, Al-Shabab in East Africa, and how Northern Ireland used to be with the IRA. All of these terrorist groups regularly kill anyone who might be a threat to the foundational argument of their cause – believing that murder and violence are the only ways to achieve one's goals.

The Zealots were no different. If you read the works of Josephus,

---

[a] Hos 13:4, Isa 43:11; see also Isa 45:5

you discover how the Zealots regularly murdered not only Romans, but also Jews who disagreed with them. There is therefore no reason to think that Yeshua` was not a threat to the Zealots. We can reasonably assume that they would have ardently sought his death, and zealously worked for it. What was stopping them was the fact that Yeshua` was respected by ordinary Galileans, and that he kept a low profile (for example, he **never** goes to the Galilean capital Sepphoris, and his only lengthy stay in Jerusalem finally gets him killed).

The Zealots knew that the Romans viewed any messianic claimant – who were two a penny at the time – as threats to Roman rule. ***The Zealots knew this***, so anyone with a modicum of intelligence (and a cold, calculating mind) would have used this deadly fact against someone they wanted out of the way, but could not do the murderous deed themselves. It is not beyond the realms of possibility that some Zealots publicly proclaimed him as a messiah while he was in Jerusalem, ***in order to get him killed.***

I would like you to look at Mt 21:6-11, and John 12:12-15. The event is the entry of Yeshua` into Jerusalem (commonly referred to as 'Palm Sunday'). We have to realise that, amidst a throng of pilgrims coming into Jerusalem, riding into Jerusalem on a donkey ***would not have been anything unusual***, unless everyone else was on foot. Everyone was also waving palm branches. The only time these conditions would have happened, would have been on the first day of the Festival of Lights (Hanukkah), when it was the custom for everyone to enter Jerusalem on foot waving palm branches. Remember, Hanukkah recalls the victory of the Jewish people over their oppressors, so it was a politically hot festival. The Romans would have been very jumpy during Hanukkah.[a]

What an ideal time for the Zealots to get Yeshua` killed! If the Zealots could encourage the crowds to proclaim him king, then the Romans would arrest him, and then crucify him. Job done! So this is what the Zealots do. They whip up people in the crowd to proclaim him 'son of David'.

But Yeshua` gets wind of this. He recalls a verse from Zechariah 9:9, which speaks of a humble and just king of peace. If the Zealots make him out to be a king, *this* is the type of king Yeshua` has to portray to the Romans. And if anyone asks who he is, his followers are to tell everyone that, rather than a king-messiah, he is actually a prophet:

---

[a] This is why I personally believe that the event known as 'Palm Sunday' actually took place on the first day of Hanukkah, not at Passover. This would mean that Yeshua` spent **far longer** between his entry into Jerusalem and his death just before Passover – a period of just over three and a half months, rather than just a week.

> *When he had entered Jerusalem, all the city was stirred, saying, "Who is this?" And the crowds were saying, "This is the prophet Jesus, from Nazareth in Galilee."*[a]

Note how Yeshua` did not tell his disciples to say, 'This is Yeshua` the king, son of David,' but rather, *'This is **the prophet Yeshua`**, from Nazareth in the Galilee'.*

This is the modern, reconstructed episode in the *Sifra d^eNissayunáyin* ('The Book of the Two Trials of Yeshua'):[b]

> **5.** *¹Now as I have already said, the Zealots had long sought a way of killing Yeshua`, but feared what the people might do, for they honoured him as a prophet of God. ²So the idea came to their leaders to let the Roman authorities do it for them. The Romans, as you know, would execute anyone who claimed to be a messiah; to proclaim someone as messiah therefore, was to pronounce a death sentence upon that man.*
>
> *³So when Yeshua` came up to Jerusalem four months before in the month of Kislev, to celebrate the Festival of Lights, some Zealots had devised a plot to proclaim him messiah as he entered Jerusalem with his followers from Bethany. ⁴They planned to do this as pilgrims entered the holy city on foot, waving palm branches, as is our custom on the first day of the festival.*
>
> *⁵But Yeshua` had come to hear of their wicked designs on him. So he devised a way of thwarting their plot, ⁶by entering Jerusalem on the back of a donkey, to show the Romans he was coming in peace, alluding to a passage in the Book of the Prophet Zekharyah.*
>
> *⁷He told his followers to proclaim him a herald of peace, over the voices of the Zealots. ⁸The Zealots called out, 'Oh Son of David, please deliver us! Welcome in the name of the LORD!' and spread their mantles in his path. ⁹But his followers waved their palm branches and called out all the louder, 'Behold,*

---

[a] Mt 21:10-11

[b] This is the fourth book of fourteen in *The Exhortations* (the modern Talmidi Israelite equivalent of the New Testament).

> *the feet of one who brings good news, who proclaims peace!' ¹⁰If anyone asked who he was, he had instructed his followers to tell them, 'This is the prophet Yeshua` from Nazareth in Galilee.'*
> *¹¹However, for the next four months, the Zealots took every opportunity to plant the seed in the minds of the Romans that Yeshua` was a claimant to the throne of Israel. ¹²He had not a day's peace, and he realised that one day he was going to be executed for sedition, and that that day was very near.*

The Zealots did not succeed in getting Yeshua` arrested at Hanukkah, but they persisted. They, rather than the Pharisees, pestered and hounded him with questions to trip him up, such as: "Should we pay taxes to Caesar?" – a question pertinent to Zealots, but not to Pharisees.

So what was Judas's part in all this? Various writers have put forward a wide range of explanations. The explanation I put forward myself, is based on the premise that Judas was a Zealot. So my question is, why did Judas betray Yeshua` to the Romans – people he hated? The logic I propose, is that initially, Judas believed Yeshua` to have been a messianic figure, but the more he spoke against violence, and the more he suppressed any talk of him being a messiah, the less Judas believed in him. Judas came to believe that Yeshua` was in fact a betrayal of Judas's *own* messianic beliefs – and therefore a betrayal of the Jewish people. As a result, Judas went along with the long-term Zealot plan to make the Roman authorities believe that Yeshua` was a messianic leader, with the full intention of having the Romans put Yeshua` to death for them. The Zealots would be rid of a thorn in their side without having spilled a drop of blood themselves.

Few modern Christians realise the nature and gravity of the crime Yeshua` was accused of and crucified for: supposedly being a Jewish king. For the Romans, this was synonymous with being 'a terrorist leader and leading a rebellion against Rome'. The Romans did not crucify Yeshua` for being a god-king who saved the human race from sin; they crucified him under the false charge of being a terrorist leader; *that* was the nature of the charge laid against Yeshua`.

Yeshua`'s death was nothing to do with salvation from sin. He was the victim of a terrorist plot to silence all critics. He was a holy man of God who was wrongly accused and put to death by a foreign, occupying power.

Most of Paul's Believers get a warm, fuzzy feeling inside when they think of a man hanging from a Roman torture stake, bleeding, disfigured and dying. As Followers of the Way of Yahveh, when we remember Yeshua`'s death, what we feel instead is sorrow and grief at the sense of injustice done to a great Jewish teacher, prophet and man of God.

> **For Yeshua` ben Yosef, of blessed memory,**
> **who died on the Friday before Passover, in the year 30 CE.**
> ***dakīr hū le-ṭab** 'May he be remembered for good',**
> *(*Aramaic words inscribed on most tombstones in the 1st century CE).*

Examining the issue of resurrection from a Jewish perspective

By the term resurrection, most people understand several, separate concepts:

- the coming back to life of someone who has obviously died, to live a normal life in this present world (return of the soul or reanimation: *chayyut mei-chadash ha-néfesh*)
- the bodily ascension of the pious into heaven (*`aliyyat ha-ts'diqim*)
- the reunification of body and soul at the end of time for final judgment (*t'chiyyah*)

In Talmidaism, all three belong to the realm of personal faith; belief or non-belief in any type of resurrection is not a requirement of adherence to the Covenant, nor of faithfulness to Yahveh (or even of membership of the Talmidi Israelite community).

1. Reanimation of the Dead

This type of resurrection belongs to the realm of miracles; it is considered a merciful act of God, who might sometimes use a holy man or woman or a prophet, to effect the raising back to life of someone who has obviously died. The best example from Hebrew Scriptures is that of Elisha` with the son of the Shunammite woman.[a] The reanimation of the dead is an act of God, and is not a sign of the divinity of the servant of God who carries it out – it is God, not the prophet, who effects the resurrection .

This is not to be confused with resuscitation; this is when someone has stopped breathing and is revived by normal medical means. In the Hebrew tradition, the soul was said to remain with the body for three

---

[a] 2Kgs 4:17-37

days before leaving the deceased body to go to God. If a body had been dead and cold, with no artificial support, for three days or more, and was then brought back to life, that was considered a resurrection.

2. Ascension of the Pious

In the Hebrew tradition, someone who is particularly beloved of God, and has shown faithfulness to God and God's ways in their lives, might be taken body and soul into heaven. In the Hebrew Bible, Elijah is the best example of this.[a] Enoch was also considered to have been someone who 'walked with God' (i.e. followed God's ways piously and faithfully, living a life pleasing to God), and was taken bodily into heaven when he died.[b] Again, in the Israelite tradition, ascension into heaven is not a sign of divinity, messiahhood or sinlessness.

It should also be mentioned at this point that most religions believe in the ascension of holy people, body and soul into heaven. Mohammed was supposed to have been taken into heaven, as were the gurus of the Sikhs, Tibetan saints, and even illustrious heroes in the myths of primitive religions. Bodily ascension into heaven does not automatically mean godhood in the Israelite tradition.

Some Talmidis accept the resurrection and ascension of the prophet Yeshua`, others do not; there is no conflict or need for argument between the two sides of Followers. It's not a sticking point, and none of our theology is dependent on it. Since no ulterior meaning is assigned to Yeshua`'s resurrection, other than that he was a holy man of God, there is no requirement in Talmidaism to believe or not to believe that Yeshua` rose from the dead. Those Talmidis who *do* believe he rose from the dead, hold that it was purely a sign that he was blessed by God, that his mission was vindicated by God, and that God chose to reward him for his faithfulness by bringing him back to life, and taking him bodily into heaven, just like Elijah and Enoch before him. Those who choose not to believe in Yeshua`'s resurrection, put forward as a reason that Paul needed to have a resurrected saviour to present to his Gentile Christian Believers, in order to compete with the traditions of pagan gods who died and resurrected to save *their* followers from their sins.

---

[a] 2Kgs 2:11
[b] Gen 5:24

3. The Final Resurrection of the Dead at the end of time

The main type of resurrection which is normally referred to when talking about the afterlife is the belief that, at the end of all time, all the dead will supposedly be resurrected whole and healthy from their graves, to be reunited with their souls. They will then be taken up into heaven. This is viewed theologically as a separate issue to reanimation of the dead and the ascension of the pious.

Some ancient Jewish sects, such as the Pharisees and Essenes, believed wholeheartedly in the Final Resurrection at the end of days as an article of faith, as do modern Orthodox Jews; others, such as the Sadducees, did not. Modern Liberal Jews do not believe in the Final Resurrection, and some Reform Jews do not either.

Talmidis agree that the prophet Yeshua` himself accepted the idea of Final Resurrection – it was, after all, the cultural environment he was raised in. However, many Talmidis today feel that, because the notion of the Final Resurrection is accompanied by the idea of a second judgment, it is therefore logically incompatible with the idea of a judgment after death, and the entry straight after of righteous souls into heaven.[a] If the souls of good people have already entered heaven, then why would they need to have their bodies? After all, Yeshua` taught us that in the afterlife, we would be like the angels in heaven[b] – that is, we would all be like spirits and have no physical bodies *anyway*. How then can we be reunited with our physical bodies and still remain incorporeal spirits? And why do we need to be judged once after death, and then again at the end of time?

Since anything to do with the afterlife belongs to the realm of personal faith, Talmidaism does not require Followers of the Way to agree with Yeshua` on this belief; after all, in the Israelite tradition, whether something happens or not is not dependent on whether someone believes in it or not. Most Talmidis do not believe in the final resurrection and judgment of the dead at the end of time, preferring instead to believe in God's judgment of the soul right after death.

Followers of the Way are generally agreed that the idea of Final

---

[a] Judaism does not believe in hell. In Massorite Talmidi belief, souls judged righteous are united with God. Unrighteous souls have to undergo a time of trial and purification in Azza Zeil, which Yeshua` called 'the Outer Darkness' (eg Mt 22:13); the statement Yeshua` makes in Mt 5:25-26 & Lk 12:57-59, about not getting out of prison until one has paid the last penny, is interpreted as the unrepentant soul not leaving the Outer Darkness until it has felt remorse and paid for all its sins; the soul then enters heaven, but in a lower, unenlightened estate.
[b] S.Yesh. 172:8; cf Mk 12:25

Resurrection belongs to the realm of personal faith. Since the original Israelite religion concentrated on how we live *this* life, we do not waste time arguing or debating it; the work and the mission that God has given to each one of us is too important for that.

4. The Resurrection of Yeshua`

In my humble opinion, I don't think that the resurrection of Yeshua` was the foremost, primary article of faith for his first Jewish Followers, as it was for Paul and his Gentile Christian Believers; realising this premise was the first major obstacle I had to overcome just over 30 years ago, when I became a Follower of the Way.

As to the factual details of what might have happened after Yeshua`'s death, I now tend to go by the earliest gospel account – that of Mark, because I think all the others are fictional accounts composed in order to back up and prove Paul's beliefs. The final section in Mark about the resurrection (Mk 16:9-21) has been proven to be from the 2nd or 3rd century, and is totally absent from the earliest texts.[a] In the earliest surviving manuscripts, Mark's gospel ends at Mk 16:8 with the women running away from the empty tomb, and doesn't even mention the post-resurrection appearances. Notably, Paul's letters don't make any attempt to prove that there was a missing body or an empty tomb.[b]

In Mark's gospel (Mk 16:7, and because of that, so also Matthew's gospel Mt 28:7), an angel gives instructions for the apostles to meet Yeshua` in the Galilee – in fact, immediately after the tomb is found empty, the apostles proceed directly to the Galilee (Mt 28:16); contrary to this, Luke's account in Acts 1:4 has 'Jesus' giving strict instructions *not* to leave Jerusalem at all – a discrepancy that cannot be dismissed.

Looking at all the other resurrection accounts, the only details that appear in two or more gospels are the appearances to the women[c] (but the specifics don't match), and the appearances to the apostles in the upper room – but again, the details don't agree.[d] Of all the remaining resurrection appearances, they are all unique to the gospels in which they appear, as are the words that 'Christ' purportedly speaks. This lack of any matching details in the accounts of the resurrection appearances,

---

[a] Bruce Metzger, 2005: *A Textual Commentary on the Greek New Testament*, p.123: "Clement of Alexandria and Origen show no knowledge of the existence of these verses; furthermore, Eusebius attests that the passage was absent from almost all Greek copies of Mark known to them."

[b] i.e. Paul *never* mentions Yeshua`'s tomb or a missing body.

[c] Mt 28:9-10, Lk 24:10-11, Jn 20:14-18

[d] Lk 24:36-43, Jn 20:19-23; the only detail that agrees in the 2 versions, Lk 24:40, has been lifted directly from Jn 20:20

suggest to me that the details are all fictionalised accounts, composed in order to justify and support a belief in the resurrection of 'Christ'.

Now, Paul talks about 'appearances' in 1Cor 15:4-8, calling his vision of 'Christ' on the road to Damascus 'an appearance'. He says that 'Christ' appeared first to Peter, then the apostles, then to 500 at one time, then James, then the apostles a second time, and then to himself.

In Paul's own mind, the appearance on the road to Damascus was not an earthly, tangible, physical 'Jesus' who appeared to Paul, but a spiritual vision.[a] If this spiritual vision was what Paul meant in his use of the verb 'appear', then there is no reason not to surmise that this type of spiritual vision is what he intended when he spoke of Yeshua` also appearing to Simon Peter, James and the others. I reiterate: Paul's letters have no details of an empty tomb, or of the lengthy physical appearances that the later gospels have.

The fact that so few details of the resurrection appearances tally up, and the fact that resurrection became so vitally essential to Paul's belief-system – and because his was also the *earliest* account of resurrection, and consistently claimed that he never received his message from any human agent[b] – all lead me to think that the various stories of resurrection, no matter how different they are from each other, can all trace their point of origin back to Paul; his claims were then back-edited onto the story of Yeshua` by later gospel writers. After all, he states that he did not get the account of the Last Supper – the Eucharist – from any human agency either, but from a vision;[c] what else in Christian doctrine also had its sole origin and invention with him?

Paul's fourteen years in Tarsus and Antioch[d] gave the Gentile Christian community ample time to develop stories to back up Paul's visions, and to make up stories to justify his beliefs. We have seen how he did everything he could to demean the reputation of the Jewish version of Yeshua`'s message, so that his Gentile Believers would never want to check his story with the original recipients of that message. If a liar wants people to believe him, then he has to lie bigly and often; eventually, *anything* that is made up will be accepted as the truth.

Paul was ultimately uninterested in anything the real Yeshua` said

---

[a] cf 1Cor 2:12

[b] eg Gal 2:6, where he claims that the apostles had nothing to contribute to him.

[c] 1Cor 11:23-25 – Paul claims that he received this story directly 'from the Lord', i.e. not from any human being); eating a man's body, and drinking his blood, if you think about it, is cannibalism. Even if it was symbolic, the story of the Last Supper does not record any distaste from his Jewish apostles; *Paul* invented the story of the ritual meal at the Last Supper.

[d] Gal 1:21, 2:1

or did while he was alive – even disparaging those who had known Yeshua` in life,[a] and who therefore could contradict Paul's version of events. He told his followers that if anyone disagreed with 'his' gospel[b] – even if the angels[c] in heaven disagreed with him – then they were cursed. He tells us that when he first met the apostles, they had nothing to contribute[d] to the gospel he received in his visions of 'Christ' – he simply wasn't interested in who or what Yeshua` really was in life, or in the experiences of James and the apostles who had actually known Yeshua`.

He never once quotes Yeshua`'s words or recounts any details of his ministry or nativity, but instead he often calls the gospel *'my Gospel'*,[e] warning against those who teach a message different to his[f] (such as the message taught by the James-community in Jerusalem); only after Paul is gone do the first gospel accounts get to be written, examining for the first time what Yeshua` might have done while he was alive – things that were irrelevant to Paul.

Nevertheless, I do think there is some substance to the idea that many Followers had some kind of 'visions' of Yeshua` after he died; after all, who hasn't had bouts of frequent dreams of a loved one after they have died?[g] I myself have had frequent dreams of my deceased grandparents, whom I loved very much, and could swear that they were real. In my dreams, they always gave me comforting words. Perhaps, in the dreams his followers had, Yeshua` gave them words of comfort and consolation too. Whether Yeshua` really was resurrected or not, would not make any difference in Talmidaism.

It is interesting to note that Paul always writes that Yeshua` ***was*** raised – the passive voice, rather than Yeshua` raised *himself*. In quite a few instances, he even explicitly says that it was God who raised Yeshua`.[h] Even in Paul's own mind, it seems, 'Christ' and God were distinct and separate entities.

---

[a] 2Cor 5:16 - 'Even if you were once familiar with Christ while he was alive, that is not how we know him any longer'. Also Gal 2:6, where he says that the apostles had nothing to contribute to him (NASB).

[b] Gal 1:8-9

[c] an odd thing to say, since according to Jewish tradition, angels cannot lie or rebel against God.

[d] Gal 2:6 – he didn't check ***any*** of his beliefs or facts with them; Christian theology begins with Paul, not Yeshua`'s apostles.

[e] Rom 2:16, 16:25, 2Tim 2:8

[f] Gal 1:6

[g] In Psychology, these are known as 'post-bereavement hallucinatory experiences'.

[h] see Rom 4:24, 8:11, 10:9, 1Cor 6:14, 15:15, 2Cor 4:14, Col 2:12, 1Thess 1:10

Moreover, the resurrection of a holy man of God does not prove that 'Jesus conquered sin and death', nor even that 'Jesus was an incarnation of God'. As I have previously mentioned, the prophet Elijah[a] and also Enoch[b] were both taken alive into heaven; the assertion in the Gospel of John[c] that *"No one has ever been taken alive into heaven"* is therefore entirely false. If that statement is demonstrably false, what other words in the Gospel of John[d] are false and made up?

I can only reiterate that Paul had to compete with the dying and resurrected gods of pagan Mystery religions – once again, we have to remember that he had 14 years[e] of personal reflection in pagan Tarsus to put together a convincing set of claims for his 'Christ' – one that equalled and even surpassed those of all pagan saviours combined. The first Gentile Christians therefore needed proof that 'Jesus Christ' had risen from the dead.

In all likelihood, genuine stories of comforting dreams and visions of Yeshua` circulated amongst his Jewish followers, and these filtered through to Paul's Gentile Believers. Like everything else Jewish which Paul transferred into a non-Jewish environment, these stories were mutated to fit the world-view of the teller. Jewish accounts of comforting dreams became Gentile accounts of incontrovertible physical appearances, and within a decade or so, had become established fact – after all, there was no way most people in Corinth, Philippi or Galatia could verify anything with the eye-witness, Jewish apostles in Jerusalem. The stories claiming that Yeshua` was seen after his death therefore grew and grew, and eventually became part of Gentile Christian canon lore. The further forward in time you go with each gospel, the more prolific, insistent and more fantastic are his resurrection appearances; also, the finer details of the stories do not match – each gospel has its own version of the appearances, which also says a great deal about their overall veracity (or lack thereof).

In summary, even if Yeshua` really was resurrected from the dead, in Jewish terms it would not suggest anything more than that Yeshua` was a holy man vindicated by God – nothing more. In all likelihood, the lengthy post-resurrection appearances recorded in Matthew, Luke and

---

[a] 2 Kgs 2:1-12
[b] Gen 5:24 – *"Enoch lived a life pleasing to God* (lit: 'walked about with God'), *and then he was no more, for God took him away."*
[c] Jn 3:13
[d] This gospel cannot have been written by the apostle John son of Zebedee; Jn 21:24 refers to the witness of the beloved disciple as '*his* testimony', not '*my* testimony'. In addition, the 'Jesus' of this gospel speaks like a Greek philosopher, rather than an authentic Jewish sage.
[e] Gal 2:1

John never happened; despite the insistence that the apostles poked at 'Christ's' wounds, I can only conclude that the resurrection stories began as the personal visions or dreams of Jewish Followers, then were elaborated upon by Paul's Gentile Believers in order to compete with the claims of the gods of pagan Mystery religions, whose adherents also believed had resurrected themselves from the dead.

The impetus behind the renewal of the Apostles' faith at Shavu`ot (Pentecost)

With regard to the spectacle led by Peter at Pentecost, such a public flurry in Roman-occupied Judea is implausible, given the historical skittishness of Rome towards messianic movements. If anyone had claimed that someone they had just executed were actually still alive, they would begin arresting all his followers. They would then have tortured them all for information, in the hopes of ascertaining his whereabouts. The public, crowd-stirring aspect of the Pentecost experience is thus unlikely; Peter's speech in Acts 2 is therefore fiction, in my opinion.

There remains the story of the 'coming of the holy spirit upon the Apostles at Pentecost'. Luke's account of the episode in Acts chapter 2, gives us the narrative that the faith of the Apostles was revitalised, because they realised Yeshua` was actually the messiah;[a] that his death was not a defeat but a victory; that his death had been prophesied, and was therefore all part of God's plan.

We know that Yahveh alone is our Saviour, that messiahs are not saviours, and that it is the Glory of God which cleanses us of our sins. So what was the real, *Jewish* impetus behind a renewed sense of mission among his apostles and first Jewish followers? At what point did Yeshua`'s Jewish followers pick themselves up, get themselves together again, and continue on with their Jewish mission?

---

[a] Peter's speech at Acts 2:25-28 quotes a psalm of David (Ps 16:8-11). Luke claims that this psalm refers to 'Jesus', but the psalm itself most definitely refers only to David, and not even one of his descendants. In the psalm, David says of **himself**, *"For you will not abandon my soul to Sheol, nor will you let your faithful one see the Pit"*. 'Sheol' and 'Pit' refer to the same place – the dark place of unknowing where souls go after death. This was the forerunner of 'the Outer Darkness' – the place of 'weeping and gnashing of teeth' (Mt 25:30) where souls go to endure the pain of their own sins in order to feel remorse for them before entering heaven (Judaism does not have a belief in a fiery Hell or 'Hades'). Luke translates *'nor will you let your Faithful One see the Pit'* as *'nor allow your holy one to undergo decay'* (NASB), which is probably taken from the inaccurate translation in the Septuagint.

One minor detail we have to get past, is that while Matthew's gospel has the apostles make their way back to the Galilee,[a] Luke's *Book of Acts* has the apostles stay in Jerusalem.[b] For the purposes of our story, I don't think it is important where the apostles were – they may even have gone first to the Galilee, and then returned to Jerusalem – who can say?

The prophet Joel[c] tells us that, before any 'Day of Yahveh' event, God will pour out God's spirit upon people to enable them to prophesy. This is so that there will be prophets to warn people of any coming calamity and tribulation. In the last days and years before the 'Day of Yahveh' event that took place in 70 CE, this turned out to be true – Yochanan the Immerser, Yeshua` of Nazareth, Jacob the Pious and Shimon bar Qlofas all had the spirit of God upon them, and they were all prophets who prophesied the destruction of Jerusalem, calling for national repentance and a return to God's ways.

As I have previously discussed, the fact that God resurrects a man and takes him bodily into heaven, in Yahwist Israelite eyes is only a sign that such a man is a holy man, blessed and favoured by God. It is not a sign that such a man has – by his own power – triumphed over death, nor that such a man is a god. Whether the appearances[d] of Yeshua` were genuinely real or merely dreams or visions, is also immaterial – either way, they *still* would not prove that Yeshua` was a god. Only in a pagan culture would such things be signs of divinity,[e] and a personal triumph over death; in a Yahwist Israelite environment, they would not. Besides, if 'Christ' triumphed over the power of death, that would mean that previous to his death, God had no power over death!

What we *can* say about what happened, is that the remaining emissaries ('apostles') and the first followers of Yeshua` were originally devastated by their Master's death; they had probably already returned

---

[a] Mt 28:16

[b] Acts 1:4

[c] see Joel 3:1-5 (Xtian bibles Joel 2:28-32), hence Peter's speech in Acts 2; this prophecy does not refer to the end of time, but to the last days before any 'Day of Yahveh' – Joel 3:4 (Xtian 2:31). Before every Day of Yahveh, God will send prophets to warn us.

[d] 1Cor 15:4-7; Paul does not say whether the appearances took place in Galilee or Jerusalem. Mark's original gospel ended at Mk 16:8, and does not say where the appearances took place either.

[e] Romulus was supposedly taken up bodily into heaven, and he was thereafter worshipped as a god. When Krishna died, he ascended into heaven and he too became a god. In the non-Jewish world, being taken up into heaven meant that one had become a god.

to their previous way of life in the Galilee.[a] Even if they hadn't openly believed he was a messiah, subconsciously they had nevertheless treated him as if he were something close to one. They had treated him as if, like a traditional messiah, he would triumph in his lifetime, and that nothing bad would ever happen to him. They had invested him with being the source of the Message – that the wisdom in his teachings was his, and his alone.

When Yeshua` was gone, they thought that so also was the Message. If they had only realised he was simply a prophet – that therefore the source of the Message was actually *Yahveh*, and that the wisdom was also from Yahveh – they would have realised that, as a prophet, it was a given that Yeshua` would suffer for God's Message, and maybe even be killed for it. ***No other complex theology has to be dreamt up to explain or justify his death.***[b] Nor would there be any need to find Yeshua``s life or ministry foretold in any prophecy of the Hebrew Bible. I say again – the Pharisees made a rod for their own backs by insisting they would only listen to a messiah; Pharisaic belief is partly responsible for the need to turn Yeshua` into a messiah in the first place.

If we look at the 'Pentecost experience', the coming of the spirit of God on the apostles at Pentecost has further implications in a Jewish context besides mere prophecy. The prophet Jeremiah[c] tells us that a time will come when people will no longer seek or miss the Ark of the Covenant. The reason for this is that, instead of the Ark, the city of Jerusalem itself will become the throne of Yahveh. This will happen, Jeremiah says, at a time when the people of Jerusalem *'no longer follow the stubbornness of their evil hearts'*. In other words, when the people of Jerusalem abandon their own desires, and follow after the will of Yahveh, then the Presence of Yahveh will be able to come and dwell openly, directly with the people; God will no longer need the Ark of the Covenant.

What this teaches us, is that the spirit of God will come and dwell with any group of people who enter upon the holy path of following God's will; the fire of God's Glory will dwell with them.

So when Yeshua``s apostles came upon the realisation that they were followers of a *Message* rather than a *man* – that this Message was directly from a living God, and that therefore this Message was ***still very much alive and relevant*** – this is what re-galvanised the community of

---

[a] The apostles were instructed to return to Galilee - Mk 16:7, Mt 28:16. John's gospel (Jn chapt. 21) has them all return to Galilee and to their original professions.
[b] in spite of what Paul says, cf Gal 2:21
[c] Jer 3:16-17, especially *"it will not come to mind, nor will they remember it, nor will they miss it, nor will it be made again"*.

Yeshua`'s followers. The Message was that the Jewish people were still very much in danger, but the good news was that living the ways of God's Kingdom would save the majority of them from the fast-approaching tribulation. They couldn't just simply accept this as an intellectual concept – they had to *feel* this understanding in their very souls, along with all its emotional implications.

This realisation – that they were followers of a heavenly Message rather than of a man, and that this Message still lived – revitalised Yeshua`'s grief-stricken followers. It was a real, tangible message that still mattered. *When* and *where* this realisation happened is not important; what matters is that it did. Yeshua`'s urgent mission became ***their*** urgent mission – to warn the Jewish people of the terrible things that were about to happen, and how they could endure and shorten the time of that tribulation – by returning to the ways of God's Kingdom, and by living the principles and teachings of the original Israelite faith given to us by Yahveh.

What re-galvanised the community of his followers, if not resurrection? The realisation that even if the messenger had died, the Message still lived, and was still very much relevant and important. This is what certainly re-galvanised me thirty years ago, once I refocussed on his teachings and message, rather than on *him*. This new realisation filled me with great joy and renewed purpose. It is that conviction in the eternal Message of Yahveh for all people that I have always tried to convey in my writings.

The Emissaries also realised that Yeshua`'s mission had not failed; for Yeshua`'s Followers and the Jewish population of the Holy Land, the 'Day of Yahveh' was still imminent, and their mission was still as important as ever – to call as many people as possible back to the true ideals and principles of God. That is what Jacob the Pious, the Emissaries and Yeshua`'s Jewish followers threw themselves back into, renewed and reinvigorated.

Their gospel – their 'good news' – was that the Jewish people could endure and survive, and that the time of that tribulation could be shortened, simply by returning to the just and compassionate ways of God's present Kingdom, and by living the wise principles and teachings of the original faith given to us by Yahveh.

Upon such a people who dedicated themselves to the living Message of God, God would pour out God's spirit among them, just as Joel said; they would prophesy, and God would save and gather in the humble and innocent of the Land.[a] God would call to Himself as many who repented, and shelter as many who returned to Yahveh. The 'coming' that the community of Followers awaited, was therefore not Yeshua`, but Yahveh.[b]

The theology of Adoptionism: how Yeshua` became a divine messiah

In theological circles, historians examining the historical Yeshua` have come up with a theory called 'adoptionism'. This is the process by which the Jewish Yeshua` became the Gentile 'Jesus Christ' – how he became the messiah, and eventually became a god. Several writers[c] have written excellent books on this subject which I encourage you to read, so for the sake of context, I will summarise 'adoptionism' for you.

Some of the earliest Jewish followers of Yeshua` felt that they needed to turn Yeshua` into a messiah. I believe that this was through force of circumstances; they felt it was the only way they were going to get followers of the Pharisees to listen to Yeshua`'s warnings about the coming tribulation, since Pharisaic teachings specified that they would only pay heed to a messiah. However, since Yeshua`'s Jewish followers had known him personally, and were therefore aware that he was not of Davidic descent, they initiated a belief that meant that he *became* a messiah through a process whereby God adopted him as God's 'anointed one',[d] when God first called him to be a prophet; personally, I believe that taking on this belief was a fatal mistake – one that modern Talmidaism has not repeated.

In the writings of Paul, written in the late 40's to 50's CE, Paul demonstrates that he is not in the least interested in Yeshua`'s life or words. As I've mentioned previously, he never once quotes Yeshua`'s teachings, and never describes any episodes from his life, apart from the Eucharist and his death. In Paul's belief-system, that's because his life wasn't important; Yeshua` only became something more than human at

---

[a] Zeph 2:3 - *'Seek Yahveh, all you humble of the Land, you who do what he commands. Seek righteousness, and seek humility; perhaps you will be sheltered on the day of Yahveh's wrath.'*

[b] Joel 2:31 – *"the great and terrible day of Yahveh's coming"*.

[c] A very good book to read on this topic is *'How Jesus Became God'*, by Bart D. Ehrman. Also, *'How Jesus Became Christian: The Early Christians And The Transformation Of A Jewish Teacher Into The Son Of God'*, by Barrie Wilson.

[d] Ps 105:15 & 1Chr 16:22 refer to God's prophets as 'anointed ones'.

the point of his death.[a]

Chronologically, the next Christian work we have is the Gospel of Mark, written in about the early 70's CE. In that gospel, Yeshua` becomes God's son at his baptism. In Mk 1:10-11 it says,

> *Just as Jesus was coming up out of the water, he saw heaven being torn open and the Spirit descending on him like a dove. And a voice came from heaven: "You are my Son, whom I love; with you I am well pleased."* (NIV translation).

The rational student of the gospels has to note here that the gospel of Mark is not interested in Yeshua`'s childhood or birth. It is sufficient for Yeshua` to have become a messiah at his baptism. The writer of Mark's gospel pushes back God's 'adoption' of Yeshua` as his son back in time, to his baptism.

Next come the gospels of Matthew and Luke, written in about the 80's CE. In their gospels, Yeshua` is special from the time of his birth. Both evangelists need to prove that Yeshua` became the 'Son of God' at his birth, so they invent fictionalised accounts of his birth. They are fictionalised, because none of their details match up, and the census of Quirinius that Luke mentions, actually took place in about 6 CE – that is, 12 years after Yeshua` was born.[b]

Last in time comes the Gospel of John. In his gospel, Yeshua` becomes the 'Son of God' even further back – at the beginning of creation:

> *'In the beginning was the Word, and the Word was with God, and the Word was God. He was with God in the beginning. . . The Word became flesh and made his dwelling among us.'* (NIV translation, Jn 1:1-2, 14).

Any rational, logically-thinking person has to see with their own eyes that as time went on, Gentile Christians pushed back the time when God supposedly adopted 'Jesus' as his 'Son'. In Paul's time, 'Jesus' became the 'Son of God' at his death; Mark's gospel has him become messiah at his baptism; and Matthew and Luke have him as the messiah

---

[a] cf Acts 13:33 – *'this he has fulfilled to us their children by raising Jesus, as also it is written in the second Psalm, "'You are my Son, **today I have begotten you**.'* (ESV translation).

[b] They also needed to place his birth in Bethlehem, because that would strengthen his claim to be the messiah. However, in John's gospel (7:41-43), some Jewish people say he cannot be the messiah, as he didn't come from Bethlehem, but rather Galilee.

at his birth. By the time of the Gospel of John in the early 2nd century however, he always was the 'Son of God'. If this process needed to happen – if Believers in fact needed to spend the next 2 or 3 centuries debating the exact nature of the divinity of someone – this logically means that there is something fundamentally amiss with the actual belief itself.

Although the modern Talmidi community is small, every single one of us has come to faith having been individually called by God. Not a single one of us has had to be converted by *any* human being. And the wondrous thing is, that we have all come to ***exactly the same belief about Yeshua`*** – that he was a fully human, Jewish prophet, and that God is One, without physical form. No one pestered us into believing this, we were not persuaded by someone screaming any message to us on street corners, and we all came to this belief, in spite of living in societies where the accepted belief was the exact opposite.

To a Yahwist Israelite – someone who thinks like Abraham, Moses, David, Solomon and all the biblical prophets – ***all*** human beings are sons and daughters of God, and all those who follow Yahveh are called the Sons and Daughters of Yahveh.[a] In Massorite Talmidi belief, we were ***all*** created in heaven,[b] and we were all given our sacred missions directly from God before we even came to earth. Yeshua` was therefore not unique – all human beings were pre-existent in heaven, and all human beings are sons and daughters of God.

What began as an attempt to make Yeshua` into a messiah ('anointed one') by virtue of him being a prophet, in order to get the Pharisees to heed his warnings on the coming tribulation, initiated the slippery and fateful process whereby he eventually became a god. I can only repeat my assertion that if the Pharisees had not declared there were no more prophets, and that they would only listen to a messiah, it would have been enough to claim that Yeshua` was a prophet, and he would never have become a god.

---

[a] cf Dt 28:10

[b] In Dt 29:14, it describes how God not only made the Covenant with those who were standing on the plains of Moab that day, but also *'with those who are not here today'* – this means that God was also making the Covenant with the souls of those not yet born, which logically means that these souls must already have existed somewhere. This is the basis of the Massorite Talmidi belief that all human beings are created as pre-existent souls in heaven, before we come to earth.

Summary

In many ways, there are certain concepts and teachings which the original Israelite religion taught as an intrinsic part of its overall philosophy, which modern Judaism has since lost, or demoted and deemed unimportant. The three biggest are first, that instead of a messiah, Yahveh is our only Saviour and Redeemer; secondly, that the promised Davidic messiah is only a servant of God, who still needs God's approval; and thirdly, that it is the Glory of Yahveh (the fire of the 'Divine Radiance') which cleanses the human soul of sin, not the blood of sacrificial offerings (or even the blood of 'Christ').

The quintessential messiah-saviour of mainstream Judaism struggles to withstand the onslaught of the Paullist god-messiah. That is because the promised Davidic messiah has been elevated in Jewish minds to a status that is already near godhood. The biblical truth is that any messiah will still be but a mortal man, someone who might sin and so be chastised by God.[a] A belief in a messiah-saviour was not and is not part of God's plan; neither Abraham, Moses or David looked forward to any messiah as their saviour, and God never gave up His title of 'Saviour' at any point, because God does not change His mind.[b]

The Davidic Covenant promises that if a messiah is obedient to God, then Israel will prosper. Biblical prophecies about the messiah are therefore built upon hopes that any future messiah will be obedient to God – after all, both the northern and southern kingdoms had already faced long successions of bad messiahs; the hope for a good messiah arose from these unpleasant experiences. Messianic prophecies are therefore consolations to the Jewish people that God will one day give us a descendant of David who is faithful to God (and that therefore the Land of Israel will have peace).

Paullist theology deliberately takes biblical passages out of context. It imposes fanciful meaning[c] on verses that are not there, and were never originally intended. Only by looking at these verses in the way that they *were* originally intended, can we arrive at a true and better understanding of what the overall concept of the Israelite faith was.

In the original Israelite religion, Yahveh was and is our ultimate

---

[a] 2Sam 7:14 - *"When he [i.e. the Messiah] does wrong, I will chastise him with the rod of men, and the affliction of mortals".*

[b] see Num 23:19 – *"God is not a man, that He should lie; nor a human being, that He should change His mind; for what He has said, will He not do? And what He has spoken, will He not fulfil?"*

[c] In Hebrew, this type of interpretation is called *pesher* – giving a biblical passage a fanciful meaning and interpretation which was never intended by the original writer.

and highest authority; in rabbinic Judaism, this power has been usurped and given over to the rabbis and the Talmud. We are told that there are no more prophets, when we are explicitly told by the prophet Joel, that God will pour out God's spirit upon us to warn us when tribulations are imminent. In mainstream Christianity, the central position of Yahveh, our heavenly Father, has been usurped by the god-man 'Christ'. Talmidaism, in seeking to restore the original Way of Yahveh, has removed everything that stands in the way of preventing us realising Yahveh God as our Saviour – the awesome Author of everything good that is written on our hearts,[a] who guides and comforts us, who gives us hope and renews us.

What's waiting for you in the next three books……

In the second book of this series, I will teach you about the various ethical principles of the Talmidi Israelite faith through the words of the *'Our Father'*. I will show you how it was not only Yeshua` who was sent to earth on a mission, but that *all* human beings are entrusted by God with a heavenly purpose, and each one of us was sent to earth with our own individual mission. I will explain how part of our spiritual journey is to get to know our inner selves – the heavenly being God created us to be – so that we can more effectively do what God sent each and every one of us here to this earth to do.

I will show you what it truly means to call God 'Father', and how we go about showing that we are sons and daughters of God; I will look at how we can hallow the Name of God in our daily lives; I will teach you how you can live the Kingdom of God in the here and now, not in some far distant future; and how we can truly do the will of our Father in heaven, and experience the living Presence of God in our daily lives.

I will look at what our faith means in practical terms for our day to day lives – I will examine what it means to look to God for our daily bread, what sin itself means in a Yahwist Israelite context, and how we can identify and resist evil. I will look at where God was in the Holocaust, explain what 'Azazel' and 'the Outer Darkness' mean, and what forgiveness and atonement are for in biblical terms; and that the future is not about apocalypse, but rather about helping God to bring about heaven on earth.

While this book taught you about the history of our past, the next book is about getting to know how to live in the present, and have hope and assurance in the future. And my greatest claim for my next book, is

---

[a] Dt 30:14, *"But the Word is very near to you, in your mouth **and in your heart**, that you may observe it."*

that by the end of it, **you will know Yahveh**! The God who loves us, whom we serve and work with, is a knowable God – an awesome Being with a knowable and recognisable personality.

In the third book of the series, I will look at how modern Talmidaism differs in the way we practice the customs and traditions of Israel, and in how we observe God's festivals. Our tradition is not based on the rabbinic Oral Law, but directly on the Hebrew Bible itself. If there is anything that is unclear or not explicit in the Bible, then we look at how the Jewish faith was practised in the Galilee and Judea in the first century CE. Our adherence to this approach, fixes our origin story firmly in time and place – not to Babylon, which is where many modern rabbinic customs come from, or from Europe, where Ashkenazi Orthodoxy comes from, but from the fields and hills of the Galilee, the home of the prophet whose teachings we so value, and the home of our spiritual forebears in whose footsteps we try to walk.

In my third book, I will be looking at how the ancient Talmidi Israelite faith can be applied to the issues and problems of the modern world. I will look at issues such as war, atheism, science, vegetarianism, the ethical treatment of animals, the environment, and how dangerous, psychopathic values have become endemic in modern society; I also offer some guidelines on how to interpret the Hebrew Bible honestly and responsibly, and the right and wrong way to be tolerant of other faiths; I will look at Talmidi mysticism, and why we reject Kabbalah as being pagan in origin; and finally, I will examine our relations with Islam and the Arab world, as well as our attitude towards Jewish extremism. In one essay, I even put forward a sensible, spiritual approach to the idea of 'space aliens'!

See you there!

APPENDICES: General Notes On The Talmidi Israelite faith

APPENDIX ONE: Main Talmidi beliefs

The Kingdom of God plays an important part in Talmidi outlook. We teach that the Reign of God exists here and now, and that we all play our small part in spreading the justice, compassion and peace of God's reign. However, there is also a hope in what the kingdom of God can become in the future – a time of universal peace,[a] where *'nations shall hammer their swords into ploughshares, and no one shall know or learn of war anymore'*.[b] It will be a time when the veil that exists between heaven and earth will fall away,[c] and the Glory of God will cover the earth.[d]

Talmidis do not believe in a personal messiah – that a messiah will come to save us. Rather, we teach that God Himself will act in human affairs to guide the future and save us, and that an anointed, faithful and righteous descendant of David will simply be one of the end-products of God's actions, together with the return of the descendants of the lost northern tribes, and the rebuilding of the Temple in Jerusalem *in peace*. In short, we accept the idea of a Davidic messiah-king, but not a messiah-saviour; we view Yahveh as our sole Saviour and Redeemer, not any messiah. We look not to a messiah, but rather to God who puts him there.

Talmidi beliefs in which there is absolutely no compromise would be: that Yahveh has no physical form;[e] that Yahveh is indivisible;[f] that Yahveh alone is our Saviour,[g] rather than a messiah; that Yeshua` was a fully human prophet,[h] not a messiah or Son of God; that we do not accept the authority of the Talmud; and that we do not accept the teachings of Paul of Tarsus. *These things are not negotiable*. If one does not accept these beliefs, then one cannot call oneself a Talmidi – a Follower of the Way of Yahveh.

The following are the most basic Talmidi beliefs and affirmations:

---

[a] Hosea 2:20 (2:18 in Xtian bibles), Isa 65:25
[b] Isaiah 2:4
[c] Isaiah 60:19-20. See also Rev 22:1-5 / Ch.Sh. 23:1-5
[d] Hab 2:14
[e] Dt 4:12-15
[f] Dt 6:4
[g] Isa 43:11
[h] Mt 13:57, 21:11; cf Num 23:19

THE WAY

Basic tenets of the Talmidi Israelite faith

The Twelve Central Attributes of Yahveh:[a]

1. the Oneness of Yahveh
2. the Incorporeality of Yahveh
3. the supreme Sovereignty of Yahveh
4. the Wisdom of Yahveh[b]
5. the Holiness[c] of Yahveh
6. the Kavodh[d] of Yahveh
7. the Davar[e] of Yahveh
8. the compassionate Love of Yahveh
9. the righteous and merciful Judgment of Yahveh
10. the Creatorship of Yahveh
11. the Saviourship of Yahveh
12. the Redeemership of Yahveh

The Four Cornerstones of Israelite Culture:

1. Torah and the commandments of Yahveh
2. the Miqra and the principles of Yahveh
3. Yahveh's eternal Covenant with Jacob and his descendants[f]
4. Houses of prayer – the Temple and the Synagogue

The Seven Pillars of Piety:

1. Faithfulness to Yahveh alone, as our only Saviour
2. Regular Prayer (directed to Yahveh alone)

---

[a] These are all intrinsic qualities of the very nature of God, not separate parts – one attribute cannot be separated from the other

[b] that not only is Yahveh the source of all wisdom and knowledge, but that Yahveh is Wisdom itself.

[c] that nothing evil, wicked, sinful or profane can approach the Glory of Yahveh, without being harmed or destroyed.

[d] *Kavodh* literally means, 'glory'. However, in the context it is most often used in Torah, it is describing the fiery, purifying and atoning radiance of God – a central concept in Israelite theology.

[e] *Davar* literally means, 'word' or 'message'. This attribute is the belief that Yahveh embodies and encapsulates the whole corpus of ethics, teachings, principles, judgments etc. The Message is not a separate entity – Yahveh IS the Message, and the Message is Yahveh.

[f] this would include things such as the Land of Israel, the people of Israel, and circumcision as a sign of the Covenant.

3. Charitable giving (*tsedaqah*) and good works
4. Observance of Shabbat
5. Fasting on Yom ha-kippurim
6. Observance of the three Pilgrim Festivals
7. Repentance for wrongdoing

The Twelve Major Negative Injunctions:

1. Do not worship any other god or name but Yahveh
2. Do not make or worship idols or graven images
3. Do not use the Holy Name for false, common or evil purposes
4. Do not consume flesh with the blood still in it
5. Do not engage in sexual immorality
6. Do not commit murder
7. Do not commit adultery
8. Do not steal
9. Do not give false testimony
10. Do not seek to have for yourself that which rightfully belongs to someone else
11. Do not follow pagan forms of religious custom or superstition
12. Do not practise witchcraft, divination, or augury

The Twelve Words of the Prophets:

1. that Yahveh alone is our Saviour and Redeemer
2. that faithfulness to God's ways will be rewarded, and widespread rejection[a] of God's ways will result in exile
3. that God will one day restore the Land, the tribes, the Temple and the Davidic monarchy
4. that one day, when God's Kingdom is fulfilled, there will be universal peace
5. that God will forgive and deal compassionately with those who return to Him
6. that to revere Yahveh in awe is the beginning of wisdom
7. that we should never forget the needs of the poor, the orphan, the widow or the alien among us
8. that religion practised with humility is the true Way
9. that ritual without intent is meaningless

---

[a] i.e. by oppressing the lowest and poorest in society, ill-treating non-Jews in the Land, allowing injustice to become commonplace, turning to other gods or other customs, corrupt ministers bringing disrepute to the good Name of God etc.

10. that personal fasts without charity are pointless
11. that we are to have just judgments in our courts
12. that we should deal and trade fairly with one another

In detail: The Basic beliefs of Talmidaism

On God:

1. that Yahveh exists, and is a living God
2. that Yahveh is One and indivisible
3. that Yahveh has no equal or opposite[a]
4. that Yahveh has no incarnation or physical form;[b] Yahveh cannot therefore be born or die
5. that Yahveh has no gender – God is neither male nor female
6. that Yahveh is holy, before whose Glory evil and wrongdoing cannot stand, and whose Presence purifies good
7. that Yahveh is different and distinctive in nature and personality to what is portrayed of pagan gods: Yahveh is a just, merciful and compassionate God; the Creator, and the Author of all the laws by which the universe functions; omniscient, omnipresent, immanent and transcendent
8. that Yahveh alone is our Saviour and Redeemer[c]
9. that all worship and prayer is directed only to Yahveh – no one and nothing else; we worship Yahveh, and *only* Yahveh
10. that we pray in Yahveh's Name alone – we use no one and nothing else's name in prayer or worship
11. that the Name of Yahveh is holy, and cannot be given to anyone or anything else
12. that we should not make any image or representation of God in any way, or for any purpose
13. It is by God's merciful love that God forgives the penitent soul
14. It is by the Glory ('Divine radiance') of Yahveh that Yahveh expiates our souls of sin (i.e. cleanses them of the stain of sin, and restores them to health and wholeness)

---

[a] Isaiah 40:25 – ' *"To whom will you compare Me? Or who is My equal?"* says the Holy One.' Also Isaiah 46:5. In practical terms, what this implies is that we reject dualism – that there is a good god and a bad god; and that we reject a belief in Satan as an evil power equal and opposite to God.
[b] Jer 17:5 warns against trusting in mortal flesh, and so by extension in human incarnations of the divine – of God incarnated in flesh. cf also Dt 4:12-15
[c] Isaiah 43:11 *'I, and I alone, am Yahveh, and besides Me there is no other saviour.'*

On Torah and the Covenant:

15. The relationship between God and the people of Israel is guided by the maintenance of the Covenant: 'If we worship Yahveh alone forever, and observe Yahveh's commandments, principles and precepts forever, then Yahveh will give us the land of Canaan forever, and preserve us as a people forever.'[a]
16. We are to follow not only the commandments of God, but also the principles of God[b]
17. The commandments and principles of our way of life are those contained in the Torah, and expanded upon in the books of the Prophets and Writings.[c]
18. The Miqra (*Torah, Prophets and Writings*) is the sole authority to our cultural, moral and ethical heritage.
19. As a sign of the Covenant – that we and our descendants have an inheritance in the Land – all Israelite males are circumcised. However, uncircumcised Godfearers are accepted as part of our wider community – the Assembly of all Israel.
20. Our holy and distinctive way of life was intended to serve as an eternal witness to the power and presence of Yahveh
21. Moses was the greatest of all the prophets, who alone spoke to God face to face[d]

On the viewpoint of the Talmidi Community:

22. We follow the Jewish teachings of the prophet Yeshua` of Nazareth, as long as they are in accord with Yahwist Israelite beliefs, values and principles
23. Yeshua` was a fully human prophet
24. His calling as a prophet was to restore the original ideals, principles and values of the 'Way of Yahveh' (the original Israelite religion), and through his call for repentance, to warn the Jewish people of the destruction of Jerusalem, and of the

---

[a] That is why gross breach of the terms of the Covenant results in exile from the Land.
[b] gleaned from Ps 119:4, Ps 103:18 – God's moral precepts are to be fully obeyed.
[c] We do however use other books to inspire and teach us, as long as they do not contradict the basic principles contained in the Miqra.
[d] that is, he spoke directly to God, not through visions; in the Mishkan, there was an opening into heaven, and God was able to speak directly to Moses. Moses was therefore able to hear God, as one human being speaks to another.

impending exile under the Romans
25. Yeshua` was born of normal human parentage, the son of Miryam and Yosef
26. Yeshua` was not a messiah, or a god, or Son of God
27. Yeshua`'s death did not serve any salvific or redemptive purpose; it was an unjust Roman punishment for a crime he did not commit (messianic rebellion against Rome)
28. After Yeshua`'s death, his cousin Ya'aqov son of Qlofas ('James the Just' / 'Jacob the Pious') was elected to serve as pre-eminent leader of the community of Followers
29. Yochanan the Immerser ('John the Baptist') was a prophet who taught in the spirit of Elijah, thus warning people of an impending 'Day of Yahveh' if wrongdoers did not repent and return to God's ways
30. Although we accept that Yahveh will set a descendant of David on the throne of Israel at some point in the future, he will not be our saviour, but a servant of God; Yahveh alone is our Saviour
31. We do not accept the authority or infallibility of the Oral Law; it is a collection of human opinions and decisions
32. We do not accept the authority of the New Testament
33. Any official record of Yeshua`'s teachings and the ancient Talmidi community, shall only have the status of 'esteemed commentary' or 'respected sermons' on the Israelite faith; it shall not overrule Torah
34. We do not accept the authority of the teachings of Paul of Tarsus, and reject the claim that he was an apostle[a] of Yeshua`
35. We follow biblical customs and traditions, as far as is possible and practical in the modern age
36. We can use God's Holy Name when speaking of faith in reverence, or in private or congregational prayer, or when teaching Followers about God, or when discussing God peacefully
37. We should not use God's Name in anger or argument, or in everyday, casual conversation (thus making it empty, profane and ordinary)
38. We do not follow Kabbalist teaching or study it, since much of it is of pagan origin and outlook

---

[a] The quintessential definition of an apostle is that they repeat verbatim the message of their Master. Since Paul clearly did not do this – he never quotes the words of Yeshua` - he cannot be called an apostle.

Some Basic Talmidi affirmations:

39. Yahveh is above all a just, loving and compassionate God
40. The Kingdom of God is here and now
41. The Kingdom of God is within us – God's ways have already been written on our hearts
42. The fulfilment of God's Kingdom won't come by watching and waiting for it; God will bring about the fulfilment of His Kingdom only with our active participation
43. The Kingdom of God will be fulfilled gradually, like a small portion of yeast leavening a large quantity of flour; even a small act of kindness furthers the cause of God's Kingdom
44. The Kingdom of God is likened not to a battlefield, but to a farmer tending his field, or to a gardener tending his garden
45. The kingdom of God is not fulfilled by violence
46. To do violence in God's Name defames the holiness of God's Name; it is an affront to God
47. Practising justice and mercy, and living a good and honorable life, are of far greater value to God than how far we go to observe the minutiae of custom and tradition
48. It is the heart and intent with which a mitzvah is carried out that matters, rather than the perfection with which it is performed
49. We show who our Heavenly Father is by the compassion, consideration and dignity that we show to others
50. By sincere repentance we are immediately forgiven by God
51. Atonement comes through prayer, reparation and good works, by which our soul is cleansed, restored and made whole
52. It is not blood or death that brings about atonement for a soul, but rather the Glory ('Divine radiance') of Yahveh
53. One cannot serve both God and wealth
54. Those who work for peace are the children of God
55. The Sabbath was created for the benefit of human beings, not human beings for the Sabbath
56. 'Seek, and you will find'[a]
57. 'The old wine is good enough' – the Israelite religion is sufficient for our spiritual needs
58. Those whom human beings have unjustly put last – the outcast and the rejected – God will put first
59. To oppress the poor is to revile God
60. Performing religious acts simply to extract praise from others is hypocrisy; such acts are meaningless, and gain no merit or

---

[a] Seek answers, and God, and you will find answers and ultimately God

favour with God
61. Spiritual defilement of the heart and soul are of greater concern than ritual defilement of the body
62. Faith without works is dead

Some Basic Talmidi values and emphases, derived from the teachings of the prophet Yeshua` and of Jacob the Pious:

63. Doing to and for others, as we would have them do to and for us
64. Doing good even to those who have wronged us
65. Helping others without want of thanks or return
66. Honesty, not swearing oaths; 'let your yes be yes, and your no be no'
67. Keeping a reign on our tongue – not being violent or malicious in speech
68. Training ourselves not to be selfish or possessive, or obsessed with our belongings
69. Storing up for ourselves treasure in heaven, rather than storing up things of this world
70. Righteousness and justice take precedence over mammon (wealth)
71. Living a good and decent life in witness to our Heavenly Father, so that we can be strengthened to endure the heat of life's trials
72. Bearing good fruit – showing the value of our ideals by our positive way of life and outlook
73. Practicing our faith with humility and compassion
74. Practicing mercy, repentance and forgiveness
75. Concern for the poor and the least of society
76. Awareness and vigilance for the stability of society
77. Being mindful of the gap between the rich and the poor
78. Not to ill-treat, oppress or exploit the poor or the weak in society
79. Treating all human beings with equal dignity and respect
80. Dealing with others without judgment or condemnation
81. Trying not to worry about things we cannot change; trying not to fret or allow evil to make us lesser people
82. Guarding our souls from the destructive effects of wrongful thought or intent
83. Guarding the tongue, not gossiping about others or spreading malicious rumours
84. Guarding against religious hypocrisy in ourselves; we should examine ourselves first before criticising others

85. Not making ostentatious or vain displays of piety
86. Guarding the fence of the mind – resisting lesser evils so that greater evils may be avoided[a]
87. Avoiding divisiveness amongst one's own, discussing differences and problems in the spirit of seeking; avoiding contentiousness for its own sake
88. Avoiding indecisiveness, wavering to and fro in our opinions
89. Not to take advantage of another's kindness
90. Mutual responsibility: each party in a given situation has their own responsibilities (host and guest, parent and child, government and citizen etc); not to take advantage of one another
91. Both rich and poor should contribute to the society from which both hope to benefit
92. If someone repents completely of the wrong they have done, amends their ways, and makes reparation to those they have wronged, then their past wrongs should not be held against them; we should rejoice over the lost who are found
93. As we are shown mercy and are forgiven, so should we also be merciful to others and forgive
94. Not treating people any differently according to their outward appearance or social status
95. Not to follow the majority when they do wrong
96. Not to follow a commandment or precept so literally that its heart and intent are lost
97. To acquire knowledge with humility, so that we might find the light of Yahveh's Wisdom

Some Voluntary Acts of Piety [b]

98. To lend to the poor, knowing that one will not get anything back
99. To live only according to one's needs
100. To seek out the company of the pious, so that we might emulate them
101. Accompanying any personal fasts with acts of charity, justice and kindness

---

[a] Such as resisting anger and hatred, so that murder may be avoided, or resisting jealousy and lust so that adultery may be avoided

[b] These are ideal acts which are not expected of everyone, but are reserved rather for those who wish to grow spiritually, and train themselves to become better servants of God and His Kingdom.

THE WAY

Some Yahwist beliefs held by Talmidis

102. God's will is knowable – not completely or perfectly, but nevertheless knowable; Yahveh is not an unknowable God
103. There is no such thing as permanent salvation; if a good man sins, then his previous good actions do not count in his favour. If a sinful man repents fully, then his previous sins do not count against him (i.e. there is no scorecard system of reward and punishment)
104. Whatever willful wrongs we do to others, God will return the same to us if we do not repent of them.
105. There are no such things as 'fallen angels'; angels cannot rebel or sin against God, since God's holiness prevents it
106. There is no such thing as 'Satan' – a supreme ruler of all evil who directs evil people and evil spirits, equal and opposite to God
107. There are no such things as demons or evil spirits – supernatural beings whose sole reason for existence is to make evil happen, or make people do evil
108. Evil comes instead from the hearts and minds of human beings; people alone are responsible and answerable for evil
109. If we return evil with evil, then we negate our own righteousness, and we turn our backs on God's help
110. God returns an unjust curse back to the one who pronounced it
111. We should not rejoice at the suffering of our enemies[a]
112. To see humanity and the world with a right mind, so that we might be led to a greater understanding of them
113. We should not seek signs of God's plans in the stars or movements of the celestial bodies
114. Places of the dead are not suitable places of worship
115. Holding that the Bible is perfect, infallible and without fault is elevating it to an equal status with God, and is therefore idolatry
116. Worshipping the Bible and putting it above God is idolatry

---

[a] Prov 24:17-18

APPENDIX TWO: About the Mission of Talmidaism

The essential mission of Talmidaism is to spread the Kingdom of God – to encourage other human beings, regardless of their religion, to live with an awareness of the nature of their heavenly Father, and change their lives accordingly. Christianity would see its mission as 'to make disciples of all nations' (i.e. to convert everyone to Christianity). However, Talmidis would see part of their mission as 'to spread the Kingdom of God to all nations' (i.e. to create peace and encourage understanding and tolerance between nations, cultures, political parties and religions).

There is a principle in the Israelite religion that God allows Gentiles their religions[a] – Yahveh does not expect everyone to become Israelites. However, what God *does* expect is that everyone should endeavour to reach a certain standard of ethical and moral behaviour within their own society. It is in this sense that all humanity will come to 'know Yahveh'. There are today many serious problems facing society, and most of them would be nipped in the bud if we simply encouraged a certain standard of respect towards our fellow human beings.

Below are the full articles of mission of the Talmidi Faith:

Articles of Mission of the Talmidi Faith

Our basic mission is to restore the best ideals and principles of the Israelite religion ('The Way of Yahveh'), and to proclaim the good news of the Kingdom of God to the House of Israel and to the Nations.

In detail:

With relation to God:

- To live a way of life that enables the holiness and power of God's Glory to dwell among us[b]

---

[a] Deut 4:19 "And when you (i.e. Israelites) look up to the sky and see the sun, the moon and the stars – all the heavenly array – do not be enticed into bowing down to them and worshipping the things that Yahveh your God *has apportioned to all the nations under heaven.*"
[b] This was the central belief and prime motivation of the Israelite Religion.

- To imitate God in God's ways, by exercising the same compassion and mercy to others that God shows to us, and thereby demonstrating who our Heavenly Father is;
- to bear witness to the power and presence of Yahveh by our holy and distinctive way of life, culturally, ethically, and in our outlook on life;[a]
- to restore the theological supremacy of Yahveh;[b]
- to restore the good reputation of God's Name, demonstrating that God is above all a loving and compassionate God;[c]
- to restore the best of the original ideals and principles of the Israelite religion;
- to make people aware that the Kingdom of God is here and now;
- to bring the good news of the peace of God's kingdom to Israel and all the nations[d]
- to sow the seeds of the fulfilment of God's Kingdom.[e]
- to make people understand the importance of the social and ethical stability of society (the 'kingship of God'), and how God is given no option but to intervene when society fails into moral lawlessness, and brings God good reputation into disrepute ('Day of Yahveh')

With relation to the Houses of Israel and Judah

- to help our people to realise why we are called to do what we do, and what our cultural and ethical distinctiveness is for;[f]

---

[a] See 1Chr 16:24, Ps 96:3 'Declare His Glory among the nations, His marvellous deeds among all peoples.' Isa 49:6 'I will also make you a light for the Gentiles, that you may bring my salvation to the ends of the earth.' We do all this by our distinctive culture, outlook, and ethical way of life.

[b] For example, by re-examining beliefs that diminish the absolute supremacy of Yahveh, such as belief in a messiah-saviour, the role of Satan as the equal of God, the rulings of rabbis overturning the rulings of God etc.

[c] not the wrathful, vengeful god of religious fundamentalism, which advocates killing and violence

[d] This does not mean converting people to one religion, but rather restoring the image of God as a loving and merciful Sovereign where Israel is concerned, encouraging our people to practice their faith with compassion; and to spread tolerance and understanding among the nations, in an attempt to bring peace between different faiths and cultures.

[e] In order to prepare humanity for the day when the veil between heaven and earth is taken away, God's Glory shines on earth (cf Isa 60:19-20), and God's will be done on earth as it is in heaven -,

[f] to be an eternal, physical, visible witness to the power and presence of Yahveh

- to encourage our people to change, to become a nation that other nations would want to be inspired by – a 'kingdom of priests and a holy nation';[a]
- to help our people to realise our collective mission, so that we as a people become better able to carry out the work that God has given us to do in the world – to minister to the nations as a kingdom of priests;
- to encourage our people to act justly in our dealings and treatment of other peoples, so that we will become a people *'set in praise, fame and high honour among the nations'*,[b] by being a people holy in our ethical behaviour and outlook, for the sake of Yahveh;
- to remind our people who are in the Land not to oppress those among us who are not of our own people;[c]
- to ever remind our people of our obligation of *ts'daqah* towards the poor;
- to encourage our people towards a living and vibrant relationship with our God;

With relation to the Gentile nations:

- to be a light to the Nations, so that by our example, they will be inspired to build just, righteous and stable societies according to their own cultures;[d]
- to be a benefit and a blessing to the Nations;
- to spread the Kingdom of God among the Nations, by encouraging them to follow a way of righteousness, and to practice tolerance and understanding between faiths and peoples;
- to remind the rich of the God-given right of the poor to social justice, since all the poor are God's people;
- to bring healing to humanity, and encourage people towards a wholeness of spirit;
- to encourage humanity to realise their stewardship of creation, and so not abuse it;

---

[a] This way the peoples of the earth will see that we are called by the Name of Yahveh, and they will respect us.
[b] Deut 26:19 – *'He has declared that he will set you in praise, fame and honour high above all the nations he has made and that you will be a people holy to Yahveh your God, as He promised.'*
[c] Ex 22:21 – *'Do not mistreat a resident foreigner or oppress him, for you were foreigners resident in Egypt.'* Also Ex 23:9
[d] It is this way that God's salvation shall be brought to the ends of the earth.

- to encourage others to work for the social, moral and spiritual stability and betterment of their society;

With relation to one another:

- to strive to love our neighbour as ourselves;
- to do to and for others that which we would want others to do to and for us;
- to encourage others to change and better themselves by not judging or condemning others;
- to so change ourselves that we become more effective citizens of God's Kingdom, and better instruments through which the Kingdom of God shall be fulfilled;

With relation to Torah:

- to promote a simple, direct approach to Torah;
- to provide a way of internalising Torah, of 'writing it on our hearts';
- to remind people of the true heart of Torah, which is justice, mercy, compassion, charity, repentance and forgiveness;
- to encourage a culture in which the Hebrew scriptures are studied and interpreted honestly and responsibly;
- to teach people the original Yahwist Israelite mind-set and outlook, so that understanding of *Torah and the Prophets* comes more easily and naturally;

With relation to Yeshua` and the Jewish tradition of his ancient followers:

- to restore his humanity, and his proper place as a Hebrew prophet;
- to help people to focus on the real Jewish aspects of his original message – that in his day he warned of the destruction of Jerusalem and eventual exile; and that this could be avoided (or if not, the time of tribulation shortened) if people changed and lived a just, merciful and compassionate life;
- to help people to refocus on his teachings, and not on him;
- to remind people of the social aspect of his message with regard to the poor, debt, charity etc;
- to make people aware of the honoured and respected place Jacob the Pious played in the ancient community of his

followers, and who he was;
- to work for and to enable the restoration of the succession of Nasis of the community one day.

APPENDIX THREE: CULTURAL DIFFERENCES WITH OTHER ISRAELITE/JEWISH COMMUNITIES

Talmidi Israelite observances are based on our understanding of the culture of 1st century Galilee and Judea, and on our understanding of Torah. Our observances therefore differ from those of rabbinic Judaism in many ways.

These are our main differences based upon our rejection of the Oral Law, and are customs shared with Karaites:

- we observe New Moon festivals (since they are biblically enjoined observances)
- our months begin on the evening of the sighting of the first sliver of the New Moon
- we observe the New Year Festival at the beginning of the first Hebrew month, not the seventh
- New Year begins in Aviv (determined biblically by the finding of *aviv* – that is, ripe barley – in Eretz Israel)
- the counting of the period of 50 days after the wave offering of omer[a] is started on the first Sabbath after the *pesach* meal[b]
- our *Shavu'ot* always falls on a Sunday,[c] and is celebrated as the 'Festival of First Fruits',[d] not of the giving of the Torah
- at *Sukkot* we don't wave a *lulav* – the bunch of 'four species' of greenery; we build our booths out of the greenery (only a palm branch is waved during the festivities)
- we wear *techelet* (blue cords) on the corner fringes of our *tallitot* (prayer shawls)
- we don't wear *t'fillin* (phylacteries or prayer boxes) on our foreheads; we feel this practise is an over-literal reading of

---

[a] Lev 23:11
[b] Lev 23:10-14
[c] Lev 23:15-16, Deut 16:9
[d] Ex 23:16, 34:22, Num 28:26; also called the Festival of Weeks, and the Festival of the Harvest

idiomatic expressions in the passages following the Great Commandment)
- the first day of the seventh month (Tishrei) is observed as *Yom Tru'ah* (Day of Shout & Trumpet), and not *Rosh ha-Shanah* (New Year); this is the day we celebrate our joy in Torah, when the whole of the Book of Deuteronomy is read in public between daybreak and noon
- we don't have *Simchat Torah* (Rejoicing of the Law) (see previous item on *Yom Tru'ah*); instead, the day after *Sukkot* is observed as 'The Eighth Day of Closed Assembly' (*Yom Shmini ha-Atseret*), when we pray for rain in Israel, and for the needs of Israel and Judah
- we do use the Holy Name of Yahveh in our private and congregational prayer
- we don't have a ban on the eating of meat and milk together; we view this as a misreading of what not to do at the Festival of First Fruits[a] – forbidding Israelites to follow a Canaanite practise of actually boiling a kid-goat in its mother's milk

The following customs are today specific to Talmidaism, based upon our understanding of 1st century Galilean and Judean custom and tradition:

- we have elders (*z'qeinim*), scribes (*soferim*) and sages (*chakhamim*), not Rabbis
- we have a *Sanhedrin ha-shalosh* (Council of Three), not a Beth Din
- we don't require *ha-tafat dam brit* (ritual cutting to draw blood) of a male convert who is already circumcised; instead, the existing circumcision is sanctified with a prayer, and thereby its purpose is reassigned and dedicated to the Covenant
- our *Miqra'ot* (bibles) do not contain the *Book of Esther*[b]
- the order of the books of the *Miqra* (Hebrew Bible) is slightly different; it follows the 1st century CE Galilean canon described

---

[a] Ex 23:19, 34:26, Dt 14:21
[b] Bibles in Eretz Israel at the time of Yeshua` did not contain the *Book of Esther*. Good examples of this situation can be found among the corpus of literature found at Qumran, which does not contain the *Book of Esther* at all. *Esther* is part of the Babylonian canon of Scripture, which mainstream Judaism uses now, but was not part of the canon used in Galilee and Judea at the time of the earliest Followers of the Way – which is the reason we don't include it. We were not part of the assembly which sat to decide on the Hebrew canon of scripture, and so stick with the one that was around in the 1st century CE.

by Josephus, rather than the later Babylonian canon of mainstream Judaism; the order is the same up until the books of the *Kethuvim* ('Writings'). In our *miqra'ot* (Bibles), the last book ends up being the *Book of Psalms*

- we don't observe non-Torah ordained festivals (apart from *Chanukkah* / the Festival of Lights, which we consider a national festival and a 'day of joy',[a] not a religious one)
- we don't observe *Purim*[b] (we believe it to have been originally a local Babylonian Jewish festival); we have no objection to the Rabbinic observance of this festival
- we count down[c] the candles at Chanukkah, not up (i.e. eight on the first night, one on the last)
- we don't wear *kippot* (or skullcaps – we view this as a Muslim practise adopted by Jews);[d] instead, conservative sects require only married men and women to cover their heads in public, women with a shawl or a woman's hat in local style, and men with either a Hebrew turban (*pe'eir*) or an ordinary hat in local style. Unmarried men and women would not be required to cover their heads. Moderate and Liberal sects tend not to observe these customs. However, we respect communal custom in wearing kippot when mixing with Rabbinic Jews.
- we don't rock when we pray, or bob when we say certain

---

[a] See Num 10:10 – 'On your days of joy, at your festivals and at the beginnings of your months, you are to sound the silver trumpets ....' Local and national festivals are permitted by Torah as 'days of joy', as long as God is remembered as the Saviour and Deliverer of the Israelite people; as the same verse concludes: 'as a reminder in God's presence that I, Yahveh am your God.'

[b] The *Book of Esther* does not mention God, and only celebrates the power of the Jewish people. It is based on the Babylonian festival of the birthday of the god Marduk, which was accompanied by outlandish costumes, heavy drinking and outrageous behaviour. It is considered by Talmidis unbecoming of the reputation and holiness of God to behave in such a manner.

[c] This is the practice followed by the School of Shammai, who followed the older Jewish tradition. They reasoned that because the festival was a second Sukkot, and since at that festival the number of offerings decreased as the festival went on, so also the number of candles should decrease. The School of Hillel decided to do something new, by increasing the number of candles as the festival proceeded. They reasoned that one increases in holiness as time passes.

[d] or possibly a leftover from the ancient Middle Eastern practice of forcing subjugated peoples to wear a corded captives' hat; see 1Kgs 20:31-32, where these hats are called *chavalim*. It is therefore the difference between the headdress of a שְׁבִי shevi (captive) and the headdress of a חָפְשִׁי chofshi (free person).

blessings;[a]
- the ancient Israelite way of having both hands raised up is seen as a valid attitude in prayer, as is being seated with the hands clasped on one's lap, or held close to one's chest
- we read Torah in three years, not one
- our synagogues would reflect the ancient layout, rather than the current mainstream trend of mimicking a church: congregants would be sat around the side and back, rather than in rows facing the front; and the prayer leader would be at the back, rather than the front; also an east-facing curtain or 'veil' [*masakh mizrachah*] would be at the front, rather than the Torah ark [which would be mobile and be brought out only during the service and kept to the side]
- the Torah scroll would be kept in a *tiq*[b] in Middle Eastern mizrachi style, rather than wrapped in a cloth in European Ashkenazi style

A note on relations with the wider Jewish Community

Talmidis do not missionise other Jewish people, because we do not see our fellow Jews as needing converting – they are already Yahwists. We are strongly opposed to the missionising of the Jewish community by Christians. In fact, Talmidis have actually assisted former lapsed Jews to return to Rabbinic or Karaite Judaism, as well as assisting Gentiles and Messianics wishing to convert to mainstream Judaism. Since Talmidaism attempts to emulate what it sees as the pluralist, non-sectarian *Common Judaism* of the 1st century CE, Talmidaism is in favour of a varied and diverse Jewish community.

Talmidis accept all Rabbinic Jews, Karaite Jews, and even secular and atheist Jews of Jewish descent as Jews, whether of matrilineal or patrilineal descent. We also respect and accept Samaritans as Israelites.

Talmidis feel a certain affinity with Karaite Jews, both our branches of Judaism being descended theologically from Common Judaism. Like Talmidis, Karaites also reject the authority of the Oral Law and Talmud. However, there are some practical differences between us: because we

---

[a] This rabbinic custom was based on a medieval rabbi making a connection between the two words 'to bless' (Hebrew *barakh*), and 'knee' (Hebrew *bérekh*). However, the two words are not connected etymologically, and have two entirely different origins.

[b] pronounced *teek*; it is a decorated wooden or metal case, in which the Torah scroll is housed.

broadly follow the ancient custom of the Land,[a] Talmidis celebrate Chanukkah but not Purim, while Karaites observe Purim but not Chanukkah. Karaites do not have any light or heat in their homes on the Sabbath;[b] Talmidis in conservative sects by contrast extinguish lights not needed, and enkindle lights needed, well before the beginning of the Sabbath. On the whole, Talmidis also have a more flexible approach to Torah.

---

[a] the customs and traditions practised in the Land of Israel up until the 1st century CE. This was our choice, our distinctive witness to Yahveh. We should not, however, berate those Jewish communities that follow customs that originated outside of the Land (unless of course, they are un-Yahwist in principle).

[b] I understand that this custom was followed by Egyptian Karaites; European Karaites in cold northern climes did not follow this for practical reasons.

APPENDIX FOUR: GLOSSARY & LIST OF ABBREVIATIONS USED IN THESE BOOKS

Word	*Definition*
Animism	the oldest human religion; the belief that spirits and gods dwell in everything around us - rivers, rocks, trees etc. All of these things are therefore worshipped and revered.
Aramaic	a Semitic language, related to Hebrew and Arabic. *Until the rise of Arabic in the 7th century CE, Aramaic was the international language of the Middle East, and there were many different varieties of it.*
Aramaicist	A person who involves him/herself in the study of the Aramaic language and its history
Asherah	main Canaanite goddess
Baal	the general title of respect for any Canaanite god; the word means 'lord'.
BCE	abbreviation: 'Before the Common Era', used with the western dating system. The academic equivalent of BC
Believers	self-appellation of the first Gentile Christians, (*Pisteuontes* in Greek); the followers of Paul of Tarsus; the Jewish followers of Yeshua` did not use this term.
CE	abbreviation: 'Common Era', used with the western dating system. The academic equivalent of AD
cf	compare with; from Latin *confero*

Ch. Sh.	*Chazoney Shim'on* (Visions of Shimon); 8th book of *The Exhortations*. It covers the Ebionite portions of the *Book of Revelation* in the New Testament
Ch. Y.	*Devarim mi-qtsat Chokhmat Yeshua` ben Sira* (Selections from the Wisdom of Yeshua` ben Sira); the 12th book of *The Exhortations*. It contains selections from the *Book of Ecclesiasticus*, on themes that would have been of interest to ancient Followers
Christianity	the religious philosophy based on the belief system of Paul of Tarsus, and the ethical teachings of Jesus of Nazareth
Convention of Jerusalem, the	known as 'Council of Jerusalem' in the Orthodox and Catholic churches. Took place in about the summer of 49 CE to discuss the status of Paul's Gentile Believers, and their relationship with the community of Followers
Coptic	modern descendant of the ancient Egyptian language.
copyist	A man whose job it was to copy existing texts.
Covenant, the	the pact made between God and Israel: 'If you will worship me alone, and follow only My laws and teachings, then I will give you the land of Canaan forever, and preserve you as a nation forever'. Everything else are terms and conditions.
Ebionite	an ancient Talmidi sect. Even in the first 40 years after Jesus's death, there were several sects. The only one whose name we still know are the Ebionites.
El (or Eil)	the highest god in the Canaanite pantheon
Essenes	ancient Jewish sect. They were opposed to the priesthood in the Jerusalem Temple,

	whom they saw as corrupt, so they formed an isolated community in the Judean desert near the Dead Sea.
Exhortations, the	The Talmidi equivalent of the New Testament, covering approximately the same period and the same kind of material. However, it does not have the same authority as the Hebrew Bible. It is used for teaching and inspirational purposes only.
Exhs	abbr. for 'The Exhortations'
Followers of the Way	self-appellation of the first Jewish followers of Jesus of Nazareth; see also: 'Way, the'
free translation	a translation that gives the sense of the original, and is not necessarily a literal, word for word translation. This also gives the nearest vernacular equivalent of otherwise misleading, idiomatic expressions.
Galilee, the	region in the north of ancient Israel. *Its population consisted mostly of farmers and fishermen. Its capital was Sepphoris*
Gnosticism	Belief system that holds that there is a good and an evil god; that this world is controlled by the evil god, and only spiritual things are good. Attainment to the spiritual realm is only possible through secret knowledge or *gnosis*.
Godfearer	Non-Jew who follows the beliefs, principles and customs of the Israelite religion, without going through full conversion (in Hebrew: *yireh elohim* [for a woman, *yirat elohim*], 'someone who reveres God in awe'). Can also be called a *nilveh / nilvah* ('one who attaches themselves' i.e. to Yahveh)
Ig. Yq.	Iggeret Ya`aqov, or 'Letter of Jacob the Pious'. The 6th book of *The Exhortations*; it is the Talmidi version of the 'Letter of James'

	in the New Testament.
immersion	the Jewish version of baptism. It is carried out, not only for conversion, but whenever one needs to be ritually prepared for attending Temple. It was therefore not a one-time-only ritual.
Inquisition	The Portuguese Inquisition (1536-1674), like the Spanish Inquisition, sought out all those who secretly practised the Jewish faith, and gave them a stark choice: convert to Christianity or face execution. There was a brief window in the early 17th century when a third choice was given: to leave Portugal.
interlinear translation	a multi-lingual text, with the original language at the top, and a literal translation word for word in the second language below each line.
Jacob the Pious	St. James the Just, author of the 'Letter of James' in the New Testament. He was the leader of the ancient Talmidi community after Jesus died. He led the community from c.30 to 62 CE, when he was executed by stoning at the orders of the High Priest.
Jerusalem Council, the	the central ruling body of the ancient Talmidi community; not to be confused with what Catholics call 'the Council of Jerusalem', which was a great meeting (or *Convention*) convened specifically to decide the position of Paul's followers in relation to the ancient Talmidi community.

Jewish Aramaic	the dialect of Aramaic spoken by Jews – more accurately, Galilean Jewish Aramaic. *It was heavily influenced by Hebrew*
Josephus	Jewish historian who lived shortly after Jesus. He was a Galilean who witnessed many of the events that led to the destruction of Jerusalem and the Temple.
Jubilee Year	the year after every 7th Sabbatical year was a Jubilee year (i.e. the year after every 49th year, or in other words, the 1st year of every 49-year cycle). In this year, land lost through debt was to be returned to its original owner.
Kabbalah	a form of mysticism which is a mixture of pagan, Gnostic and Jewish thought. Not accepted in Talmidaism as being of pagan origin.
Karaism	The religious philosophy of Karaite Jews. They do not accept the authority of the Oral law, and rely on the freedom to interpret Scripture according to one's own learning and understanding.
Kavodh	lit. 'glory'; refers to the fire of the 'Divine Radiance' - the powerful and purifying aspect of God's nature.
kheruvim	(pronounced khair-oo-VEEM) a form of angel that, according to tradition, supports God's throne. They have the back end of an ox, the front end of a lion, the wings of an eagle, and the torso and head of a man. The Christian version of these angels are cherubs; Israelite *kheruvim* look nothing like the baby-faced Christian cherubs.

Koine Greek	the everyday form of Greek spoken by ordinary people *(in contrast to classical or literary Greek). The gospels were probably written in this form of Greek to make them easy to read by ordinary people.*
literal translation	a translation that gives a word-for-word translation of the original language. Literal translations don't give the real sense of idiomatic expressions, only the literal rendering of them.
marpei	the ancient Israelite art of healing, the using of plants and herbs alongside prayer and human care; it dealt with the human mind, body and soul as a whole unit.
Marranos	Jews who were forcibly converted to Christianity in Spain and Portugal in the 16th - 17th centuries.
merappei	(female: *merappah*) healer who practises the Israelite healing art of *marpei*.
Mg. M.	*Megillat ha-Musar* (Scroll of the Preaching); 2nd book of *The Exhortations*
minuscules	small Greek letters *(the opposite of capital letters)*
Miqra, the	the Hebrew Bible or 'Old Testament'. Sometimes called Tanakh, after the rabbinic abbreviation for the 3 parts of the Miqra (T.N.K. - Torah, Nevi'im Ketuvim (Torah, Prophets & Writings).
miqveh	ritual immersion pool
Mishkan	Hebrew for the Tabernacle, the covered tent that was the central place of worship in the

	Sinai, and also in the Land of Israel until the Temple was built.
mitzvah	a religious commandment
Miz. E.	*Mizmorey ha-Evyonim* (Hymns of the Pious Poor); 10th book of *The Exhortations*
Molekh	Ammonite god, whose followers believed that the sacrificial death of one's child, especially an only-begotten son, could 'save' them from their sins, and bestow upon them permanent salvation.
Nazirite	a man or woman who has taken a particular vow not to consume anything derived from grapes, and to avoid contact with the dead. During the time of their vow, they had to live a life of piety, in accordance with the laws and principles of the Israelite religion.
Oral Law	a corpus of books that contain the debates and decisions of the ancient rabbis. It has greater authority in modern Rabbinic Judaism than the Hebrew Bible.
Outer Darkness	in Massorite Talmidi theology, a term used by Yeshua` to describe a place after death where the soul goes to dwell apart from God (also known as *Sheol* and *Azza Zel*). Here one has to work through one's sins by reliving what one has done to others as if they were happening to oneself. Once one has experienced and repented of all the sins one did not repent of in life, one then goes on to heaven.

Parallel panels	a particular form of Hebrew poetry. You have two lists of lines of poetry. The first lines of the lists will parallel each other in either ideas, form or language; then the second two, then the third two, and so on.
Paul of Tarsus	St Paul. His teachings and beliefs form the basis of modern Christianity (the atoning death of Jesus on the cross, original sin etc). He was not accepted by the ancient Jewish followers of Yeshua`
Paullist	adjective, describing a particular theology and outlook that originates from the teaching of Paul of Tarsus (or 'St Paul'), and not Jesus.
Pharisees	ancient Jewish sect from which the majority of modern Jewish sects (i.e. Rabbinic Judaism) are descended. They held the Oral Law in greater esteem than the Hebrew Bible
Q-Gospel, the (or simply, *Q*)	earliest hypothetical gospel, containing only the sayings of Jesus; it would have predated the Gospels of Matthew and Luke, and possibly even Mark.
Qin. Y.	*Qinot Lirushalayim* (Laments for Jerusalem); 9th book of *The Exhortations*
Roman alphabet	the alphabet that English and most European languages are written in; also called 'Latin script'.
S. Kit.	*Sefer ha-Kitbey ha-vney ha-Derekh* (Book of Talmidi Writings); 14th book of *The Exhortations*
S. Niss.	*Sefer Nissayunayin* (Book of the Two Trials of Yeshua`); 4th book of *The Exhortations*. It contains the stories of the trials of Jesus before the Jewish Sanhedrin and the Roman

	governor, Pontius Pilate, and of his death by crucifixion.
S. Yaq.	*Sefer Ya'aqov* (Book of James the Just); 7th book of *The Exhortations*
S. Yesh.	*Sefer Yeshua`* (Book of the Prophet Yeshua`); 3rd book of *The Exhortations*. It contains the detailed Jewish sayings and stories of Jesus.
S. Yoch.	*Sefer Yochanan* (Book of the Prophet John the Baptist); 1st book of *The Exhortations*
Sabbatical Year	every 7th year was a Sabbatical year. The land was not to be tilled or harvested, and all debts were to be forgiven.
Sadducees	ancient Jewish sect consisting mostly of aristocratic priests. They only accepted the first 5 books of the Hebrew Bible, and did not believe in life after death.
Samaritans	Israelite sect descended from the northern tribes of Israel. In Jesus's day, Jews and Samaritans hated each other, and there were regular intercommunal clashes.
scribe	generally a professional who is paid to write or copy anything. In Yeshua`'s time, they were also trained, learned interpreters of Torah.
Second Temple period	Jewish historical period from 530 BCE to 70 CE. The period in which Jesus lived is referred to as the Late Second Temple period, or the Herodian period (after King Herod the Great, and the dynasty he founded).
seraphim	(pronounced sair-raff-FEEM); fiery, winged, serpent-like angels who are traditionally thought to exist in the immediate presence of God. In Jewish tradition they are gigantic, flying serpents, the colour of copper or bronze. They have three sets of wings, one

	with which they fly, another with which they cover their faces, and the third with which they cover their middle.
Shem Tov Matthew	rabbinic Hebrew translation of the Gospel of Matthew, dated 1385. The translator was Ibn Shaprut, who lived in Aragon, Spain.
She'ol	the underworld, place of the dead. *Before the Israelites believed in heaven, they used to believe that the dead went to a dark, unknowing underworld called She'ol. This later evolved into belief in a place Yeshua` called 'the Outer Darkness'.*
sidra	a portion of Torah. Differs from a *parashah*. A *sidra* is short, and the division of the Torah into *sidra'ot* enables the Torah to be read in 3 years (the division of Torah into longer *parashot* enables Torah to be read in 1 year). The *sidra'ot* represent the older custom.
sukkah	(pronounced soo-KAA, plural *sukkot*); a simple, rectangular structure, made with 4 poles, connected at the top by 4 pieces of wood. Used during the festival of Sukkot to dwell in. The roof is made of date palm branches, and the sides are decorated by fragrant or leafy branches and fruits.
Syriac	the Syrian dialect of Aramaic. *It is heavily influenced by Greek, and is used by Aramaic-speaking Christians. It is distinct from the dialect that Yeshua` spoke, Galilean Jewish Aramaic.*
T. Sh.	*Torat ha-Shlichim* (Teaching of the Emissaries); 5th book of *The Exhortations*

Tabernacle	the covered tent that was the central place of worship in the Sinai, and also in the Land of Israel until the Temple was built.
Talmidaism	modern term for 'Jewish-Christianity' (pronounced taal-mee-DAY-izzm, from the Aramaic *talmida*, 'follower', 'disciple'), and is synonymous with 'the Way'. It is an umbrella term for any Jewish sect that follows Jesus of Nazareth as a fully human prophet.
Talmidi	modern term for 'Jewish-Christian', (pronounced taal-MEE-dee; plural: Talmidis), and is synonymous with 'Follower of the Way'. *This term refers to those Jewish followers of Jesus of Nazareth who believe he was a fully human prophet. Although the word was only coined in 1996, the term is used retrospectively by modern 'Jewish Christians' to refer to ancient Jewish Christians too.*
Talmud	the Oral Law. *This is the collected debates and decisions of the ancient rabbis, and contains material which is often contradictory to books of the Hebrew Bible, and even with itself. For modern rabbinic Judaism, it has greater authority than the Hebrew Bible.*
Targum Onqelos	An Aramaic translation of the Hebrew Bible. *Targum* means translation, and Onqelos (or Onkelos) is the name of the translator. It literally means, 'translation by Onqelos'.
tithe	ten per cent of one's income before tax. This was given to pay the clergy, the upkeep of the Temple, and to help the poor.
trinitarian	adj. pertaining to belief in the Trinity.

Trinity, the	Christian belief that holds that God is made of three persons: Father, Son and Holy Spirit. Each person of this trinity is considered the same as each other, yet at the same time distinct from each other.
Ts. Y.	*Tsava'at Yehudah* (The Testament of Judah the Nasi); the 13th book of *The Exhortations*
uncials	the capital form of Greek letters. *In the 1st century, all Greek was written in capitals*
Unitarian	Liberal Christian denomination which believes Jesus was a human being, and that God is indivisible and without bodily form.
Way, the	short for 'the Way of Yahveh'. It was the original name of the Israelite religion, but came to be associated with the faith of the first Jewish followers of Jesus of Nazareth.
Yahwism	the pure form of Israelite theology, before it was affected by the beliefs of other religions. Yahveh is held supreme, without equal. Yahveh alone is Saviour (i.e. not a messiah), and has no equal (so Satan is not the 'ruler of evil').
Yahwist	someone who adheres to the purest form of Israelite theology; also adj., to describe the purest form of Israelite theology
Yeshua`	Jesus of Nazareth. This was his original Aramaic name (from Hebrew *Yehoshua`*, which means 'Yahveh saves'). Talmidis use it to emphasise the difference between the Christian 'Jesus' and the Jewish 'Yeshua`', and to point out that they are two distinct entities.

Yochanan the Immerser	John the Baptist. He actually led his own sect, the Nazorayyans. The Mandeans of Iraq claim descent from these Nazorayyans.
Zoroastrianism	The old religion of Persia (now Iran). It was founded by a man called Zoroaster (*Zardusht*). It believed in a good god (*Ahura Mazda*) and an evil god (*Ahriman*), and that a saviour from the world of light would come to save humanity. This religion influenced Judaism after the Babylonian Exile in the 6th century BCE, and introduced new beliefs such as a king-saviour, Satan, fallen angels and battles in heaven.

SELECT BIBLIOGRAPHY & RESOURCES

This list is by no means a complete record of every single book that has ever had influence over the material contained within these books. However, it is a list of those books which have had the most impact on the contents of this work. I apologise for the omission of any book.

GRAMMARS:

Grammatik des Jüdisch-Palästinischen Aramäisch
Gustaf Dalman
J C Hinrichsische Buchhandlung, Leipzig 1905

Manual of the Aramaic of the Palestinian Talmud
J T Marshall
E J Brill Ltd, Leiden 1929

A Short Grammar of Biblical Aramaic
Alger F Johns
Andrews University Monographs 1972

A Grammar of Galilean Aramaic
Caspar Levias
Jewish Theological Seminary of America, New York 1986

Grammar of Palestinian Jewish Aramaic
William Stevenson
Clarendon Press, Oxford 1987

A Grammar of Biblical Aramaic
Franz Rosenthal
Harassowitz Verlag, Wiesbaden 1995

An Introduction to Aramaic
Frederick E Greenspahn
Scholars' Press, Atlanta 1999

DICTIONARIES

A Manual of the Chaldee Language
D M Turpie
Williams and Norgate 1879

An Aramaic Handbook Part 1
Franz Rosenthal
Otto Harassowitz, Wiesbaden 1967

Hebrew-Chaldee Lexicon to the Old Testament Scriptures
Gesenius
Baker Book House, Grand Rapids 1988

A Dictionary of Jewish Palestinian Aramaic
Michael Sokoloff
Bar Ilan University Press 1992

Practical Talmudic Dictionary
Yitzhak Frank
The Ariel Institute 1994

A Dictionary of Judean Aramaic
Michael Sokoloff
Bar Ilan University Press 2003

The Comprehensive Aramaic Lexicon Project
http://cal1.cn.huc.edu/

DISCUSSIONS AND RESOURCES ON ARAMAIC

A Manual of Palestinian Aramaic Texts
J Fitzmeyer, D J Harrington
Biblical Institute Press, Rome 1978

An Aramaic Approach to the Gospels and Acts
Matthew Black
Clarendon Press, Oxford 1979

ANCIENT TEXTS *(related to the study of Aramaic)*

Gospel of Mark (Koine Greek text)
(Synopsis of the Four Gospels, Kurt Aland, German Bible Society 1984)

Gospel of Matthew (Koine Greek text)
(Synopsis of the Four Gospels, Kurt Aland, German Bible Society 1984)

Gospel of Luke (Koine Greek text)
(Synopsis of the Four Gospels, Kurt Aland, German Bible Society 1984)
Book of Revelation (Koine Greek text)
(NIV Interlinear Greek-English New Testament, Rev. A Marshall, Zondervan 1976)

Book of Daniel
(NIV Interlinear Hebrew-English Old Testament, J R Kohlenberger III, Zondervan 1987)

Book of Ezra
(NIV Interlinear Hebrew-English Old Testament, J R Kohlenberger III, Zondervan 1987)

Aramaic Targum of the Torah (Onqelos)
(Alexander Sperber, Brill Paperbacks 1992)

Aramaic Targum of the Prophets (Jonathan)
(Alexander Sperber, Brill Paperbacks 1992)

COMMENTARIES ON THE MIQRA & THE NEW TESTAMENT
I have not included every single commentary I have ever read on every book of scripture; I have merely listed those that have had a direct influence on the current manuscript.

Book of Exodus
N M Sarna,
JPS Torah Commentaries 1991

Book of Joshua
Trent C Butler
Word Biblical Commentary, 1983

The Book of Isaiah
S B Freehof
UAHC Press 1972

The Book of Jeremiah
S B Freehof
UAHC Press 1972

A Critical and Exegetical Commentary on the Book of Daniel
J A Montgomery
T&T Clark 1926

Gospel of Saint Mark
D E Nineham
Pelican NT Commentaries, 1986

Gospel of Saint Matthew
J C Fenton
Pelican NT Commentaries, 1985

The Gospel of Luke
E Earle Ellis
New Century Bible Commentary, 1983

The Book of Revelation
R H Mounce
Eerdmans Publishing 1997

CULTURE, HISTORY AND EVERYDAY LIFE IN JUDEA AND THE GALILEE

Wars of the Jews
Flavius Josephus
Milner & Sowerby, 1864

Life In Palestine When Jesus Lived
J Estlin Carpenter
The Lindsay Press, London 1949

Manners and Customs of Bible Lands
Fred H Wight
Moody Press, Chicago 1953

Everyday Life in New Testament Times
A C Bouquet,
B T Batsdord Ltd, 1953

New Testament History
F F Bruce
Pickering & Inglis, Basingstoke 1969

Jerusalem in the Time of Jesus
Joachim Jeremias
Fortress Press, Philadelphia 1975

Everyday Life in the Holy Land
James Neil
The Olive Press, London 1976

Jesus and the World of Judaism
Geza Vermes
SCM Press, London 1983

The New Manners and Customs of Bible Times
Ralph Gower
Moody Press, Chicago 1987

Jesus Within Judaism
James H Charlesworth
SPCK 1989

Judaism – Practice and Belief 63 BCE – 66 CE
E P Sanders
SCM Press, London 1994

Galilee – History, Politics, People
Richard A Horsley
Trinity Press International, Pennsylvania 1995

Archaeology, History & Society in Galilee
Richard A Horsley
Trinity Press International, Pennsylvania 1996

The Meaning of Jesus
NT Wright, Marcus Borg
SPCK 1999

Jesus the Jewish Theologian
Brad H Young
Hendrickson Publishers 1999

THE ISRAELITE RELIGION

Antiquities of the Jews
Flavius Josephus
Milner & Sowerby, 1864

The Jewish Encyclopedia
(online and printed versions)
1901-1906

Hebrew Religion – Its Origin and Development
W Oesterley, T H Robinson
SPCK 1952

Israel's Prophetic Heritage
B W Anderson, W Harrelson
SCM Press, 1962

Everyday Life in Old Testament Times
E W Heaton
BT Batsford Ltd, London 1966

Ancient Judaism
Max Weber
Free Press 1967

Ancient Israelite Religion
Susan Niditch
Oxford University Press 1997

Ancient Israel – Its Life and Institutions
Roland de Vaux
Eerdmans Publishing, 1997

Families in Ancient Israel
L G Perdue, J Blenkinsopp, J J Collins, C Meyers
Westminster John Knox Press 1997

Reconstructing the Society of Ancient Israel
P McNutt
Westminster John Knox Press 1999

Life in Biblical Israel
P J King, L E Stager
Westminster John Knox Press 2001

The Lost Testament
David Rohl
Century Random House Ltd 2002

A Final Note from the Author

Any good thing that I have written here which has lifted your spirits and taught you wisdom has come from Yahveh, not me. And if you find here anything base and distasteful, then it has come from my simple and imperfect human heart.

It was never my intent to criticise any sect, denomination or religion, or make enemies of any religion. My job is and always has been to criticise negative attitudes and ways of thinking, that are an active hindrance to God and God's Kingdom. Sometimes it will seem as though I am criticising a specific belief, but I only say what I say because all beliefs have consequences, and some beliefs have distinctly unhealthy consequences.

If you have any constructive criticism of these books, or any useful comments, suggestions or information, I would be happy to hear from you. If you think I have made any factual errors, *please tell me*, so that I can correct them in the next edition. Genuine enquiries about the Talmidi faith can also be sent to the same email address. I can be contacted at:

shmuliq.parzal@googlemail.com

Please be aware that any hateful or missionising emails will be filtered out, and will not be read; similarly with junk or spam email.

Our important work needs your support. Please help us by sending a donation through PayPal to

talmidi-donations@hotmail.co.uk

or visit my Patreon page and support my work by pledging a monthly amount:
www.patreon.com/shmuelparzal

Printed in Great Britain
by Amazon